C000075487

# WATER ON

In the 1990s and mid 2000s, turbulent political and social protests surrounded the issue of private sector involvement in providing urban water services in both the developed and the developing world. *Water on Tap* explores examples of such conflicts in six national settings (France, Bolivia, Chile, Argentina, South Africa and New Zealand), focusing on a central question: how were rights and regulation mobilised to address the demands of redistribution and recognition? Two modes of governance emerged: managed liberalisation and participatory democracy, often in hybrid forms that complicated simple oppositions between public and private, commodity and human right. The case studies examine the effects of transnational and domestic regulatory frameworks shaping the provision of urban water services, bilateral investment treaties and the contributions of non-state actors such as transnational corporations, civil society organisations and social movement activists. The conceptual framework developed can be applied to a wide range of transnational governance contexts.

BRONWEN MORGAN is Professor of Socio-Legal Studies in the School of Law at the Faculty of Social Sciences and Law, University of Bristol, and an Associate Research Fellow of the Centre for Socio-Legal Studies, University of Oxford. Her research focuses on the political economy of regulatory reform, the intersection between regulation and social and economic human rights, and global governance.

# CAMBRIDGE STUDIES IN LAW AND SOCIETY

*Cambridge Studies in Law and Society* aims to publish the best scholarly work on legal discourse and practice in its social and institutional contexts, combining theoretical insights and empirical research.

The fields that it covers are: studies of law in action; the sociology of law; the anthropology of law; cultural studies of law, including the role of legal discourses in social formations; law and economics; law and politics; and studies of governance. The books consider all forms of legal discourse across societies, rather than being limited to lawyers' discourses alone.

The series editors come from a range of disciplines: academic law; socio-legal studies; sociology; and anthropology. All have been actively involved in teaching and writing about law in context.

*Series editors*

Chris Arup *Monash University, Victoria*
Martin Chanock *La Trobe University, Melbourne*
Pat O'Malley *University of Sydney*
Sally Engle Merry *New York University*
Susan Silbey *Massachusetts Institute of Technology*

*Books in the Series*

*Diseases of the Will*
Mariana Valverde

*The Politics of Truth and Reconciliation in South Africa: Legitimizing the Post-Apartheid State*
Richard A. Wilson

*Modernism and the Grounds of Law*
Peter Fitzpatrick

*Unemployment and Government: Genealogies of the Social*
William Walters

*Autonomy and Ethnicity: Negotiating Competing Claims in Multi-Ethnic States*
Yash Ghai

*Constituting Democracy: Law, Globalism and South Africa's Political Reconstruction*
Heinz Klug

*The Ritual of Rights in Japan: Law, Society, and Health Policy*
Eric A. Feldman

*The Invention of the Passport: Surveillance, Citizenship and the State*
John Torpey

*Governing Morals: A Social History of Moral Regulation*
Alan Hunt

*Series list continues after the Index.*

# WATER ON TAP

## Rights and Regulation in the Transnational Governance of Urban Water Services

BRONWEN MORGAN

CAMBRIDGE
UNIVERSITY PRESS

CAMBRIDGE UNIVERSITY PRESS
Cambridge, New York, Melbourne, Madrid, Cape Town,
Singapore, São Paulo, Delhi, Mexico City

Cambridge University Press
The Edinburgh Building, Cambridge CB2 8RU, UK

Published in the United States of America by Cambridge University Press, New York

www.cambridge.org
Information on this title: www.cambridge.org/9781107411838

First published 2011
First paperback edition 2012

*A catalogue record for this publication is available from the British Library*

*Library of Congress Cataloguing in Publication Data*
Morgan, Bronwen, 1966–
Water on tap : rights and regulation in the transnational governance of
urban water services / Bronwen Morgan.
p.   cm. – (Cambridge studies in law and society)
ISBN 978-1-107-00894-6 (hardback)
1. Water utilities–Law and legislation.   2. International business enterprises–
Law and legislation.   3. Privatization–Law and legislation.
4. Right to water.   I. Title.   II. Series.
K3984.M67   2011
343.09′24–dc22
2011002697

ISBN 978-1-107-00894-6 Hardback
ISBN 978-1-107-41183-8 Paperback

To Jim

# CONTENTS

# FIGURES

# TABLES

# ACKNOWLEDGEMENTS

This book germinated, developed and flowered in three stages over the years. It would not have been possible without the opportunity opened up by the Harry Woods Research Fellowship, which I held at Wadham College and the Centre for Socio-Legal Studies, University of Oxford, from 2002 to 2005. Early pilot work was supported by a small grant from the UK Socio-Legal Studies Association, for which I remain grateful. The core fieldwork was generously funded by the ESRC-AHRC Research Programme 'Cultures of Consumption' (ESRC Grant RES-143–25–0031), and Frank Trentmann's remarkable leadership of that programme, together with the intellectual vibrancy of the Centre for Socio-Legal Studies, created fertile growing conditions for the project's roots.

In the second stage, an important influence was the 2005–7 series of Law and Society Association Summer Institutes on the intersection of rights and regulation, particularly the one hosted by Oxford University in 2005. These were shaped by the input of my co-organisers and colleagues, Jonathan Klaaren and Eve Darian-Smith, and funded by the US National Science Foundation, the US Law and Society Association, and the UK Socio-Legal Studies Association. The project came to final writing fruition in its third stage at the University of Bristol, where the stimulating intellectual support of my socio-legal colleagues provided the ideal environment for completing the manuscript, in combination with the generous research leave policy of the Law School, for which I remain strongly appreciative.

Along the way, the project benefited enormously from the input of those who worked with me. For research assistance, I thank most of all the inimitable Carolina Fairstein, who was an indispensable partner and colleague in Latin America, as was Annabelle Littoz-Monnet in France. Thanks also for the valuable research support from Susan Buell, Elaine Deegan, Russell Hitchings, Julia Labeta, Alison McPherson, Tina Piper, Min Shu, Elen Stokes and Oisin Tansey. For invaluable feedback on the manuscript and critical conversations, I thank in particular Karen

Bakker, Esteban Castro, John Clarke, Dave Cowan, John Gillespie, Terence Halliday, Emanuel Lobina, Simon Halliday, Tim Lang, Morag McDermont, Pip Nicholson, Tony Prosser, Greg Shaffer, Keith Syrett and Frank Trentmann. Finola O'Sullivan at Cambridge University Press has been a supportive and congenial editor.

The original fieldwork was carried out in 2003 and 2004, with desk-based updating in 2007 and 2009. I owe a debt to those who provided academic homes, as well as much supportive enjoyment, while I was carrying out the fieldwork, especially Michael Taggart at the University of Auckland, New Zealand; Jonathan Klaaren at Wits University, Johannesburg; and Javier Couso at Diego Portales University, Chile. I am deeply indebted to the communities and professionals whose daily work in the struggle to provide basic needs has an urgency and salience that writing can never attain, and I thank in particular Maria Alegria, Penny Bright, Danielle Morley, Innocent Nojiyeza, Jean-Louis Olivier, Robin Simpson, Laila Smith and Miguel Solanes.

Finally, I want to voice my heartfelt appreciation for Jim, Cassidy and five-week-old Brooklyn, whose cumulative appearance in my life as the project unfolded marked its beginning, middle and end, creating the joy and support which nourished this book, and so much else.

# Introduction

## The field of global water policy: struggles over redistribution and recognition

This is a book about water: water as a basic good, an essential resource and a life need that is deeply embedded in relations of power, meaning and identity. But it is also a book about collective institution-building, about governing in a world of rapidly shifting power dynamics between governments, businesses and 'ordinary' people. From this second perspective, struggles over access to water are emblematic. They are an instance – a particularly intense instance – of conflicts over how to provide collective goods and services. The questions about provision and governance of water services explored in this book resonate with the provision and governance of other basic goods too – education, health, transport, communications, energy. These are all areas where the scope of state-led capitalism is especially contested, and many of them also echo the question that water raises most intensely: how far should economic principles of market-based delivery govern the provision of collective goods? What is the fate of 'the social' as state–market relations are ever more intensively reconfigured? Where, if not with respect to water, can we find, define and make real the limits of a market-based political economy?

These substantive political questions are deeply linked to the reconfiguration of state–market relations in a context of global governance, where the role of the nation-state in collective provision of essential services is increasingly supplemented and re-shaped by transnational institutions. 'Globalisation' is of course, by no means a new phenomenon, but Frank Munger has argued (Munger 2008) that in contrast to earlier periods of global interconnection,[1] contemporary 'third wave' globalisation is distinctively about transnational influence on governance through exporting institutions, organisation, and technology. Although much of what is seen as new in those patterns of export relates to the influence of *non-state* actors such as multinational corporations and NGOs, patterns of

---

[1] Namely, those that were accelerated by revolutions in transportation (from the sixteenth to the nineteenth century) and global finance (post-World War II).

transnational influence are also clearly linked to particular state interests. Indeed, there is a persistent strand of literature that suggests that globalisation is in fact an analogue for Americanisation (Shapiro 2001).

Struggles over how to provide access to water challenge the equation of globalisation and Americanisation. At least in relation to the issue of providing drinking water for domestic, household use, the powerful actors in transnational governance debates have been not US companies or the USA, but French and British companies, and in particular the French state. The historical resonance of colonisation – an earlier 'wave' of globalisation if ever there is one – is here profoundly relevant: as the 'market for water services delivery' increasingly extended beyond national borders, so too did the direction of foreign investment by British and French companies into water service delivery in former colonies. This growth – particularly marked in the 1990s but still highly politically salient – catalysed transnational trajectories of resistance and routinisation. Activists challenged market-led capitalism, embodied in the cry of 'water is a human right, not a commodity'. In response, the global water policy field has increasingly attempted to embed social facets into the expansion of transnational markets: part of the incremental growth of 'globalisation with a human face'.

This book tells the story of these struggles – of how they are both deeply local and yet also embedded in relationships that cross and re-cross national borders. It focuses on the turbulent upheavals of 1990–2005 that held up two models of governance as answers to the urgent questions posed by the provision of collective and essential goods such as water. One was managed liberalisation, the other a reinvigorated image of public provision that aspired to infuse or even supersede bureaucratic state management with participatory democracy. The core message of the evolving struggles between these models is that the striking contrast between 'water as a commodity' and 'water as a human right' makes considerable sense at a macro-political level, but is deeply ambiguous at the micro-institutional level. This ambiguity is reflected in the hybrid solutions which have emerged across and within the case studies explored in forthcoming chapters, a complication of the initial dichotomy which has intensified since 2005.

On the one hand, the underlying political tensions over the limits of a market-led way of life are remarkably resilient: especially at a macro-political level they continue to be expressed in terms of a tension between commodification and notions of fundamental rights in relation to basic essential needs. On the other hand, it is increasingly clear that as aspects of the public participatory model are institutionalised at the micro level, they tend to be colonised by managed liberalisation. Without support from an alternative structural development pathway from that of market-led capitalism, micro-level dynamics of governance are likely to continue to reflect the absorption of fundamental rights into trajectories of commodification.

The tension between commodification and notions of fundamental rights in relation to basic essential needs has a broader resonance that goes beyond water, as does the clash between managed liberalisation and public participatory governance. Challenges arise, however, in moving between these different registers. While the tension between commodification and fundamental rights is often articulated with reference to the ideological clashes of 'high politics', debates about different governance models tend to leach out politics altogether. This makes it difficult to work through the specific implications of the ideological tensions for everyday governance. Paradoxically, perhaps, a special emphasis on the role of law can help to re-insert politics in constructive ways at the level of debates over governance. This book aims to do just this, and in so doing make a distinctively socio-legal contribution to the debate over global water governance. In many strands of this debate, even where struggle and contestation are at the forefront of the analysis, law nonetheless appears as the background structure, or the final glue, of a deal elsewhere formed in the crucible of politics. This book presents law as a crucial lens for understanding the struggle and contestation.

Legality, I argue, is a particularly fertile site for bridging the macro and micro dimensions of transnational governance: a role best illuminated by means of a series of dispute-centred snapshots of struggles over access to water. Law, understood as disputes articulated under frameworks of formal rules allocating entitlements and obligations, freezes politics, routinises conflicts and establishes order. But law in this sense is also a resource for challenging the status quo, for articulating alternative visions of collective justice, and for embedding such visions in concrete institutions and practical rules. Law is the place where aspirations for justice, consensus and stability can crystallise in a form more enduring than most other formal institutional spaces, particularly in a secular society. Because law's form is enduring, and also because it is backed ultimately by violence, however legitimated, the high stakes of struggles over and through law illuminate vividly – almost paradoxically – the ineradicably political, fluid and contested nature of aspirations for justice, consensus and stability. In each of the six case studies that follow, the settlements that flow from struggles over access to water, however provisional they may be in the long run, give a glimpse of the concrete ways in which the local mobilisation of law is increasingly incorporating responses to global pressures.

The remainder of this introduction has two parts. In the first, I paint a picture of the global water policy field which provides the setting for the struggles over access to water at the heart of the book. That struggle is at its core concerned with the politics of distributive justice between the global North and South, focusing in particular on 'social' dimensions of access to water. 'Social' dimensions of water services policy encompass both *material* redistribution (in terms, for example, of the tariffs charged for access to water and for connecting to networks, or the basis of disconnection for inability to pay) and *recognition* (in terms of the subjective and symbolic dimensions of identity, respect and belonging that are linked to access to a basic essential good such as water). The fate of the 'social' understood in these terms is shaped by a transnational politics that is influenced in particular by international financial institutions and transnational advocacy networks. The influence of these actors reflects a double decentring of both law and nation-state that is central to my theoretical approach, one which constructs transnational governance at the intersection of regulation and rights.

In the second part of the introduction, I summarise the research that underpins the rest of the book and the questions that it will help to answer. The core question is: how have rights and regulation been mobilised to address the demands of redistribution and recognition that are at the core of social protests around access to drinking water? This question, which is linked to the centrality of law and disputes to the politics of necessity, emerges from dialogue with a recent important book by Ken Conca (2005). The framing of the research in the introduction is mainly addressed to readers who aim primarily to learn more on the debates about governing access to water, while Chapter 1 is addressed more directly to socio-legal scholars and those interested in conceptual frameworks of relevance to global social policy on basic needs and essential services more broadly.

## 0.1   The global water policy field

The global water policy field of urban water services delivery emerges from the activities of four types of institutions shaping the problem of access to water at a transnational level: water-specific policy fora and transnational water services corporations (together key to a double decentring of both law and nation-state), and international financial institutions and transnational advocacy networks (together key to the construction of transnational governance at the intersection of regulation and rights). Before describing these institutions in more detail, I should emphasise that the struggles over access to water at the heart of this book concern the production and distribution of domestic drinking water as a service in urban settings: this could be termed the 'micro' water cycle. This is a much narrower and more specific issue than questions of access to water resources in relation to the 'macro' water cycle, such as in the context of irrigation, transport, ecological river basin health and industrial water usage. Obviously, the macro and micro water cycles are related: indeed, pressures on access to water in the context of the macro cycle are emblematic of a crisis of rapid urbanisation and access by the poor to essential services that is at the heart of the North/South politics of necessity. But my focus on the micro water cycle informs the picture of the global water policy field I draw below. Although many of the actors and institutions I describe may deal with both the micro and macro water cycles, the detail I highlight is relevant only to the former.

### 0.1.1 *Transnational institutions*

The field of global water policy in relation to urban water service delivery refers to the regulation, provision and policymaking environment of urban water services. Narrowly understood, the regulatory framework for delivery of water services is carried out by domestic institutions. Indeed, as the case studies presented in forthcoming chapters will show, national and local regulatory dynamics are the most crucial aspects of water service delivery on the ground. However, despite the absence of any formal international institutions responsible for the regulation of water services at the global level, transnational influence in the provision and policymaking environment of urban water services is now substantial.

Both state and non-state actors have created transnational organisations that debate and shape water policy initiatives in a global context. The most important of these is the World Water Council, created by non-state actors. Indeed, a striking feature of the global water policy field has been the degree to which non-state actors have taken the lead in this respect, particularly in relation to the micro water cycle. The United Nations has never succeeded in creating a single coherent organisation to deal with  water (Conca 2005), although access to water in the context of the macro water cycle does have a long history of treaty-based and United Nations activity. But a policy space in relation to the micro water cycle existed, and its political salience first became urgently visible at the transnational level in the setting of the World Water Forum, a triennial event convened by the World Water Council. The World Water Council is effectively a transnational 'think-tank'. The Council is legally a French-based NGO but in practice is composed of a curious amalgam of business-based NGOs and large corporations.[2] The Council is a site for debates over access to water and for the formulation of influential position papers on key issues, and the Forum (the most recent of which was in Istanbul in 2009) hosts the most prominent of these debates, generating principles and policy documents for guiding water governance. Though not sponsored by the United Nations, each World Water Forum also hosts a formal intergovernmental Ministerial Meeting whose declarations are scrutinised by key actors in the policy field for clues to transnational political trends, making the Forum a powerful site of non-state actor influence on global water policy trajectories.[3]

From the state actor angle, intergovernmental initiatives and United Nations activity have a long history in the transnational policy environment around urban water services delivery, notably during the UN International Drinking Water and Sanitation Decade during the 1980s. But beginning in the 1990s, as non-state actors began to take agenda-leading roles of the kind described above, UN activity increasingly focused on including private sector water providers and non-state actors as key partners in global water policy formulation. This activity included endorsing the principle that water be treated as an economic good (International Conference on Water and the Environment 1992), supporting public–private partnerships (Kara and Quarless 2002)[4] and eventually convening a multi-stakeholder taskforce (United Nations Millennium Project Task Force on Water and Sanitation 2005) that led to the establishment of the United Nations Secretary General's Advisory Board on Water and Sanitation, focusing to date on Water Operator Partnerships, monitoring and reporting activities, and capacity-building activities to support a focus on access to sanitation.

---

[2] Members include Suez, Severn Trent, Vivendi, Mitsubishi, Evian, Électricité de France, Japan Dam Engineering Centre, Mitsubishi Heavy Industries, PricewaterhouseCoopers, US Army Corps of Engineers.

[3] Additional important non-state transnational initiatives in the global water policy field include those that provide technical assistance (Global Water Partnership), design voluntary management standards (Technical Committee 224 of the International Standards Organization) or form trade associations that lobby directly on behalf of water service providers (Aquafed).

[4] Elaborating on GA Res. 56/226 (28 February 2002).

In essence, these developments reflect a shift over the last ten years from heated and highly polarised debates pitting 'public' against 'private' in the provision of water services, to a more nuanced approach that foregrounds complex ranges of mixed public–private structures. For example, the UN Advisory Board works with UN-HABITAT to create North–South technical assistance partnerships for utility companies, working with both the public and private sectors.[5] This hybrid approach reflects developments in the involvement of the second important institutional actor: transnational corporations.

### 0.1.2 Private sector participation: the wax and wane of multinational corporations

Multinational water companies, in particular from the UK and France, grew substantially during the 1980s and started investing heavily in cross-border service provision during the 1990s. The transnational markets for water services delivery were led by British and French companies Suez (now Ondeo), Vivendi (now Veolia) and Thames. In the 1990s, these three companies were three of the largest water service operators globally, in absolute terms as well as in terms of foreign investment.[6] Along with the controversial multinational Bechtel, whose involvement in the Bolivian city of Cochabamba has become an iconic instance of conflict over access to water, these companies' involvement in South Africa, Chile, New Zealand, Bolivia, Argentina and France structured the selection of case studies explored in forthcoming chapters. Each case study, with the exception of Chile which was used as a 'control' case study, focused on specific projects that catalysed major disputes ending in a change in the ownership or control structure regarding the delivery of water services. The significance of more recent changes in foreign investment patterns in the first decade of the new century is discussed below.

Significant shifts in the last ten to fifteen years have occurred both in the polarised nature of the debate over public and private involvement in water service delivery and in the quantitative levels of investment in water service delivery by transnational water companies. The year 1997

---

[5] See the Hashimoto Action Plan (UNSGAB 2006) and the Global Water Operators' Partnership Alliance (UN-HABITAT n.d.).

[6] Of the developing world population served by private operators between 1990 and 2000, Suez served 36 per cent, Vivendi 12 per cent and Thames 6 per cent. By 2007 this had changed to 12 per cent, 19 per cent and 0 per cent (Thames withdrew from the international market in 2006) (Marin 2009).

represented an unprecedented peak in private sector investment in water and sanitation: in the seven years leading up to the peak, investment increased by 7,300 per cent compared to the previous sixteen years (Silva *et al.* 1998), but eight years later peak investment had halved (Simpson 2006). Since then, where private sector involvement has continued, it has largely avoided long-term concession contracts in favour of short-term management contracts involving little private sector capital investment (Marin and Izaguirre 2006). Private sector investment has also shifted geographical focus: while Latin America took almost 50 per cent of global private sector investment in water services in the 1990s, it has been replaced by East Asia as the major recipient in the 2000s (Kerf and Izaguirre 2007).

But I would argue that neither institutional interest in hybrid public–private solutions nor muted private sector investment levels alter the ongoing salience of the case studies chronicled in future chapters. There are several reasons for this. First, reduced levels of multinational investment do not necessarily mean less interest by the private sector. Rather, more local private sector firms are involved, and private sector actors in general are focusing on shorter-term, less-expensive projects (Marin and Izaguirre 2006).[7] But the urban population served by the private sector in the developing world has continued to grow since 1990, reaching 160 million in 2007 (Marin 2009). Second, the withdrawal of multinational corporations from long-term cross-border concession contracts has not altered the enduring importance of the commercialisation of water service delivery, as recent reports emphasise, arguing that successful public utilities require the same structural reforms as private sector participation brings (Marin 2009). Thus it is really commercialisation that is at the core of the political conflict in struggles over access to water, as the case studies in New Zealand and South Africa illustrate (Chapter 5). Water service provision, when it is structured along commercial lines (and whether or not it is actually delivered by private sector actors), continues to exist at a troublesome intersection of competitive markets and resource-blind universal need, an intersection that animates the bedrock political dynamics of many areas of global governance, as contemporary debates over appropriate responses to climate change vividly illustrate. Finally, the large transnational providers and the political conflict their presence engendered between 1990 and 2005 had an important shaping influence on the

---

[7] This is exemplified by the fact that even though quantitative levels of overall investment have reduced sharply since the 1990s, 2005 was a record year for growth in new contracts: forty-one projects were concluded in 2005, the most since 1990.

governance architecture that has emerged thus far in the global water policy field. The extensive involvement of private sector providers in Latin America in the 1990s, for example, is being drawn upon for lessons in the currently more popular investment area of East Asia (Kirkpatrick and Parker 2004). And although customised, hybrid solutions that draw on both public and private involvement are increasingly popular in the water services policy field (Marin and Izaguirre 2006), the experiences chronicled in this book are crucial to understanding the political implications of these nuanced, hybrid solutions. As the case study chapters will demonstrate, the dilemmas presented by those solutions complicate, rather than efface, the underlying politics of struggles over access to water.

### 0.1.3 International financial institutions and regulatory frameworks

The double decentring of state and law that is at stake in the changes in the structure of water service provision discussed above means that the politics of access to water, especially in relation to the micro cycle, are increasingly regulatory politics. Whether water services are delivered by public or private entities, they operate more and more at arm's length from traditional representative politics and under the supervision of some kind of regulatory body. Yet the politics of access to water are also a passionate flashpoint for popular social and cultural concerns, often expressed in the language of human rights or through the action of direct protest. This bifocal centrality of regulation and rights structures the remaining exposition of the global water policy field in this and the next part of Section 0.1, as well as the theoretical framework introduced in Section 0.2.

The World Bank and regional international financial institutions (the most important of which, in this book, is the Inter-American Development Bank) funded the provision of water services during the 1990s and early 2000s on the assumption of a commercial model of delivery, and strongly encouraged borrowing states to directly involve the private sector. While not all of these loans necessarily came with formal conditionality, the provision of expertise, advice and support powerfully shaped national trajectories, as future chapters will illustrate – promoting in particular a regulatory model centred on politically insulated autonomous agencies controlling commercially structured operators.

In practice, this regulatory model was mainly taken up in the Latin American region, with significant variation and dilution, while case studies from New Zealand and South Africa foreshadow the regulatory pluralism that has become much more marked since the post-1990s decrease in direct private sector investment in water services. Debates around regulation now emphasise content over institutional form: the need to control tariff-setting, to set equity targets for service operators with non-compliance sanctions, and to accommodate differing service and quality standards for small-scale informal providers without entrenching a two-tier service (Bakker 2009).

These debates take place in the shadow of an enduring feature of the transnational legal landscape that potentially undermines any national-level regulatory regime: investment protection agreements that provide for any disputes to be resolved by arbitration processes that tend to exclude broader public interest issues or even to view national regulation as potentially expropriatory. The case studies in Bolivia and Argentina illuminate the powerful political shadow that one particular arbitration forum – the International Centre for the Settlement of Investment Disputes, housed at the World Bank – casts over the water policy field. Arbitration also shows how, in counterpoint to debates over regulatory form and content, articulations of conflict around access to water have increasingly engaged with the issue in terms of rights: in this case the property and contract rights of investors protected by the legal framework of international arbitration. But rights have also come to dominate the debate over access from a very different political perspective: that of social and economic human rights, increasingly the lingua franca of a diverse range of efforts to ameliorate or temper the effects of global market integration.

### 0.1.4 Transnational advocacy networks and the trajectory of the human right to water

During the 1990s patterns of sustained political protest occurred in countries of all income levels, uniting organised labour, consumers, environmentalists, women's groups and in some cases farmers, in strategies that ranged from street protests to lobbying campaigns, court cases and civil disobedience, including bill payment boycotts and illegal connections to water networks. The case study chapters document the variations and local contexts of these, but what is notable here is that by 2005 they had acquired sufficient transnational visibility that even the World Bank painted them as part of the global policy field, noting that 'the frequent (not inevitable) result [of water privatisation] was popular protests, dissatisfied governments, and unhappy investors' (World Bank 2005: 22). During this polarised period, the notion of a human right to water became an important site for embedding, communicating and – particularly recently – institution-alising the demands articulated by activists and social movements.

Radical social movements and alter-globalisation NGOs (Attac in France, Food and Water Watch and Public Citizen in the US, the Council of Canadians in Canada) tend to use the human right to water as a rhet-orical device, contrasting it with the notion of water as an economic com-modity, and as a rallying cry for political mobilisation. In contrast, service delivery NGOs (WaterAid in the UK, PS-Eau in France) and more mod-erate reformist NGOs (COHRE in Switzerland), even if they support the broad political thrust of the more radical wing, have in practice worked more closely with the growing legal institutionalisation of the right to water at the transnational level, as well as with forging links between this level and national and local legislative and regulatory responses to the problem of access to water.

The legal institutionalisation of the right to water at the trans-national level can focus on November 2002 as an important watershed point, when General Comment 15 of the United Nations Committee on Social, Economic and Cultural Rights (a 'soft' form of international law) elaborated the obligations and responsibilities entailed by such a right. Since then, a series of UN-affiliated activities have led most recently to the appointment by the UN Human Rights Council of an Independent Expert to provide a study on the implementation of the right to drinking water and sanitation.[8] Thus far, the Independent Expert has resolved that, in a thematically structured approach to her mandate, she will spend 2010 focusing on privatisation and the private sector (De Albuquerque 2009), which vividly illustrates the ongoing resilience of this issue despite the shifts that have occurred since the more turbulent 1990–2005 period.

Reflecting the move in the regulatory debate towards a more nuanced approach and the advocacy of hybrid solutions, over time the notion of the human right to water has acquired a political open texture that belies any simple dichotomy between water as human right and water as commod-ity. Both the basic concept of a human right to water, and even the central-ity of the General Comment have, after initial suspicion, been embraced by transnational corporations (Russell 2009; Suez Environnement 2007) and the World Water Council (Dubreuil 2006).

It is also important to note that, due in part to suspicion engendered by the perhaps too broad church that now supports the human right to water,

---

[8]  See OHCR (n.d.(a)), noting the appointment of Ms Catarina de Albuquerque in November 2008.

and in part by well-founded concerns regarding the limits of rights as a conceptual and political device to counter market-based policies, there is a healthy debate over alternative conceptualisations for articulating concerns over the commodification of water, most importantly via notions of the commons. The conclusion of the book touches upon this alternative possibility, but the centrality of rights to current strategies and mindmaps of the key actors in the global water policy field is reflected in the theoretical approach I take, which I now summarise.

## 0.2   Research questions, approach and context

The brief account sketched above of the global policy field in relation to urban water service delivery highlights trajectories of rights and regulation, putting them at the centre of my approach to unpacking the dynamics of transnational governance in the field. My central question is: how have rights and regulation been mobilised to address the demands of redistribution and recognition that are at the core of social protests around access to drinking water? My approach foregrounds the way in which fluid social relations interact with, constitute and are shaped by formal institutions. The physical and technical dimensions of the 'problem of access to water' are not the primary focus, although their salience will emerge in specific case studies. But I highlight instead an agency-centred interpretive approach to governance consistent with a post-positivist social constructionist view of the world (Bevir 2007).

Interpretive governance approaches burrow inside formal institutional structures and reject reified conceptions of their existence, with two important effects. First, by focusing on the practices of locally situated actors, and how *they* understand the meaning of those practices, community boundaries that cut across formal political boundaries become much more visible, allowing us to complicate and break up notions of multiple vertical 'levels' of governance that currently dominate discussions of global governance. Second, tracking messy, contingent, micro-level trajectories of agent-centred choices, ideas and beliefs helps us understand how agency is possible in what may seem sometimes paralysing trajectories of global governance.[9] For Bevir, this encourages a dual focus on how agents *transform the traditions* in which they are embedded, and how

---

[9] Alternative, more structural approaches, which aim to relieve this sense of paralysis by generating explanations and even predictions at the macro level, can often intensify the sense of determinism attached to global governance that my approach explicitly seeks to challenge.

they *respond to dilemmas* which require them to integrate new beliefs into existing ones. My socio-legal perspective on this agenda works outwards from the centre of disputes, to explore how actors engaged with water policy transform traditions and respond to dilemmas by engaging with rights discourses and regulatory dynamics.

As Chapter 1 will elaborate, viewing governance through the lens of two triads – 'naming, claiming and blaming', and 'rulemaking, monitoring and enforcement' – facilitates a transposition of the dynamics of bilateral individual disputing into the context of collective political conflict. This transposition helps explore in a dynamic and fluid way the struggles over the content and sites of rights and regulation, which become the two principal axes of the institutional architecture of the global water policy field. Out of these struggles emerge two competing models of transnational water governance: managed liberalisation and public participatory governance. Both models exist against the important background of the existing status quo, which is national state governance. Each model decentres different aspects of that state governance. Managed liberalisation transposes state functions of protecting property and contract rights to the transnational level. Public participatory governance transposes the representation of ordinary citizens' needs from formal democratic government institutions into a locally situated – but globally oriented – more directly participatory mode that aims to build a counter-hegemonic model of development.

Below I briefly review the array of recent literature in relation to the global policy field of urban water service delivery, with an emphasis on what my approach adds that is distinctive. As a whole, my approach takes forward a recent call for research on the practices of non-state actors as possible sources of 'alternative' mechanisms of global governance to shift focus:

> One striking aspect of research on the nonstate is how little its chroniclers have had to say about institutionalisation. The emphasis is on movements, actors, networks, and relationships, but not on embedded, enduring sets of roles and rules that give shape and form to a whole array of struggles over time.
>
> (Conca 2005: 24)

A wide range of literature has emerged in very recent years that engages with the political and institutional dimensions of private sector involvement in urban water service delivery. Geographers have engaged with water sector reforms from the standpoints of political ecology (Bakker

2004; Swyngedouw 2004), postcolonial governmentality (Kooy and Bakker 2008) and sociological citizenship (Castro 2005), crafting richly detailed empirical accounts of institutional trajectories, spatial variability and political dynamics. Although I draw on this valuable work to inform the more detailed case study chapters that follow, its primary orientation to water scholars differs from the socio-legal approach I advocate, which is intended to be capable of extension beyond water to other domains of global social policy. For this purpose, two admirable recent contributors provide a more fertile starting point for situating my approach: Rutgerd Boelens in anthropology (Boelens 2008; 2009; Roth *et al.* 2005) and Ken Conca in international relations (Conca 2005). Conca's primary aim is to explore political struggles over governing water as a lens for demonstrating the limitations of 'regime' approaches to problems of global governance more generally. I build on this point, pointing out how the alternative epistemology he advocates resonates with the commitments of significant strands of socio-legal literature in rights and regulation. But I take his approach one step further, arguing that a socio-legal approach illuminates law and disputing as critical and neglected sites of the dynamics of transnational governance. Boelens' work is helpful here, but in building on his work I add not only a focus on the micro rather than macro water cycle, but also a distinctive approach on disputes.

Conca's (2005) magisterial mapping of four spheres of the global water policy field[10] challenges a particular vision of transnational governance that I would argue resonates across many policy sectors beyond water. That vision, for Conca, is epitomised by the regime approach in international relations, but would be equally true of a formal legal positivist approach. In both, transnational governance centres on building effective global agreements through intergovernmental bargaining that legally codifies cooperative means and ends, sets international standards and articulates the sovereign (state) responsibilities necessary to implement these standards. But as Conca argues, this approach has little traction on many, if not most, problems related to water, including river basin governance, soil degradation and access to water for domestic uses. In part this is because of the centrality of non-state actors in tracking responses to these problems, and Conca's emphasis on the practices of networks of technical experts (Litfin *et al.* 1995) and coalitions of value-driven activists (Keck

---

[10] Conca explores transnational river basin governance; the diffusion of integrated water resource management policy; struggles over the building of large dams; and the building of a global market for the delivery of water services. The last of these four is my direct concern in this book.

and Sikkink 1998) in the water policy field is confirmed and extended by the material in this book.

But the limits of regime approaches or of formal positivism are also epistemological. Foregrounding messier, 'bottom-up' forms of institutionalisation involves a shift of focus from top-down centralised perspectives to looking at how socially and politically embedded rules, roles and practices at the local level gradually diffuse across borders. It replaces institutional development as a question of instrumental design with a conception that grows from 'embeddedness, routinization and normalization ... institutions ... not as something to be designed but rather *as something to be nurtured*' (Conca 2005: 384). Conca argues that these alternative forms of institutionalisation should be an important focus for global governance researchers, and emphasises the ways in which they confound core assumptions about territorial stability, the efficacy of formal state authority and the explanatory and predictive power of scientific knowledge that are embedded in, and assumed by, regime approaches.

The reconfigured conceptions of territoriality, authority and knowledge that Conca welds together into an alternative epistemology for international relations are familiar territory for interpretive socio-legal approaches. Like Conca, an interpretive socio-legal exploration of the field of global water policy would not extract predictable patterns from the data explored, but would aim instead to make visible, understand and to nurture 'messy', bottom-up trajectories of institutionalising global governance. More specifically, rights, regulation and disputing are conceptual tools familiar to territorially oriented formal legal scholars, but equally capable of drawing upon a rich heritage of interpretive socio-legal literature that *already* recognises the constructed and contingent nature of authority and knowledge and (to a lesser extent) territoriality.

While Conca emphasises the bottom-up diffusion of norms and practices, he also wants to avoid conveying 'a deterministic process of norm reproduction' (Conca 2005: 69), arguing that instead, 'we need to see institution building [in global governance] as a site of struggle with no predetermined outcome' (Conca 2005: 69). So far, this is also resonant with a socio-legal interpretive governance approach – but Conca then structures the empirical scope of his book with reference to normative struggles in *multiple* sites: administrative structures, legal systems, project enterprises, policy networks and social movements. In this list, legal systems appear more as the formal container for policy content and project-based actions than as a site for actually resolving conflict – in other words, as a rough proxy for policy rather than a place of dispute resolution.

This approach has limits that suggest that one further step is needed: a focus on the socio-legal dimension of global governance. Law and legal systems are crucial sites for the convergence of the micro and macro dynamics of global governance, conceptually and in collective social imaginaries, even when they are instrumentally marginal to the everyday rhythms of global governance. They combine a normative pull that administrative structures and project enterprises lack, and an institutional bite that policy networks and social movements lack. This book therefore reinserts law not in terms of circulating norms, but in terms of the channelling of political conflict into formal legal dispute. Judicialisation, rather than juridification, tells us most about the emerging direction of, and forces shaping, enduring transnational patterns of governance.

For Boelens (2008; 2009), law is conceptually central. Through the lens of legal pluralism, he traces the ways in which local normative orders of rural water user communities in the Andes intersect with state-embedded market governance, highlighting how actors resist or sidestep incorporation into market governance though legal, illegal and non-legal strategies. He contends that 'non-legal' strategies – those which manage to stay out of the way of legal frameworks – are the most important resource for constituting pathways of an alternative political economy of water. Boelens' research focuses only on the macro water cycle in a rural context,[11] making his substantive focus less immediately salient to my concerns. But his perspective on how actors' multifaceted relationship to legality engages with different levels of struggle[12] is deeply illuminating in showing how 'movements, actors, networks, and relationships … [congeal into] embedded, enduring sets of roles and rules that give shape and form to a whole array of struggles over time' – the goal advocated by Conca. My aspiration for this book is that it will bring together the spirit of Boelens' approach, the substance of Conca's important pioneering work, and my own distinctive socio-legal approach. My core argument has three facets, each exploring a dimension of transnational legal governance.

First, in relation to the *transnational* dimension, regulation and rights are two of the most important building blocks of the architecture of transnational governance. Both tend towards counter-majoritarianism.

---

[11] As such, his work is in fact especially illuminating in relation to the important Bolivian case study, where the political dynamics of rural water access were centrally important, as Chapter 2 will show.

[12] He argues that four levels of struggle are salient and often co-present: struggle over resources, rules, regulatory frameworks and regimes of representation.

Although both rights and regulation have their roots in felt wrongs which could as easily be channelled into democratic political processes, their systemic institutionalisation tends to link them to processes and interpretive communities that erect boundaries between them and democratic political institutions. This is intensified by the inbuilt trajectories of communities of expertise that elaborate detailed rulemaking, monitoring and enforcement regimes for rights and regulation. Combined with the absence of democratic institutions at the level of global governance, these tendencies create at least partial systemic closure.

Second, in relation to *governance*, the most interesting place to explore trajectories of regulation and rights is their *intersection*. Systemic closure tends to seal regulation and rights off from each other, but under certain conditions they come into contact with each other in very interesting ways: primarily in either situations of intense political contestation, or when a policy problem emerges in a novel arena with little existing institutional architecture. Their intersection is helpfully explored through the double triad of 'naming, claiming and blaming', and 'rulemaking, monitoring and enforcement'.

Third, in relation to *legality*, the double triad has especially important ramifications in the context of major infrastructure-based provision of basic needs. In such contexts, the stage of activism – naming and blaming – tends to blur civil, political and socio-economic rights. But even when claiming, and especially in the context of rulemaking, monitoring and enforcement, socio-economic rights and civil and political rights take separate trajectories. At this stage, unless socio-economic rights claims engage with regulation, they risk remaining 'mere rhetoric'. But if they step too close to regulation, they lose their critical edge and political force.

The combined import of this argument aims to generate a conceptual framework that has resonance beyond water, illuminating multiple dimensions of basic human need in a world of increasingly globalised social policy. The final part of this introduction summarises the steps that will lead the reader along that pathway.

## 0.3   Summary of chapters

In Chapter 1, I elaborate the analytical lens that brings together rights and regulation, locating the approach in relation to broader trends of socio-legal approaches to transnational governance and illustrating it by linking selected aspects of the detailed case studies to the sketch of the global policy field given in this Introduction. As Chapter 1 argues, regulation needs normative life (whether it promotes consensus or conflict) and rights need routinisation (whether they institutionalise or co-opt social movement energy). Where these pathways intersect, a constructive interdependency can arise.

Chapters 2–5 each focus on a different national setting, drawing on fieldwork into the practices of water activists across different scales – local, national and transnational – in six different national settings: South Africa, Chile, New Zealand, Bolivia, Argentina and France. The structure of these four central chapters rests on comparative case studies carried out in the context of a multilevel sectoral perspective. The integration of a comparative and sectoral perspective on transnational governance enables me to complicate assumptions about scale and 'levels' in governance without losing an empirical sense of the everyday microdynamics of global governance. Detailed comparative case studies are critical given that global governance institutions still stand substantially on the shoulders of national state institutions, certainly in water but in other fields too. But retaining an understanding of the ways in which this *co-exists* with the dispersal and limits of formal state power is important: thus the overall picture of the book traces, in relation to a single policy sector (in this case, urban water service delivery), the relationships between local practices, national-comparative traditions and global norms and structures.

In short, although the chapters are structured as national case studies, each charts a deep interpenetration of the global water policy field as described in this Introduction within that national setting. Each focuses on particular disputes that make sense primarily in a highly localised setting which is at the same time moulded by the global water policy field. Thus the 'national stage' in each chapter is just that and no more: a setting in which to chart the complex, multilayered picture of transnational governance that is emerging in urban water services delivery policy. In all but one of these settings, the participation of a major private transnational company in the delivery of urban water services catalysed significant social protest culminating in a dispute that resulted, however temporarily, in a change of formal ownership or structure of provision for water services. The Chilean case, as the exception to the pattern of major disputes, functions as a kind of 'control' case where patterns of governance in the absence of disputing dynamics can be explored. Table 1 summarises this:

Table 1 *Comparative case study structure and focus*

| Water company | Country context | Project | Main focus of social conflict | Endpoint of social conflict |
|---|---|---|---|---|
| Suez and Vivendi (France) | France | Concession contract to private sector for Grenoble water services | Corruption | Remunicipalisation 1999 after corruption-related social conflict |
| International Waters Ltd: Bechtel/ Edison SpA (USA/Italy) | Bolivia | Concession contract to deliver water to residents of Cochabamba | Steep increases in tariffs; disconnections; illegal connections; martial law and violence | Government rescission of concession in 2000; arbitration hearing formally settled January 2006 |
| Thames (UK), Biwater (UK), Suez (France) | Chile | Privatisation of regional corporatised water services | Political and social resistance to the general policy but without effect | Privatisation proceeds as planned |
| Vivendi (France) | Argentina | Concession contract to deliver Tucumán water services | Steep increases in tariffs; disconnections; illegal connections | Company rescission of concession 1997; remunicipalisation 2001; compensation awarded by arbitration panel 2007 |

Table 1 (*cont.*)

| Water company | Country context | Project | Main focus of social conflict | Endpoint of social conflict |
|---|---|---|---|---|
| Suez (France) | South Africa | Management contract to deliver water to residents of Johannesburg; also strategies of corporatised public company in Durban | Introduction of pre-payment meters (Johannesburg); restriction of water services beyond the Free Basic Water limit for non-payment (Durban) | Non-renewal of management contract in 2005 |
| Thames (UK) and Vivendi (France) | New Zealand | Public–private partnership to manage delivery of Auckland water services | Increases in tariffs; disconnections; illegal connections | Amendment of Local Government Act to facilitate private sector participation in the municipal water sector |

One chapter is devoted to France (Chapter 2) and one to Bolivia (Chapter 3), as they represent core instances of the two principal competing governance models: managed liberalisation (France) and public participatory governance (Bolivia). Although both France and Bolivia have had a vitally important influence on the model in question, as stressed above, the images of governance emerging from those national settings are not straightforward extensions of national interests. Rather, the ideal-typical models I sketch are pulled, tugged and modified by actors from many different geographical settings and levels of governance. Chapters 4 and 5 explore the resulting complexities in two sets of paired case studies, each of which initially foregrounds regulation (Chapter 4) and rights (Chapter 5).

Chapter 4, comparing Argentina and Chile, highlights two countries that both created semi-independent regulatory agencies in the water sector, in accordance with predominant Latin American trends, but in strikingly different political cultures. Despite the adoption of a seemingly similar policy template, the much stronger emphasis on neoliberal conceptions of property and contract rights in Chile, combined with much more extensive mobilisation of consumer and human rights in Argentina, produced fascinating divergence in the resulting regulatory dynamics. Chapter 5, comparing New Zealand and South Africa, takes two cases where water service delivery policy is carried out primarily at the level of local government in the absence of any centralised regulatory agency, and where the human right to water, in very different ways, has shaped the clash between activists and local governments. It shows how less formal, quasi-judicial procedures at local levels can play an important role in channelling direct protest into sustained and more routine political leverage.

Chapter 6 returns to the case studies from a sectoral perspective, pulling together actor-related threads across the six settings with a particular focus on law. The chapter charts three images of the role that law has played in the case study narratives: law as a support structure for markets, law as a way of keeping open political space, and law as (ambiguously) constitutive of partnership. The three images co-exist across multiple levels of governance, and it is in their interplay that the specifics of transnational governance settlements can be found: settlements that are the focus of struggle not only in relation to water, but also in the context of other fundamental human needs in education, health, transport and communications. Chapter 1 provides the bridge between this more general aim and its grounding in the intricacies of the global water policy field. To this terrain I now move.

# Rights, regulation and disputing: a conflict-centred approach to transnational governance

## 1.1 Introduction

This chapter aims to elaborate an analytical framework that can integrate the dynamics of social protest into understandings of the transnational governance of a particular kind of social policy problem. These are issues of social policy provision that involve significant capital investment but also directly impact the basic needs of individuals, of which access to water is an example. Transnational governance is now the subject of an extensive literature, ranging through anthropology, law, sociology and politics. The different strands of literature have two observations in common: first, that forms of transnational governance, including substantive social policy initiatives in a transnational context, increasingly focus on rules and standards rather than, or in addition to, legally mandated redistributive settlements. Second, transnational governance is shaped as much by non-state actors as by national state interests.

This second commonality in the literature obscures an important double decentring – that of national states and national laws. Literature from politics and the world systems approach in sociology tends to focus on the decentring of states, expressed in a burgeoning interest in regulation, networks and norm transmission. Anthropological and more micro-sociological literature by contrast is more concerned with the decentring of law by extending long traditions of enquiry into legal pluralism into the transnational sphere. This double decentring is particularly challenging for (formal) law, given law's layered relationship with the state – both part of the state and independent from it. A socio-legal approach attuned to analysing the flows of money, ideas and practices that constitute transnational governance needs to be attuned but not tied to traditional conceptions of the state.

A small but growing field of socio-legal transnational governance does take seriously the partial nature of this double decentring. One strand, addressed more to audiences within politics and world systems sociology, explores how different understandings of law circulate between national and international levels of governance (Halliday and Oskinksy 2006). Another, located more in the anthropological literature, is more interested in the circulation of understandings of law between state and non-state actors, albeit across levels of governance (Merry 2003). This book is intended as a contribution to that literature, by means of an analytical framework that brings together rights and regulation as a lens for understanding the dynamics of transnational governance. Struggles over access to water provide the material for animating the framework.

Access to water, as explored in this book, is an area of social policy provision that involves significant capital investment, but also directly impacts on the basic needs of individuals. Such a combination, which can also arise with respect to education, health, transport or housing, can foster a combination of technocratic and populist patterns that can and often do collide, creating significant political turbulence and catalysing intractable disputes. All too often, academic literature in these areas tends to explore either the social activist dynamics or the technocratic regulatory dynamics but rarely brings them together. The benefit of bringing them together in one analysis is two-fold. First, it addresses a political and policy issue of real significance. On the one hand, the gulfs between these two worlds need bridging if stable policy trajectories are to emerge in these globalising areas of social policy. Alternatively, it may be just as important to make visible the depth of conflict at stake between these two worlds. In either situation, a common language for articulating the issues from both sets of perspectives is critical for productive debate.

Second, from a scholarly perspective, melding social activist and technocratic regulatory dynamics provides a framework for an interpretive socio-legal approach to governance that captures everyday micro-sociological dynamics without losing purchase on the structural dimensions of power and authority. A framework centred on rights and regulation is particularly apt for building this bridge. This is because both rights and regulation can be viewed either in terms of fluid social practices or as part of the formal apparatus of governing. As fluid social practices, rights are a powerful language in which to make moral claims, while regulation is an oft-demanded buffer against arbitrary fate or the pervasiveness of risk. As part of the formal apparatus of governing, states and international organisations routinely administer regulation, or define and enforce rights. Yet unlike direct executive administration, budget allocations or legislative control, rights and regulation are, as formal governance mechanisms, both partially insulated from political control, which may account for their particular ubiquity in fields of transnational governance. Rights and regulation, therefore, are both fertile sites for exploring the interdependency of formal institutionalisation and more tacit practice-shaped dynamics of transnational governance, an interdependency crucial to an appreciation of the character of that governance.

## 1.2    Rights and regulation

An analytical framework centred on rights and regulation has both formal and substantive advantages as an approach for studying the socio-legal politics of transnational governance. Substantively, the shifting political resonance of rights and regulation captures important contemporary political tensions around the limits of a market-centred political economy. Formally, rights and regulation capture notions of legality that are not necessarily tied to the state, making them peculiarly suitable tools for a decentred enquiry in a context of transnational governance. This allows, to an extent, rights and regulation to function as translation concepts from one geographical, political or cultural setting to another. I will elaborate on each of these points in more detail.

### 1.2.1    Shifting politics of rights and regulation

The political resonance of rights and regulation in policymaking discourses has shifted considerably in the past few decades. A staple consensus of the post-war welfare state in industrialised countries was, as Orly Lobel puts it, 'the divide between the administrative impulse to regulate the market and the adjudicative impulse to protect individual rights' (Lobel 2007: 23). This makes most sense when understood as a contingent claim made in the context of a basic commitment to Lockean liberalism and a free market, possibly tempered by an interventionist welfare state. Rights, in this context, are common law rights: contract and property rights classically protected by courts and invoked to restrain the state. Regulation is something the state does that interferes with such rights. This dichotomisation fits comfortably with the homilies, now markedly threadbare, of the deregulationist politics of 1980s neoliberalism and the 'Washington Consensus' on development. The evolution of neoliberalism and development policies in the 1990s has altered the resonance of both rights and regulation.

As Tickell and Peck argue (2003), in the 1990s neoliberalism entered a 'normalisation' phase when its earlier polemical deregulatory emphasis became more technocratic, managerial and active, particularly in managing the negative side-effects of earlier neoliberal policies. This led to a greater rhetorical stress on participatory politics and more engagement with anti-poverty agendas, while the detail of policy initiatives increasingly contained activist, even authoritarian, social and penal policy agendas. In this phase, regulation is actively compatible with the project of extending market and market-like arrangements across national borders – it becomes a strategy for facilitating individual choice and exchange, rather than directly promoting substantively defined collective goals.

Meanwhile rights, once bastions of individualisation, are now commonly invoked to make socio-economic and collective claims. Margaret Somers has recently argued (2008) that human rights has become the dominant mode of expressing human suffering and social injustice throughout the world, and that this makes building a sociology of rights a vital collective project, notwithstanding admitted obstacles both conceptual (philosophical normativity, abstract universalism, individualism) and sociological (racism in the US, cultural relativism, national sovereignty and the privileging of civil rights over socio-economic rights). The long-term agenda of supporters of social and economic rights, recently expressed as 'respect for and fulfillment of social and economic rights through development and poverty eradication' (ICHRP 2008: 86) is increasingly coterminous with the post-Washington Consensus in development and a 1990s neoliberalism that integrates social goals into its economic agendas. Of course there are also tensions between them: in particular, rights, when invoked to defend collective socio-economic claims, may well undermine contract and property claims, bringing the political resonance in the policymaking context full circle back to regulation: 'Social and economic rights can be viewed as the values that underpin the regulatory interventions of the 20th century ... as a modern way of expressing the collectivist values that were formerly described in the language of utility and welfare' (Collins 2007: 20).

The plural political resonance of rights and regulation leads to complex overlapping layers of debate, as can be illustrated by policy debates over the provision of access to safe drinking water. The idea of regulation might once have invoked mainly the administrative allocation of water resources by river basin agencies, or certain aspects of nationalised water service provision. Of late, it is more tightly associated with the spread of independent regulatory agencies in the context of privatisation: indeed, the most recent *Oxford Handbook of Public Policy* lists regulation only as a companion to privatisation, in a section discussing rationales of policy intervention (Scott 2006). From this perspective, regulation connotes a stable and predictable means for protecting the individual property and contract rights of private investors and for taming arbitrary state discretion. Rights, meanwhile, could refer to 'water rights' in the sense of tradable property entitlements to water resources, to contractual rights to water under long-term investment plans based on concession contracts, or, in the context of a human right to water, to a socio-economic and collective rights claim that is likely to be fleshed out by positive programmes of state intervention.

This last formulation of rights leads potentially to regulatory norms that establish minimum standards of provision – standards that may encroach upon existing contractual and property rights of the kind already specified. Indeed, Gesellschaft für Technische Zusammenarb (GTZ), the German development finance organisation, now frames its approach to embedding human rights into its approach to water service provision explicitly in regulatory terms:

> The raison d'etre of the human right to water is to facilitate access to sustainable and safe water services, especially for the poor and marginalised. What do we need for this to happen? ... We need institutions like an autonomous regulator who has the responsibility to protect consumers. We need instruments: guidelines, tariff negotiation procedures and publicly available benchmarks of water services (especially in relation to the human rights' criteria of availability, quality, access and affordability. In addition to transparency we also need enhanced participation and accountability [from] groups that represent the connected and the underserved, and [which] have the authority to negotiate with the service providers and provide feedback to the regulators ... By doing this, we move from a system of constant confrontation between consumers and state institutions to a situation of constructive dialogue. Instead of going to court to solve isolated cases, it is possible to scale up affordable quality service provision on the ground.
>
> (Levin and Kampf 2009)

Clearly, then, even within one policy domain, the political resonance of general terms such as 'regulatory strategies' or 'rights-based approaches' can be unclear. Consequently it is important when framing transnational governance debates in terms of rights and regulation to clarify the political stakes attached to different specific forms of both rights and regulation. This can only be done in a contextually specific way, and hence lends itself to drawing upon socio-legal (rather than economic, legal-doctrinal or philosophical) approaches to rights and regulation. The advantage of such approaches goes beyond their attunement to specific micro-level empirical settings. Analytically they can incorporate a broad spectrum of linkage to state institutions, ranging from weak to strong. This makes them peculiarly suitable for a decentred enquiry into transnational forms of legality.

### 1.2.2 Decentred transnational legality

Domestic-level socio-legal literature on regulation has long focused on non-legal forms of control, and has also paid sustained attention to the crucial roles of non-state actors, giving rise to lively debates around collaborative governance (Freeman 2000), responsive regulation (Ayres and Braithwaite 1992), democratic experimentalism (Dorf and Sabel 1998) and post-regulatory law (Teubner 1983). More recently, Braithwaite and Drahos (2005) extended these foci to global business regulation, arguing that the rise of the 'new regulatory state' in a transnational context has conferred great power on self-regulatory organisations, as well as on the Organisation for Economic Co-operation and Development (OECD), which build and support epistemic communities for regulatory change. In this fluid context, they argue, regulation emerges from 'contests of principles' that are deployed principally by non-state actors in webs of dialogue that build models of regulation, both from bottom-up shifts in practice and top-down elaborations of agreed-upon principles. Although more coercive mechanisms than dialogue-based modelling are given sway in Braithwaite and Drahos's approach,[1] theirs is predominantly a world of discursively built consensus and negotiated settlements. The state exists as a background coercive shadow useful for breaking negotiation bottlenecks and correcting implementation deficits. Not only the state, but also 'law' in a formal technical sense is decentred – key political conflicts are not over specific technical rules but over open-ended principles, non-legal codifications of core competing values that are weighed and balanced against each other in the webs of dialogue.

Socio-legal rights scholarship, like that on regulation, is sensitive to micro-political empirical contexts but also steps away from both state and law. Somers points to rights scholarship that traces 'the social practices through which claims are fought for and institutionalised' (Somers 2009: 409) as a productive way of avoiding both the 'foundationalism that

---

[1] Namely, military coercion, economic coercion, capacity-building, and systems of reward, all of which also matter for Braithwaite and Drahos (and have all been important in the global water policy field).

searches for nonempirical, philosophical origins of rights and a strict legal positivist perspective in which rights are merely "entitlements recognised in law" ' (Somers 2009: 409). Approaches from legal anthropology, legal consciousness and social movements are, she argues, particularly well suited to this. De Sousa Santos and Rodriguez-Garavito (2005: 2) reject the conventional focus of accounts of global legal transformations on 'top-down processes of diffusion of economic and legal models from the global North to the global South', which inherently tends towards highlighting the roles of states and formal international organisations. They argue instead in favour of a conception of 'subaltern cosmopolitan legality' that foregrounds the political agency of the most disadvantaged groups in the global economy. This agency is, they insist, embedded not only in sustained political mobilisation but also in 'new notions of rights that go beyond the liberal ideal of individual autonomy, and incorporate solidaristic understandings of entitlements grounded on alternative forms of legal knowledge'. Law and rights, they argue, are 'elements of struggles that need to be politicised before they are legalised' (De Sousa Santos and Rodriguez-Garavito 2005: 16).

A notable feature of these decentred concepts of rights and regulation is that rights-based or regulatory initiatives that act as pathways for the emergence of transnational legality have a troubled relationship with democratically controlled institutions. Regulatory initiatives in a transnational setting that lacks any landscape of institutionalised representative democracy can easily become highly technocratic, magnifying the inherently non-majoritarian nature of regulation as a technique of domestic governance. Conversely, rights-based activism in an analogous context can tend towards a form of hyper-majoritarianism, slipping into a populism that resists institutionalisation or routinisation of any kind. These two trajectories, technocratic and populist, can and often do collide in particular policy areas, creating significant political turbulence and catalysing intractable disputes.

### 1.2.3   Combining two triads

The essence of my argument is that rights and regulation form overlapping and complementary aspects of processes of disputing and rule-elaboration that can be captured by two well-known triads in socio-legal studies – 'naming, blaming and claiming' (Felstiner *et al.* 1981) and 'rule-making, monitoring and enforcement'. Rather than two distinct and sometimes incompatible sets of practices, I suggest there is a powerful, albeit varying, interdependency between rights and regulation. Fresh insights can be gained by encouraging more work in regulatory scholarship on 'naming, claiming and blaming', and more work in rights scholarship on 'rulemaking, monitoring and implementation'. In particular, we can ask: how does an understanding of regulatory dynamics inform the process of institutionalising the rights-based activism of social movements? And, conversely, how can transnational regulatory policies better incorporate the sense of a compelling collective moral vision that so often energises 'rights' talk?

Viewing rights and regulation as part of broader patterns of disputing involves a focus upon them as *social practices* articulating generalised claims upon the social order. It is a perspective that acknowledges the irreducible inevitability of conflict in building governance institutions. These generalised claims upon the social order may or may not have specific legal implications, but rather constitute at most a call – sometimes an implicit one – for some kind of institutionalised response. Felstiner *et al.*'s triad captures the importance of the set of social practices that precedes the formal articulation of a grievance. 'Naming' refers to the articulation of a felt injury, 'blaming' to the identification of a specific actor, process or institution that is felt to be responsible for the injury, and 'claiming' to the explicit request for a remedy from the actor or institution identified as having wrongly caused the perceived injury. Claiming as a separate stage highlights the fact that attribution of responsibility in formal legal terms is a distinctive step in itself.

In the original work on disputing, these three steps are essentially cognitive steps experienced by individuals in the process leading up to bilateral disputes. Their use here translates the sequence into a different context: that of activist groups, political constituencies and social policy claims. The changed context makes it possible to inject both agency and conflict into understandings of changing governance patterns, which are too often portrayed as a set of functionally driven institutional reforms. However, the institutional context is more naturally implicated when the second triad is invoked. For once groups and actors enter a dispute in a field of global social policy over a particular issue, the resolution of that issue at a systemic level engages a second triad: that of rulemaking, monitoring and enforcement. This triad is often closely associated with regulatory trajectories (Black 2005; Murray and Scott 2002),[2] and there

---

[2] Black refers to standard-setting, information-gathering and behaviour-modification. Murray and Scott (2002: 502) argue that three components are common to a wide range of

is a relatively easy link made between 'naming, blaming and claiming' processes and the articulation of rights-based claims. However, I argue that both triads have an equal and combined applicability to both rights and regulation.

From the combined perspective, social responses to struggles over access to water in a context of global governance emerge through the lens of a roughly chronological six-fold process (naming, blaming, claiming, rulemaking, monitoring and enforcing). This process allows us to see regulation and rights as species of a common genre, rather than as distinctive sets of practices. The formal articulation of a claim after a process of 'naming and blaming' could emerge either as a rights claim or as a demand for regulation. And the systemic resolution of the problem underlying specific disputes will engage rulemaking, monitoring and enforcement, whether the claim is a rights-based one or embedded in regulation. True, this move depends to a certain degree on a rather functional understanding of these social practices, one that uses arguably unfamiliar terminology to describe empirical phenomena that we are used to speaking of much more contextually. It appears to strip away a historical and contextual sense of the specificity of rights claims or the emergence of regulatory regimes. But this stripping is an analytical move that distances us from taken-for-granted assumptions regarding relationships between state and non-state institutions, as well as between local, national and international dimensions of governance.

The approach has two advantages. First, it allows us to analyse law and development without any embedded reliance on neat images of nested, vertical 'levels' of governance. Rather, both rights and regulation are increasingly institutionalised in ways that cut across state institutions. This creates interpretive communities whose capacity to govern legal and social change rests less on the lines of accountability connecting them to electoral or other nationally based accountability systems, and more in their shared epistemic and moral commitments to particular forms of naming, claiming, blaming, rulemaking, monitoring and enforcement. Second, the framework makes it possible to explore, *with the same analytic tools*, both the normative internalisation and the formal institutionalisation of transnational governance without falling into the trap of seeing 'local culture' as the normative lifeblood of cold, technical

'regulatory modalities': a goal, standard, rule or norm to which the system refers; a mechanism for monitoring or feeding back information about performance; and a mechanism for realigning the system when its operation deviates from its intended goal.

transnational pressures. When regulation orders a field of activity, we can explore whether 'naming/blaming/claiming' processes can animate 'rulemaking/monitoring/enforcement' processes as a way of internalising normativity, or whether they expose the exclusory dimensions of such processes. When rights strategies challenge and re-map social relations, the study of rulemaking/monitoring/enforcement processes can shed light on how routinisation can institutionalise the gains – or co-opt the political energies of those who mobilised to 'name and claim'.

In short, the approach argued for here allows social and legal perspectives on transnational governance to be held in productive tension, which in turn allows regulation to acquire normative life (whether by confronting challenge or internalisation), and rights to be productively routinised (whether by technocratic means or by fostering new social and political spaces for community-building). In the next section, I illustrate the application of the two triads, using a simplified and stylised illustration of competing models for governing struggles over access to water.

## 1.3   Competition for the rules

This section will sketch stylised accounts of managed liberalisation and public participatory governance, each elaborated through strands of rights and regulation, and drawing on brief examples from the case studies elaborated in this book. The aim is to link the sketch of the transnational dimensions of the global water policy field from the Introduction to selected aspects of the local and national trajectories that future chapters will explore in detail. Juxtaposing two stylised accounts will help to guide the reader through future chapters, as the more detailed accounts in those chapters highlight the variability, contingency and multiple layers that characterise the applicability of each model in real-world contexts.

The fate of the social is decided through competition for the rules. Institutions and rules compete to establish a legitimate transnational public sphere for the governance of water. This sphere is shaped by a mix of regulation and rights that are sites for political struggles over the commodification of water. *Rights* affecting access to basic water services increasingly operate at a transnational level, even in formal terms. As the descriptive sketch of the global water policy field in the Introduction showed, there is a strong tension between the property and contract rights protected by international legal trade and investment regimes, and socio-economic rights laws protected by human rights institutions. Even though formally speaking a legal socio-economic 'human right to water' is still relatively incipient, transnational networks increasingly draw on this claim as a rights-based one that advances their political struggles in the global debate over access to water.

While rights frame the basic value conflicts of the global water policy field, the detailed operational reality of water service provision is shaped by sector-specific services *regulation*. Here the status quo state-centred political control is under pressure in many countries to shift to an arm's-length regulatory regime (at the extreme involving an independent agency). While the formal structure of regulation remains resolutely national, its content and orientation are powerfully influenced by transnational flows of money and ideas. International financial institutions have, using these flows, strongly promoted an essentially transactional model of regulation, one that facilitates major transactions (such as long-term concession contracts) between government and private provider as the key focus of regulation. This approach leaves the relationship between private providers and individual citizens largely within the purview of managerial discretion, although at national level labour and consumer groups have been able to influence selected aspects of regulatory regimes, primarily in relation to participation and grievance mechanisms. As noted in the Introduction, however, although a 'one-size-fits-all' regulatory model influenced by economic theory and Anglo-American practice initially dominated, regulatory approaches to water service provision advocated in the transnational field have recently become more pluralistic, reflecting a degree of experimental learning responding to specific aspects of developing country contexts (such as the importance of small-scale informal water provision).

Thus far, I have reinvoked the picture of the global water policy field sketched in the Introduction by linking rights to value conflicts and regulation to detailed operational management. If value conflicts are elaborated in terms of 'naming, blaming, and claiming' and detailed operational management in terms of 'rulemaking, monitoring and enforcement', models of water services governance can be sketched by interweaving the two triads. By this I mean that a model of governance is built up by cross-linking the triads: 'naming' practices are linked to 'rulemaking' practices, 'blaming' to 'monitoring', and 'claiming' to 'enforcement'. This cross-linking shows the relevance of rights and regulation across both triads. In the rest of this section I will sketch the two models that, at the time of the research explored in future chapters, polarised the global water policy field: managed liberalisation and public participatory governance. The detailed case studies, and particularly the cumulative cross-national effects of the case studies, show that the conflict and polarisation suggested by these dichotomous models have mutated into a more nuanced debate over more layered, hybrid responses to the problem of access to water. But painting the initial landscape in polarised terms helps to illuminate the complex mix of rights and regulation that characterise these more recent hybrid responses, and to clarify the deep political divides that continue to haunt these complexities.

### 1.3.1  *Managed liberalisation*

Naming and rulemaking

At the heart of managed liberalisation is a naming of the 'problem' of access to water as one of scarcity understood in terms of commodity value. Water is scarce, water costs money to provide, water should be understood as a precious commodity: this was the core framing value articulated in a number of global fora that emerged in the 1990s as important sites in the global water policy field. These fora, discussed in more detail in the Introduction and in Chapter 2, were dominated by non-state actors such as the World Water Council and private sector water providers who were expanding their operations across borders. The notion of water as a scarce commodity was also endorsed by states in the 1992 Dublin Statement (International Conference on Water and the Environment 1992), albeit accompanied by additional core principles relating to the importance of participatory approaches in water development and management, the importance of the role of women, and the status of water as a finite, essential and vulnerable resource. The mixed agenda of principles in the intergovernmental arena is typical of an attempt to balance multiple pressures from constituent interests: as we shall see in the next section, gender and participation are highly salient to the public participatory model. But for non-state actors the centrality of the notion of 'scarce commodity' in the naming of the problem of access to water was clear.

Articulating this emphasis as a cognitive transformation along a pathway of disputing highlights the contentious nature of what was involved in this process of naming. For water, often more 'naturally' seen as a fundamental need insulated from the structures of commodity frameworks, significant work had to be done to reframe its salience in terms of a scarce commodity (Mehta 2008). This was not only done through incremental communicative persuasion: there was also a certain amount of hostility expressed towards alternative conceptions of water that drew more on affective, religious or cultural values. As the director of one of the major multinational water companies was often quoted as saying, trying to make the point with a certain levity: 'Water may be a gift from God but he forgot to lay the pipes' (CBC Canada 2004).[3] In this sense, when the naming of water as a 'scarce commodity' is experienced or conceived as an injury, it brings to the foreground the ways in which the work of naming was political and intended to reframe social relations.

Beyond communicative persuasion and rhetorical conflicts, significant rule making reforms were an important part of according institutional flesh to the naming process. At its core, this involved the instantiation of cost-recovery frameworks and the protection and promotion of contract and property rights. For example, cost-recovery was a crucial dimension of the contractual rights at the centre of long-term concessions granted to private water service operators in the case studies in Bolivia, Argentina and France (Chapters 2, 3 and 4). Moreover, illustrating the point made in the Introduction that declining private sector involvement does not of itself reduce the salience of this emerging contention, rules that ensured cost-recovery were just as important in the processes of commercialising public service water operators that characterised Chile in the 1990s (Chapter 4), New Zealand and South Africa (Chapter 5).

Contractual responsibilities to pay for water, often enforced by local municipal government, were also rulemaking dimensions central to the protestors who staged mass payment boycotts in Argentina, South Africa and New Zealand (Chapters 4 and 5), as were the property rights of private sector investors protected by international investor–state treaty frameworks and recourse to arbitration, which emerged as important aspects of the case studies in Bolivia (Chapter 2) and Argentina (Chapter 4). Overall, rules that gave institutional flesh to the vision of water as a scarce commodity existed at multiple levels of governance, from international (investor–state treaties), to transnational (cross-border contracts), to national (regulatory frameworks supporting cost-recovery) and local (enforcement of debt collection).

## Blaming and monitoring

Once water was named as a scarce commodity, links were then made to a 'blaming' process in order to create political space for the rulemaking goals

---

[3] This quote is taken from a transcript of an interview with Antoine Frerot, then Managing Director of the Water Division of Veolia Environnement, from the CBC Canada documentary *Dead in the Water* (2004).

alluded to above. For managed liberalisation, the 'blaming' processes targeted arbitrary political discretion allied to state control and the inefficiencies of public ownership as the key barriers to reframing access to water services as a problem involving a scarce commodity. In Bolivia (Chapter 3), Chile and Argentina (Chapter 4) this form of blaming was part of an economy-wide drive towards privatisation that usually reformed water in the wake of earlier infrastructure reforms to gas, electricity and transport. In New Zealand a prominent strand of critique levelled by business actors at the water service delivery policy framework was precisely that it had remained untouched by the neoliberal reforms of the 1980s that had privatised so much other critical infrastructure in New Zealand. This relative immunity of the water sector reflects the greater space for a public participatory model. In South Africa too, the blaming critique was much more muted, reflecting the overall greater commitment to a public participatory model nationally, mixed with exposure to pressures from transnational actors to experiment with private sector involvement.

In France, interestingly, there was relatively little of either the naming or the blaming processes, yet the concomitant rulemaking and monitoring mechanisms of managed liberalisation were well developed. This illustrates the powerful role of France in generating aspects of this model in the first place, as discussed in Chapter 2, and the long-established historical role of the private sector in water service delivery within France. It also shows how the process of diffusing that model across borders requires considerably more explicit rationalisation than does the incremental evolution of governance domestically, at least from the 'bird's-eye' view of comparative transnational developments taken in this chapter. Conflict still subsists domestically, of course, as we shall see in the detailed chapter on France (Chapter 2).

A palpable sense of anger and entitlement often accompanied these blaming narratives, though it could be driven by quite contrasting motives. For international financial institutions, it was often expressed as public-spirited frustration at the perceived inefficiencies of local governmental control, while transnational private companies might be more obviously motivated by self-interest in securing greater market access for their cross-border expansion. International financial institutions were especially involved in linking this blaming rhetoric, however implicitly, to processes of monitoring. Primarily through their capacity to impose conditions on the loans made to improve access to water, they designed mechanisms to 'monitor' the rulemaking push towards cost-recovery and reliance on private property and contract rights. Transnational financial conditionality is, however, by no means the whole story. The rulemaking reforms referred to above included the introduction of monitoring mechanisms at national level, particularly through regulatory agencies. The pictorial representation in Figures 1 and 2 is drawn from a World Bank paper on regulation in Latin American water services (Foster 2005) and shows how a regulatory agency is envisaged as a monitoring cure for the perceived injuries wrought by clientelist politics. The 'reformed' model of regulation (an ideal-type transactional view in my argument) seeks to eliminate 'dole handouts and partisan loans'. The vision is one of purifying clientelism: politicians become policymakers giving strategic guidance; the creation of a regulatory agency replaces political favours with a focus on technical decisions about quality and price, introduces competition and improves cost-recovery and labour efficiency. As a consequence, the unconnected are drawn into the circle of connection (see Figures 1 and 2).

It is important to stress that, as all the case studies demonstrate, there were powerful sections of national political elites who supported these trends, and who participated in the projects to design monitoring institutions. This typically led to significant internal conflict within states, often between departments of treasury, the economy or business who supported managed liberalisation, and departments of public works or the environment, who resisted the changes that resulted. Sometimes the conflict was ideological in nature: this was more common when national elites supporting managed liberalisation did so in the context of having been extensively trained and professionally acculturated in transnational epistemic communities supporting this approach, as in the example of the 'Chicago boys' in Chile (Chapter 4) or in the fractions of the New Zealand state that supported privatisation as a general policy option (Chapter 5). But national political support may not necessarily internalise the 'naming and blaming' process: some elites may support reforms simply because they cohere with their short-term interests and prospects of electoral success, as was arguably the case in Bolivia and Argentina (Chapters 3 and 4). Reform may also suit other kinds of internal conflicts such as those between central and local authorities: this was likely an important factor in both Argentina, where regulatory agencies were effectively imposed by fiat via federal reforms (Chapter 4), and in France where, in the absence of regulatory agencies, model contracts imposed by the central state performed an important monitoring function for private sector involvement, at least until the 1980s. In short, the managed liberalisation model should not be viewed as simplistically imposed by the North upon the South, nor simply by powerful transnational interests upon domestic national settings.

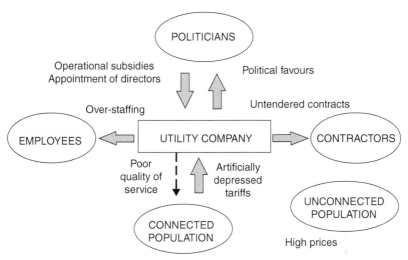

**Figure 1** 'Clientelist' model of governance framework for water service delivery
Source: Adapted from Foster (Foster 2005).

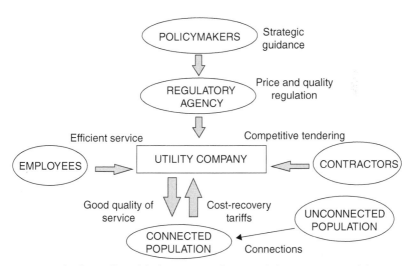

**Figure 2** 'Reformed' model of governance framework for water service delivery
Source: Adapted from Foster (Foster 2005).

## Claiming and enforcing

The last paired interweaving of the two triads relates to the processes of 'claiming' and 'enforcing'. The core claim that is made in managed liberalisation is one that instantiates a vision of water as a scarce commodity in need of protection, but threatened by clientelist political control and inefficient state delivery. The solution to the threat, framed in this way, is depoliticisation. The organisations and groups that have promoted managed liberalisation consistently call for independence and neutral expertise to dominate the governance of water service delivery. From a variety of different perspectives, they urge that access to water be depoliticised and managed as a technocratic problem, albeit one of great social urgency. This claim often takes the form, particularly in the policy papers produced at the World Water Forum, that 'governance' provides the appropriate solution to managing access to water: governance defined in ways that prioritise the role of non-state actors and dilute the capacity of political actors to shape crucial decisions.

Clearly, such a claim is very diffuse, and arguably not distinct from the common strategic move made by any hegemonic discourse to naturalise the inherently political nature of its claims. For the purposes of fleshing out a model of governance, the more formal institutional terms of 'enforcement' from the second triad are of crucial importance. For international financial institutions and national governments in the Latin American case studies, enforcement often occurred through the medium of independent regulatory agencies. Interestingly, in the case studies where there was greater penetration of loan conditionality by international financial institutions (Argentina and Bolivia), transnational arbitration was an additional vital enforcement tool for imposing a managed liberalisation model of governance – although, as Chapter 3 will explore, unsuccessfully in the long run in Bolivia. Chile's reliance on a regulatory agency for enforcement was not paired with the salience of transnational arbitration, reflecting the fact that its genesis was much less shaped by external transnational pressures than in Bolivia and Argentina.

Countries more reliant on local government for the delivery of water services (South Africa, New Zealand and France) in general retained more political control over the detailed operational implementation of managing water as a scarce commodity. In South Africa and New Zealand (Chapter 5), where regulatory agencies were not established for water, enforcement of managed liberalisation was not strongly embedded, reflecting their limited efforts to insulate their water policy frameworks from the penetration of managed liberalisation. For France, this apparent contradiction, given its broad support for all other aspects of the model, related to the expansionist vision of the country in diffusing a 'French' model of water management across national borders, as explored in Chapter 2. The greater the space for local political control of water services, the more visible is the inherently political and conflictual environment that exists internally within managed liberalisation – conflicts that point towards aspects of the competing model discussed in the next section.

The stylised account of managed liberalisation given here makes clear that both the ideological and ethical commitments animating 'naming, blaming and claiming' and the formal institutional flesh secured by rule-making, monitoring and enforcement draw on tenets and techniques familiar from the broader policy trends of the Washington Consensus. The detailed case studies in Chapters 2–5 illustrate how national political elites and domestic political dynamics shape the particular combinations of rights and regulation that emerged in variations of managed liberalisation. But just as managed liberalisation emerged from coalitions that cross levels of governance, so too did the competing model that stimulates political conflicts over access to water.

### 1.3.2   Public participatory governance

I have called this competing model public participatory governance in full cognisance of the ambiguous implications of the word 'public', which can signal either governmental involvement or refer to more direct participation of the citizenry. On the one hand, the link between 'public' and 'state' refers to the undeniable fact that national state management of administration remains a powerful default model, not least in the empirical sense that some 95 per cent of the world's networked water services are still delivered by state or local governments. From an ideological perspective, there is also still a significant attachment to the importance of state responsibility in relation to a basic essential need such as water.

However, ideological emphases on the importance of state responsibility for basic services include a significant emphasis on the more participatory implications of the notion of 'public'. This resonance is often in tension with notions of state control, particularly given the practical realities of the downsides of national state control, which include clientelism, remoteness from everyday needs, and a failure to connect unserved populations. Governmental failures certainly persist even – perhaps particularly – in the countries where the most intractable disputes over water service delivery reforms have emerged. Resistance to the harsh redistributive impacts of private sector participation and anxieties over its implications for natural resource sovereignty thus generated a deeply ambiguous call for the return of 'public' control. As we shall see in elaborating this model through the interlinked triads, the naming, blaming and claiming triad can, up to a point, bridge the implicit tensions inherent in the notion of 'public'. However, the ambiguity emerges strongly in the rulemaking, monitoring and enforcement triad.

## Naming and rulemaking

For the public participatory model, a variety of disparate approaches to naming the problem of access to safe water have coalesced around a common sentiment: the avowal of water as a crucial basic necessity, a fundamental human right that should be accessible by all on universal and equitable terms. This form of naming tends to dominate debates at the transnational level but arguably emerged as a way of uniting the range of disparate approaches embedded in different national and local contexts as explored in the case study chapters. These disparate approaches ranged from a visceral sense of water as territory located in long-standing indigenous 'uses and customs' (explored in Chapter 3 in relation to Bolivia), to claims for equal access to water as a crucial constituent of a new democratic constitution (in South Africa, Chapter 5), to arguments that water is a 'prime necessity' under the common law (in New Zealand, Chapter 5).

There is an inherent tension in suggesting that the broad array of different conceptualisations of water referred to above can be encapsulated by a single generic notion of water as a human right, particularly given the very disparate local historical, political and cultural worldviews held by actors in the various case studies. While local actors may not have used the language of human rights in the context of particular disputes, the language often appears as a framing device in post hoc accounts of these same disputes, particularly when circulated by NGOs and activists in the context of debates in the global water policy field. This could be viewed as a counter-effort to the persistent portrayal of water as a scarce commodity: an effort to find a common term that would pose a clear contrast to this contested conception. The simplification and even suppression of local variety was, from this perspective, part of what has been called 'the continual discursive boundary work necessary to … preserve the privileged status of particular resource definitions in the face of alternative claims' (Bakker and Bridge 2006: 226).

The underlying diversity of the various conceptions of water that compete with its status as scarce commodity was, however, well reflected in the broad range of rulemaking projects that emerged through the lens of the case studies as the institutional flesh of this naming process. Some of these rulemaking projects did focus specifically on institutionalising water as a human right, both at the international level (General Comment 15 issued in November 2002 by the United Nations Committee on Economic, Social and Cultural Human Rights) and nationally (as in the South African constitution of 1995, or in French statute law in 2000). In 2009 Bolivia too moved towards the constitutional protection of water as a human right, but led up to this with a very different approach that aimed to reconfigure the broad macro-political economy of governing water. As explored in more detail in Chapter 3, this involved a combination of enacting a new water rights law at national level, instantiating community-based governance through 'social control' of the remunicipalised Cochabamba water services operator, and withdrawing from international investor–state treaty frameworks. More pragmatic 'bricolage' approaches to rulemaking also existed, sitting somewhere between this specific rights-based approach and broader political economy approaches to rulemaking. In New Zealand (Chapter 5), activists relied on a patchwork of legal claims in administrative law, consumer law, commercial law and electoral law, while in Tucumán, Argentina (Chapter 4) a mix of regulatory rulings, small claims activity and legislative amendments sought to institutionalise a vision of water as a crucial basic necessity accessible to all on universal and equitable terms.

## Blaming and monitoring

The 'blaming' axis of the public participatory model was most clearly visible in hostility to the private sector involvement in the delivery of water services. Although, as noted earlier, the contours of the broad debate in the global water policy field have become increasingly less polarised in the sense of pitting public provision directly against private provision, hostility to the commercialisation of publicly delivered services remains undimmed, as we see particularly in the South Africa and New Zealand cases (Chapter 5).

This hostility was caused by a wide range of reasons, from ideological opposition to governing a basic fundamental need by reference to the profit motive to concerns about the harsh redistributive impacts of private sector participation and anxieties over its implications for natural resource sovereignty. Activists and social movements expressed this hostility in all the case studies, with the greatest depth and breadth of hostility occurring in Bolivia (Chapter 3), and the least in Chile (Chapter 4). To varying extents, other key actors shared the hostility: most often these were legislators, but some local governments (in France, South Africa and New Zealand) and even regulators (in Tucumán, Argentina) shared the hostility.

Interestingly, two different types of pathways developed for 'monitoring' this blaming process: a legalised pathway and a pathway through electoral politics. The ambiguity inherent in the notion of 'public' is reflected in the contrast between these two pathways. The legalised pathway seeks to pressure the *existing* governmental authorities to implement more effectively the various rulemaking structures noted above which help to institutionalise water as a crucial basic need and fundamental human right. Electoral politics, by contrast, consists of the citizenry seeking to intervene directly to *replace* current state structures in order to pursue those aims.

Several of the case studies show how the introduction of the managed liberalisation model led to electoral backlash and an alteration of the rules governing water service delivery. For example, in two cases the disputing dynamics triggered the success of a new political coalition at local government level along with a change of rules. In Grenoble in France (Chapter 2), the remunicipalisation of water service delivery occurred,[4] and in Auckland in New Zealand (Chapter 5), local government rules governing procurement were amended. In Bolivia (Chapter 3), the struggle over access to water infused electoral politics into the governing board structure of the newly remunicipalised water company for the first time, also indirectly contributing to the election of Evo Morales, Bolivia's first indigenous president, who was directly involved in the 'water wars'.

An example of the contrasting legalised pathway for monitoring is the reporting system used by the UN Committee on Economic, Cultural and Social Rights, where states are required to report to the Committee on progress made against the standards of the General Comment, notwithstanding its uncertain status legally within the UN system (OHCR n.d.(a)); UNCESCR 2002). Not quite as legal, but still invoking the underlying logic of legality in seeking objective recommendations from an arm's-length 'expert' third party, is the commissioning by the UN Council on Human Rights of an Independent Expert to provide a study on the implementation of the right to drinking water and sanitation (HRC 2008).[5]

---

[4] See, more broadly, Corporate Europe Observatory and Transnational Institute (2010).
[5] Human Rights Council Resolution A/HRC/7/L.16 appointed Catarina de Albuquerque from November 2008.

Other possibilities also exist at the national level, such as the tentative monitoring of progress on access to water and sanitation undertaken by the South African Human Rights Commission (Chapter 5), and at the local/provincial level, such as the use of the legal *amparo* action by the Tucumán Ombudsman explored in Chapter 5.

### Claiming and enforcing

Dual pathways of legalised and political approaches also characterise the final linkages between the triads, which is the link between processes of claiming and enforcing. Strikingly, the legalised pathway for enforcing a public participatory model of governance effectively conflates claiming and enforcement, particularly in relation to monitoring strategies that rely directly on litigation. Litigation is a salient tool in a wide range of the case studies (New Zealand, South Africa, France and Argentina), primarily relying on public-law embedded rights at the national level. The results, as explored in Chapters 2, 4 and 5, are only ambiguous successes for the public.

The political pathway for articulating the claim that access to water should be protected as a basic human right emerged most vividly in mass direct action. This was especially significant in South Africa, Bolivia and Argentina, sometimes coupled with civil disobedience actions such as illegal reconnections to the network and payment boycotts. Mass direct action embodies an urgent form of claiming that is temporarily self-enforcing: at its most intense, as for example in the riots provoked in response to the private sector concession contract in Cochabamba, Bolivia, it forces a response from those in power (in this case the cancellation of the contract). As the case study chapters explore, however, this particular political strategy for claiming the right to instantiate the vision of water underpinning public participatory governance does not easily generate any routinised ongoing sense of enforcement. This comes, instead, from complex feedback effects between the two models, discussed briefly in the final section of this chapter.

Overall, the two pathways, legalised and political, that develop in the interstice of the linked triads constituting public participatory governance, pull in different directions. This means that, on the one hand, the model opens up directly to politics much more explicitly than the managed liberalisation model. That model, as discussed in the previous section, places a high premium on apoliticism and independence from politics. Although recent work on Latin America has shown the ongoing salience of politics even within managed liberalisation responses (Murillo

2009), the public participatory model explicitly seeks, and celebrates, the re-opening of political space that its interwoven techniques seek to achieve. Yet the legalised pathways it relies on, while they sometimes keep open that political space, also often lead back to a hybrid dependence on managed liberalisation. Chapter 6 explores this issue in more detail from a cross-case sector perspective: in the meantime the interweaving of the two triads used to illustrate competing models is illustrated in summary form in Tables 2 and 3.

Table 2 *Managed liberalisation*

---
---

*Naming* – Water is scarce! Water costs money! Water is a precious commodity!
　　　　*Rulemaking* – cost recovery, property and contract rights
*Blaming* – Out with government interference!
　　　　*Monitoring* – regulation via loan conditionality
*Claiming* – We need independent, expert input
　　　　*Enforcement* – independent regulatory agency, enforcement of
　　　　property rights by international arbitration

---
---

Table 3 *Participatory public governance*

---
---

*Naming* – Water is life! Access to all! Water is a human right!
　　　　*Rulemaking* – UN General Comment 15, community governance,
　　　　retreat to nationalist protectionism
*Blaming* – Out with the large-scale commercial private sector!
　　　　*Monitoring* – UN reporting system, elections
*Claiming* – Let's go onto the street! Or go to court!
　　　　*Enforcement* – Optional Protocol to UN International Covenant on
　　　　Economic, Social and Cultural Rights, constitutional litigation

---
---

### 1.3.3    Moving away from nested governance: feedback loops and hybridity

The two triads are linked along two different dimensions: temporal and ontological. Temporally, 'naming, blaming and claiming' could be viewed as the sequence of tacit practice-shaped dynamics that precedes a sequence of formal institutionalisation through rulemaking, monitoring and enforcement. Looked at in this way, the first advantage of this framework emerges: it allows us to analyse law and development without any embedded reliance on neat images of nested, vertical 'levels' of governance. Rather, both rights and regulation are increasingly institutionalised in ways that cut across state institutions. The economic experts who staff independent regulatory agencies, the activists who organise mass payment boycotts and illegal reconnections, the consultants who design regulatory policy frameworks funded by heavily conditioned loans – all these are examples of the horizontal interpretive communities created by the intersection of rights and regulation in the global water policy field.

This capacity of these interpretive communities to govern legal and social change rests less on the lines of accountability connecting them to electoral or other nationally based accountability systems, and more in their shared epistemic and moral commitments to particular forms of naming, claiming, blaming, rulemaking, monitoring and enforcement. This creates a form of governing that is curiously insulated from democratic accountability, even when reporting lines to democratic institutions exist. This is because productive governing work done by these communities, particularly at the micro level of implementation, proceeds only on the community's own terms. When an issue becomes visible in the discourse of that interpretive community, only then are resources and power devoted to it. Combined with the functional specialisation which tends to characterise transnational policy fields, transnational governance is, even at its most political, in a sense almost forced to operate at one step removed, through the expert discourses of the different functional groups in the policy network. The fact that the public participatory model of governance deliberately creates more openings to politics, yet struggles with implementation issues related to monitoring and enforcement, is consistent with this, as is the fact that public participatory governance is much less institutionalised than managed liberalisation at the transnational level.

The temporal relationship between the two triads sketched above helps to describe how a transnational policy field challenges notions of nested, vertical levels of governance. But this is only necessary, and not sufficient, to understand how transnational governance in a particular policy field works, for the temporal angle on the two triads belies the fact that formal institutionalisation and tacit practice are in fact mutually constitutive. Without both, the policy field would not exist. Without a felt sense of the social ethics that animate the naming, blaming and claiming process, rules are unlikely to be elaborated, monitored and enforced with any efficacy. Conversely, at least in transnational settings where strangers must coordinate over significant distances, without the techniques and mechanisms afforded by rulemaking, monitoring and enforcement, the energy of naming, blaming and claiming is likely to dissipate. In short, rights and regulation provide a bridge for Conca's call to make what he describes as a critically important move: the move from studying 'movements, actors, networks, and relationships' to 'embedded, enduring sets of roles and rules that give shape and form to a whole array of struggles over time' (Conca 2005: 24). In the context of law and development, this move reinjects agency into what is all too often an overly structural account of legal transfer. The capacity to move productively between agency and structure is given specificity and purchase by viewing rights and regulation through the lens of the two triads: 'naming, blaming and claiming' and 'rulemaking, monitoring, enforcement'.

In exploring this mutually constitutive relationship, it is easy but misleading to view transnational governance in terms of cold, technical transnational pressures that acquire their normative lifeblood from 'local culture'. Rather, the mutually constitutive relationship between the two triads leads to feedback effects. In the context of competing models such as managed liberalisation and public participatory governance, this creates complex hybrids that display a curious mix of political compromise (on the substantive policy issues that are in dispute) and epistemic closure (on the terms in which those policy issues are acknowledged and their solutions diagnosed). Let me explain briefly what I mean by this mix of political compromise and epistemic closure.

A persistent thread that emerges through the case studies is that water's status as a basic necessity and fundamental human right for which public collective responsibility must be taken *does* feed back into the managed liberalisation model. But it is accommodated using the rulemaking, monitoring and enforcement techniques of that model, rather than of the public participatory model of which it is the core. When accommodated in this way, its importance, from the perspective of activists and social movements who have struggled for that recognition, appears in *translated* form, and (more contentiously) is diluted and distorted as a result of that translation. For example, the subsidy scheme grafted onto Chile's water service delivery model (Chapter 4), or the guarantee of a minimal amount of 'Free Basic Water' in South Africa's policy framework (Chapter 5): do these policies distort and dilute, or do they appropriately recognise, the values and social ethics embedded in the call to recognise 'water as life'? Or, drawing from the Tucumán case study in Chapter 4, when mass direct action demands a 'place at the table' in transnational settings that control crucial aspects of water services policy, is the ability to submit an amicus curiae brief in international arbitration hearings a co-optation or a recognition of this demand?

The above examples resemble what Liu and Halliday have recently called a 'diagnostic struggle' in recursive cycles of legal change (Liu and Halliday 2009: 933–44). But the challenge represented by the feedback effect operates at an even more complex level caused by another of the factors highlighted in Liu and Halliday's framework for illuminating the recursivity inherent in cycles of legal change. That factor is the mismatch between actors involved in formal enactment and those involved in day-to-day implementation, a mismatch that can lead to feedback effects becoming visible only in the implementation phase, complicating what appeared to be a straightforward victory at the enactment phase. For example, as we shall see in Chapter 3, the Bolivian activists succeeded in enacting a new legal framework for water resources that instantiated a vision of public participatory governance they had long struggled for. But its detailed implementation ended up deeply dependent on the regulatory framework for monitoring and enforcing managed liberalisation, and as the reforms have unfolded, their original distinctiveness has been increasingly challenged.

What is at stake here is a deep divergence between a specific rights-based approach to the problem of access to water, and a broader approach that seeks to reform the broader political economy at a much more structural level. This divergence is often obscured at the 'macro' level of the contentious politics, which is captured by a combination of the naming, blaming and rulemaking stages of the triads. But once the micro politics of claiming, monitoring and enforcement are implicated, challenges emerge for the integrity of the rights-based approach, which flow from the different implications of the dual pathways (legalised and political) that develop at this stage. Rights-based approaches, at this point, unless they engage closely with the challenges of claiming, monitoring and enforcement, risk remaining 'mere rhetoric'. The political pathway bears this risk – but if these approaches depend too closely on the frameworks provided by managed liberalisation (all too easy a result in the legalised pathway) they lose their critical edge and political force.

These challenges will be explored in the chapters that follow. The Introduction outlined the growing problem of access to water, and this chapter has argued that out of the narratives that swirled around solving this problem in the 1990s, two different institutional visions emerged: *managed liberalisation* and *public participatory governance*. Chapters 2–5 of the book show how different threads of the web of transnational governance emerge in response to nationally inflected interests, identities and communities. Each chapter focuses on the pivotal role played by a specific country, while continuing to emphasise that the roles of national actors and institutions are embedded in a web of transnational governance relationships and institutions. Read together, they gradually build an increasingly complete picture of the transnational frameworks and coalitions that give each model of governance its full range of expressive meaning and strategic power. Drawing on the models sketched in this chapter, Chapter 2 builds a layered account of managed liberalisation with a particular focus on France, while Chapter 3 elaborates the vision of public participatory governance with a particular focus on Bolivia. Across the two chapters, a sense of the feedback effects between the models will emerge: effects which are cumulatively leading to complex hybrids that try to bridge the gulf between the two models of managed liberalisation and public participatory governance and the political conflicts that underlie them.

# Managed liberalisation and the dual face of French water services provision

## 2.1 Introduction

This chapter tells the story of how the French state and French actors responded to the problem of access to water by promoting the diffusion of 'managed liberalisation' as a governance model. The story is primarily one of changing institutions, both domestically and internationally. France is both an exemplar of the European 'social model' and a major force in shaping the global field of urban water services delivery in an international development context. As a result, the French role in constructing a 'human face' for a globalising water policy sector has both 'inside' and 'outside' aspects, grounded not only on long-standing colonial links between developed and developing countries but also on a two-faced conception of 'le service public'. Internally, French water services policy uneasily reconciled private sector delivery of water services with a constitutional vision of equal access for all citizens by means of a vision of 'le service public' secured by political regulation and individual citizen rights under administrative law. Externally, in a global context lacking any overarching controlling state, securing 'le service public' for disadvantaged citizens became a much more peripheral aspect of the overall policy framework, and the French approach became embedded in the broader policies and practices of international organisations including the World Bank and the UN, as summarised in the Introduction. This linked water services delivery to institutions more readily associated with liberal market economies such as that of the UK – arm's-length quasi-independent regulatory agencies, discretionary 'solidarity' mechanisms, and an overarching legal framework for the global economy that prioritises property and contract rights.

Despite the differences between the internal and external faces of French water services policy, both are consistent with the notion that building a market economy is a state project, orchestrated rather than undermined by targeted political management. If the state controls the formulation and codification of the 'rules of the game', cohesive political community and a national market economy can be seen as synergistic rather than antithetical projects. This is what Peter Lindseth (2005) has argued is central to understanding French traditions of governance, tracing how from the seventeenth to the nineteenth century France conducted a sustained political effort to make the state a more effective agent for the construction of both a national market economy and a cohesive national political community, and linking *both* objectives to the projection of state power on the international level, particularly in competition with the British and, later, the Germans. Thus citizenship and a market economy in France are *both* ultimately products of a state-centred ethos.[1] This is an interpretation that Lindseth links to a reinterpretation of Polanyi's double movement (Polanyi 2001) by emphasising the relative neutrality of the state in historical terms, so that in France the administrative state was linked to the movement seeking to create a self-regulating market economy, while in the UK the later-emerging administrative state was associated more strongly with the counter-movement seeking to re-impose on that economy a public-regulatory regime.

Urban water services policy in France exemplifies this view of the connection between politics and markets. Superficially, water service delivery occupies an apparently paradoxical position within received understandings of the French 'variety of administration'. France has long been characterised as *étatiste* and uneasy with liberal market approaches, committed instead to a state-led centralist system and a strong conception of 'le service public' embodied in a robust and universal welfare state. Often, especially in relation to welfare state and essential services, the French commitment to 'le service public' has been linked with government ownership and nationalisation (e.g. of electricity, gas, health, education and transport). But water is an exception to this trend: in water service provision, France is and always has been an exemplary regulatory state: over 70 per cent of French people receive their water services from private sector companies who have long-term contracts with local municipalities.

---

[1] Lindseth in effect separates the question of the role of the state from the political substance of Polanyi's 'double movement'. Britain offers the relevant contrast: here, Lindseth argues that the development of the modern administrative state at the end of the nineteenth century, came *after* the establishment of a liberal market economy and was consequently seen more as a counter-struggle – an attempt to subject the economy to political control rather than to support the construction of a well-functioning market – a difference that has implications for the comparative role of France and the UK in the diffusion of regulatory models: see p. 64.

However, this can be seen as consistent with centralist *étatisme* once the specificities of regulation and rights in the policy area are understood.

To illustrate this, the chapter traces how, given that water service delivery has always been the legal responsibility of local municipalities, the delegation of delivery to large private infrastructure companies has facilitated central control, whether by state-endorsed model contracts (prior to the 1980s) or by procedural state regulation of competitive tender (since the 1980s). This control has been contested at the local level by citizen protest, lobbying and litigation, sometimes with strong effects at the local political level that led to remunicipalisation, and which over time have built a social safety net at the legislative level that acknowledges the status of water as a basic need to which all citizens are entitled.

In short, water service delivery within France lays bare some crucial underpinnings of the European social model, illuminating a relationship between public and private that posits the state as a crucial determinant of a *nationalised* market economy which is not just an engine for economic growth but simultaneously a crucial instrument of social cohesion in constructing national political community. In the transnational context, however, the exclusory dimension of state-based support of a market economy becomes much more visible. As we shall see, in the absence of a global market economy embedded in a global government, the diffusion of managed liberalisation responsibilities to extra-national citizens is embodied in, at best, charitable and voluntary programmes existing in the context of a set of deeply fragmented and unequal market relations with governments and actors in the developing world. Those market relations are constructed by four concrete transnational regulatory initiatives in which the French state and large multinational companies have played a strong role, but which have also been influenced by other global players, and in water particularly by the regulatory model of the UK. Together these initiatives have, through political orchestration in concert with powerful private sector actors, embedded contract (through contract modelling), market conditions (via international trade rules relating to water services), property rights (via bilateral investment treaties), and self-regulatory standards (via the International Standards Organization, ISO) into the institutional space for addressing the problem of access to safe drinking water. The cumulative result is a model of managed liberalisation as a vision for responding to that problem.

The bulk of this chapter lays out in more detail the contrasting approaches of the transnational and domestic faces of French urban water services policy, each structured in terms of regulation and rights. But I preface this with the story of an early political struggle *internal* to managed liberalisation, which illustrates the political dynamics of both the normative impulses that activated 'naming, claiming and blaming' by local citizens and the rules, monitoring and enforcement mechanisms that they engaged with as a result.

## 2.2   The story of water in Grenoble

In the early 1980s, the provincial city of Grenoble in the east of France was at the centre of a struggle to take back local water services into public hands that unseated a politically powerful national minister and led to prominent criminal litigation. The success of this struggle was a product of local political coalitions, grassroots consumer advocacy and historical specificity. But it is a struggle that also typifies the configuration of rights, regulation and disputing that characterises French water services provision in transnational perspective. Those broader links will be highlighted in the sections that follow on rights and regulation. For now, I highlight the narrative of the dispute in its simplest contours.

In 1989 the city of Grenoble decided to delegate the provision of its water services to Suez des Eaux, the world's largest water company (now called Ondeo). This decision was highly contentious and sparked three trajectories of opposition. First, it catalysed the political energy of the Greens at local government level, often acting in a Red–Green coalition, who challenged the local municipality's decision to delegate the water services. Second, a Green councillor, Raymond Avrillier, organised a campaign for the 'legal asphyxiation'[2] of the contract by challenging delegation decisions and tariff clauses in administrative courts. Third, the battle was also waged by citizens who formed a non-profit association called Eau Secours in 1994 and brought many civil (private law) actions challenging the cost of water as an indirect way of challenging the management structure.[3] Direct action also existed, albeit in muted form. Overall, therefore, public mobilisation and political dynamics, supported by legal actions, were all vital to the change.[4]

---

[2] Vincent Comparat, member of the Association Démocratie Écologie Solidarité, interviewed by Bronwen Morgan, Grenoble, 14 September 2004.

[3] Comparat interview. Like others, Comparat withdrew his civil suit the day the contract was cancelled.

[4] Raymond Avrillier, founder member of the Association Démocratie Écologie Solidarité, interviewed by Bronwen Morgan, Grenoble, 17 September 2004.

The Greens in Grenoble have long focused on public services as 'the hardwire issues for the environment'.[5] The strength of the Greens in Grenoble has specific historical roots, but was able to secure real leverage at the local level after important decentralisation reforms were passed by the French government in 1982. As Avrillier explains:

> Here there was a green movement that existed before the Green Party, an extra-parliamentary movement between 67 and 68 – we focused on issues like pollution, nuclear plants, work accidents … This movement was extra-parliamentary. In 1977 there was a list for municipal elections, it was before decentralisation in 1982, so there was no real opposition at local level. [At that time] the list called 'Grenoblois for Self-managing the City' got more than 10 per cent of the votes, but was unable to secure any representation on the council.

After decentralisation, the Greens formed a Red–Green coalition with the Socialists, and within three years doubled their share (from 8.5 per cent to 19.7 per cent) of the city vote in municipal elections. Avrillier continues:

> Decentralisation allowed us to access institutions. It allowed this extra-parliamentary movement to find support within institutions, and as far as this dispute is concerned it was essential. Usually councillors have a very limited political life and that might explain the lack of political will. Fighting for eighteen years on the same dispute in order to win is just impossible: life is short and there are other things to do.

In fact, it took eleven years of struggle from 1989 to 2000 to achieve remunicipalisation of the Grenoble water services. Crucial to this was a successful criminal prosecution of the then mayor Alain Carignon in 1995 for corruption in relation to the water concession contract.[6] The detailed entanglement of litigation, political lobbying and direct action is discussed later in the chapter. But by 2001 the city's water services had been remunicipalised under the control of a municipal company, Régie des Eaux de Grenoble (REG). REG is an autonomous legal entity, whose board of administration is two-thirds elected and one-third appointed by the municipal council. Tariffs must be approved by the vote of the council's advisory board but the board of administration could in principle privatise or delegate without the council being able to do anything. However, the board includes many who fought for remunicipalisation: local councillors, water activists, water consumers and a lawyer (Raymond Avrillier).

---

[5] Comparat interview.
[6] Tribunal correctionnel de Lyon (6ème chambre du tribunal de grande instance) jugement du 16 novembre 1995 n° 7579.

REG is also monitored by La Gestion Déléguée, an independent commission which annually and retrospectively audits the accounts for water, electricity and gas. A memorandum of understanding also exists between REG and the consumers' committee set up by the mayor in 1996.

To summarise, the Grenoble case demonstrates elements of regulation and rights that typify the French landscape of provision of water services. It depicts a regulatory landscape that shifted from a complex concession contract between a private firm and local government, the fate of which was shaped by political dynamics but also by litigation, to a municipally owned company monitored by a semi-independent public consultative commission. The case narrative suggests that local political dynamics were of crucial importance in the trajectory of the dispute, in particular the Red–Green coalition's successes in the 1995 and 2001 Grenoble local elections. However, mobilisation of the legal system by civil society was also important, at least when buttressed by the support of a keen activist and local Green councillor, Raymond Avrillier. Civil society and Green councillor activists were rights-conscious actors driven by a desire for local democratic accountability and a concept of citizenship premised on equality of access to public services. In the following parts of the chapter, the regulatory and rights dimensions of French water service provision are placed in broader context.

## 2.3   Regulation

### 2.3.1   Regulation: the internal face of the French model

The central feature of French water service provision is that its historical roots have always included a model of delegated management, where private sector firms provide water services under delegation from local government authority. This is the current situation in the UK, and we shall see in the next section that both the UK and France are major players externally in transnational provision of water services. But unlike the UK, France has resolutely avoided creating a national independent regulatory agency to supervise delegated management. Repeated debates, the most recent being in 2004, have regularly stalled.[7] Echoing the comparative

---

[7] In 1998 a proposal on the reform of water agencies called for the standardisation of water management systems on a European level, as well as allowing the water companies to be brought before the Competition Council. The report of the High Council on Public Services (1999) called for a slightly stronger form of national regulation. Dominique Voynet of the Jospin government proposed the creation of a Haut Conseil des Services

insights of Peter Lindseth discussed earlier, one could argue that the UK frames private sector provision of water services as an activity which requires the *constraint* of water service provider economic activity by an independent regulatory agency. By contrast, the French frame private sector provision of this public service as an activity *facilitated* by state and political involvement.

French water provision has, since its inception, been based on the model of *gestion déléguée*, or delegated management. Private companies have run French waterworks under delegated management to one degree or another since the Napoleonic era.[8] Four large companies (Suez-Ondeo, Vivendi-Veolia, Bouygues-Saur, Cise (since 1997 part of Saur)) and ten to fifteen smaller companies compete for the contemporary market.[9] This has always sat slightly oddly under France's famous 'public service' ethos, but the French do not view delegation to the private sector as diluting the notion of 'le service public'. Rather, it is viewed as rooted in the Roman law notion of usufructuary rights, empowering actors to use something that does not belong to them. Moreover, the government argues that the

Publics de l'Eau et de l'Assainissement, which was to regulate the price, quality and per-formance quality of water and wastewater services. This was again rejected, and after years of conflict and debate, a less regulatory, more information-based, alternative emerged – the National Office for Water and the Aquatic Environment. Formally established in 2007, but in practice still in the process of being institutionalised, the Office will collect and make publicly available data from water service providers on a range of performance indicators that dovetail with ISO standards on water management: see Guérin-Schneider and Nakhla (2010). See also ONEMA (1999). Although the regulation of water resources in the aquatic environment has become more formalised (with the creation of ONEMA, the National Office of Water and the Aquatic Environment), the framework for water service provision is still essentially supported self-regulation. Resistance to more comprehensive regulation comes primarily from local elected representatives, who fear centralised enforcement and loss of water basin agency fees (Michel Desmars, Fédération Nationale des Collectivités Concédantes et Régies, interviewed by Bronwen Morgan and Annabelle Littoz-Monet, Paris, 21 September 2004; Monsieur Mescheriakoff of the Mayors' Association, representa-tive for the Municipality of Isère, interviewed by Bronwen Morgan, Grenoble, 17 September 2004; Jacques Sironneau, director of the Regulation and Litigation Department, and Jean-Claude Riveau, director of the Department for Economic Aspects of Water, both from the Ministry of Environment and Sustainable Development, interviewed by Bronwen Morgan in Paris, 20 September 2004).

[8] The pedigree of Suez Lyonnaise des Eaux dates to the 1858 founding of a company by the visionary French engineer Ferdinand de Lesseps to dig and manage the Suez Canal. Générale des Eaux, the corporate ancestor of Vivendi and Veolia, created by an imperial decree of Napoleon III in 1853, won the concessions to supply Paris and Lyon, and later Venice and Constantinople, with drinking water. Another critical juncture for the com-panies came after the liberation of France from the Nazis.

[9] Vivendi had 36 per cent of the French market in 1989; Suez 21 per cent, Saur 9.4 per cent and Cise 5.7 per cent. See International Office of Water (2009).

public service ethos is retained because the state retains the ultimate responsibility both for service organisation and for re-tendering at contract's end.[10]

France's water services are most directly under the control of local municipalities. France has 36,763 municipalities, of which 75 per cent currently delegate water services to the private sector, and 25 per cent manage them as public services.[11] Four levels of delegation of different intensity have emerged: subcontracting,[12] management contracts,[13] lease contracts[14] and concession contracts.[15] But, over time, the mix of public and private provision, as well as the related regulatory role of the state, has gone through several shifts, summarised by Table 4.

Table 4 shows two striking trends. First, although private providers dominated the initial introduction of household piped water services, municipal provision contributed significantly to the achievement of universal access, but the 'last mile' of that access has returned dominance to private providers. Second, state responsibility has had two primary roles over this period: substantive provision of standard contracts during the 1950s to 1970s, and procedural statutory regulation of the tendering process during the 1990s. In addition, administrative courts have always played a regulatory role.

The primary regulatory role of the contract between municipality and operator deserves further elaboration. Although contract-based regulation is inherently decentralised, the model contracts for leases and

---

[10] Sironneau and Riveau interview.

[11] Because the majority of small municipalities collaborate in syndicates for providing water services there are 15,244 water supply services and 11,992 sanitation services for these 36,763 communities (International Office of Water 2009).

[12] The municipality contracts out a specific part of the operation and management, such as reading meters or billing, for a flat-rate fee, with a typical duration of up to ten years.

[13] The municipality hires a private firm to provide specific services, such as day-to-day operation and pipe maintenance, typically for five to ten years. The Johannesburg case study in Chapter 5 concerns this kind of contract.

[14] The municipality leases the water supply system to a private firm, which is responsible for operating and managing the water system. The private firm provides working capital only, as operating costs and profits are covered by water consumption charges, paid by the water users. A municipal surcharge to finance capital investments and infrastructural improvements is levied by the municipality. This was the type of contract signed in the Grenoble case.

[15] The private company is responsible for financing, building, operating and maintaining all installations, as well as overseeing billing and consumer relations. The contract establishes the water tariff to be paid by consumers directly to the private company, which bears all the financial risks. Contracts last twenty to thirty years: the Chile and Argentina case studies discussed in Chapter 4 concerned this type of contract.

Table 4 *Evolutionary snapshot of French modes of water service provision and regulation*

| Access to household water | Provision | Principal legal form | Regulation | Coverage |
|---|---|---|---|---|
| Late nineteenth century | 100 per cent private provision | Concession contracts | Jurisprudential regulation (Conseil d'État supervision) | By 1900 2 per cent of population with household connections |
| Early twentieth century | Much more municipal | 'Régie' (local government direct provision) | Conseil d'État supervision focused on price caps | |
| 1945 decree nationalised gas and electricity but not water, with multi-sector utilities reinvesting their compensation into water and thereby growing substantially | | | | |
| By the mid 1950s | 30/70 private/public provision | Rise of the 'régie' | Subsidies to local municipalities | |
| By the mid 1970s | 50/50 private/public provision | Co-existence of 'régie' and private provision, but latter moving to lease contracts (state bears more of the risk) | Regulation by model contract from 1951, endorsed by central state (Ministry of the Interior); Conseil de'État supervision focuses on cost of service rather than price caps | By mid 1970s, 90 per cent of population with household connections |
| Mid 1970s to 2006 | 75/25 private/ public provision: competitive tensions | Lease contract continues as principal model, but with increasingly shorter contractual terms | Deregulation in the 1980s + return of central state regulation in the 1990s but procedural | By 2006, 100 per cent of population with household connections |

concessions provided by the national state added an element of centralisation. Indeed, until 1982, a municipality wanting to modify the model contract required permission from the Department of the Interior in Paris.[16] Furthermore, the Conseil d'État pre-approved any major new contractual developments. And while the model contract gave substantial design discretion to the operator, it allocated price control powers to the national prefecture within a cost-recovery framework whereby the state would pick up any budgetary slack.

In 1982, the newly elected left-wing government of France passed 'decentralisation laws' giving considerably greater autonomy to municipal governments. These reforms diluted the substantive contractual modelling and allowed more discretion for varying contractual terms, and from this period dates the extensive growth of France's largest water companies.[17] The introduction of decentralisation also brought great anxiety about water prices into the political spotlight. In late 1983, parliament wrestled over a bill that capped water prices for a year and tied them in the future to negotiated agreement between the national government, municipalities, the Association of Mayors and the trade association of professional water companies. The bill was rejected twice by the Senate and ultimately had to be referred to the Constitutional Court, who approved its legality even while remarking that it would make municipal budgets difficult to balance.[18] In practice, however, the bargaining power of the large water companies grew very substantially in the 1980s. It was in 1989 that Grenoble's water services were delegated, and there is widespread support for the view that the Grenoble case catalysed political support for re-regulation in the 1990s.[19]

This re-regulation, however, differed markedly from the substantive control imposed by contract modelling. It was primarily procedural, focusing on regulating the process of contractual delegation of water services in France by requiring public competitive tenders. The Sapin Law of 1993[20] refers explicitly in its title to corruption and transparency,

---

[16] Jean-Louis Olivier, French Water Academy, interviewed by Bronwen Morgan and Annabelle Littoz-Monet, Paris, 29 July 2004.

[17] Olivier interview.

[18] Le conseil constitutionnel, Décision n° 83–166 DC du 29 décembre 1983 concernant la Loi relative au prix de l'eau en 1984, available at: www.conseil-constitutionnel.fr/decision/1983/83166dc.htm.

[19] Marc Laimé, independent journalist, interviewed by Bronwen Morgan, Paris, 20 September 2004.

[20] Art. 38, Loi no 93–122 du 29 janvier 1993 relative à la prévention de la corruption et à la transparence de la vie économique et des procédures publiques, Journal Officiel n° 25 du

foreshadowing the focus of the Alain Carignon corruption case of 1995. Indeed, the law as initially drafted applied only to private companies, although a constitutional challenge to this resulted in an extension of its scope to apply equally to public companies.[21] The Sapin Law defined a delegation more clearly, removing the need to rely on the cumulative knowledge of many different and unclear administrative judgements, and laid out clearly the steps required in calling for a new competitive tender.[22] In 1995, the Mazeaud Law[23] followed, imposing large fines and imprisonment for any public official procuring public services in any way that harmed free and equal access to the tendering process. The Mazeaud Law also required more precise financial reporting by delegated water service operators, giving municipalities the capacity to double-check documentation, and thus avoid manipulation of accounts by operators. Also in 1995, the Barnier Law banned 'market entry' fees in water services delegations, placed a twenty-year limit on the length of the contractual delegation of water services (unless the delegating authority acquires treasury approval), and required mayors to present to their municipality an annual report on water quality and prices suitable for transmitting to ordinary citizens.[24]

All of the features rendered illegal by this package of laws existed in the Grenoble case study: a contract of twenty-five years, allocated with no competitive tender or public transparency, accompanied by the payment of market entry fees to the municipality which subsequently distorted the tariffs charged to consumers, and with poor financial reporting, often consisting of a single page (Lobina and Hall 2007(b)). Whether or not the Sapin, Barnier and Mazeaud laws were a direct response to Grenoble, data from the early 2000s indicates a growing downward trend

---

30 janvier 1993, available at: www.legifrance.gouv.fr/WAspad/UnTexteDeJorf?numjo=PRMX9200148L.

[21] Décision n° 92–316 DC du 20 janvier 1993, available at: www.conseil-constitutionnel.fr/decision/1992/92316dc.htm.

[22] See Madalena de Faria, a lawyer for Service Public 2000, interviewed by Bronwen Morgan, Paris, 20 September 2004, for discussion of the series of steps legally required: (i) writing a report on the principle of the delegation transmitted to the councillors, (ii) a meeting of the municipal council where deliberations are taken, (iii) the transmission of a publicity notice, (iv) candidates send in their applications, etc.

[23] Loi no 95–127 du 8 fevrier 1995, relative aux marché public et délégations de service public, proposed 15 December 1994.

[24] Arts 73, 75 and 76, Loi no 95–101 du 2 février 1995 relative au renforcement de la protection de l'environnement, Journal Officiel n° 29 du 3 février 1995, p. 1840: www.legifrance.gouv.fr/WAspad/UnTexteDeJorf?numjo=ENVX9400049L, amending the Sapin Law.

in renegotiated prices in water service delegations.[25] Of course, the procedural re-regulation had limits: it did not force a municipality to choose in favour of the 'best' or 'cheapest' supplier, nor did it prevent suppliers from indirectly inflating prices by other methods (e.g. through meter installation fees or connection fees).[26] But other regulatory resources exist in the landscape of French water services policy: in particular, regional audit courts, an innovative non-profit consultancy service, and local consultative commissions of public service users.

Regional audit courts complement the role of administrative courts by means of their power to issue public reports when a delegated service operator commits irregularities in financial reporting and accounting. Publicity from the Grenoble dispute (in which regional audit courts were able to verify that Suez had paid a fee to the local municipality for the 'right to enter' that local market, and had subsequently distorted their tariffs as a means of recouping that fee) catalysed a more general tendency for audit courts to examine water service delegation contracts more closely.[27] The Grenoble dispute, and others like it, also encouraged the development of other monitoring bodies with a broader scope. First, a 1992 law[28] created mandatory local consultative commissions for the users of public services in towns with over 10,000 inhabitants or groups of towns with over 50,000 inhabitants. These commissions represent councillors and users and must be consulted every six months by public service operators in relation to the annual report, tariff-setting and the effectiveness of the service.

There have, however, been extensive problems in practice with these consultative commissions: in particular, low consumer participation due to the complexity of the issues, an absence of financial support and lack of expertise.[29] There is also a structural problem: citizens usually focus on practical problems which the municipality rarely has control over, but the private operator, who can affect these issues, is not represented on the commission.[30] So while these commissions may improve citizens'

---

[25] Just before the Sapin Law was signed in 1993, 60–70 per cent of existing contracts were extended to avoid its effects. These extensions are now expiring and urban water services contracts are now renewed at an average of 15 per cent lower water rates (Pezon and Bonnet 2006; Pezon 2007).

[26] Monsieur Mangermont, Secretary General for the Public Services Union for Veolia, interviewed by Bronwen Morgan and Annabelle Littoz-Monet, Paris, 21 September 2004.

[27] Mescheriakoff interview.

[28] La loi d'orientation du 6 fevrier 1992 relative à l'administration de la territoriale de la République.

[29] Desmars interview.    [30] De Faria interview.

perceptions of legitimacy, they have little influence on who writes the rules of the game. They also failed to stem the continuing rise in water prices, which rose by an average of 56 per cent between 1991 and 1996.[31]

In 2002, a further law[32] required the formation of water consumers' consultative committees, which mayors must consult when they want to change the municipality's form of management for water and sanitation. While this was meant to undermine a too easy reliance on the status quo, it seems not to have achieved this objective: 'Each year, there are about 700 decisions taken; in 96 per cent of the cases, there was no change of system, in 3 per cent of the cases, the change was in favour of delegated private management and although 20 per cent consider shifting to public management ("régie"), only 1 per cent of the cases do so' (Smets 2007: 10).

In response to the limited efficacy of these locally embedded monitoring mechanisms, French local government officials devised an innovative response which aimed to retrieve the expertise that centralised contract modelling had once drawn on,[33] and make it available in the newly decentralised landscape of contracting that has prevailed since the 1980s. A growing power disparity accompanied the growth of the large private water companies over the 1980s.[34] Service Public 2000 (SP2000) is a non-profit consultancy service which aims to mitigate that bargaining power disparity while still providing a flexibility that model contracts could not achieve. It was established in 1996, by the Mayors' Association of France together with the National Federation of Municipal Syndicates (FNNCR or Fédération Nationale des Collectivités Concédantes et Régies).

The non-profit consultancy has forty employees of three kinds: engineers, financial experts and legal experts. Each employee handles between ten and fifteen negotiations of contracts for municipalities at any one time, with each negotiation lasting six months on average. They are prohibited from working for any organisation other than municipalities (including private companies), and only operate in towns of between 10,000 and 50,000 people. SP2000 assists municipalities in negotiating new contracts

---

[31] Rapport de la Direction générale de la concurrence, de la consommation et de la répression des fraudes (DGCCRF), noted at: www.vie-publique.fr/dossier_polpublic/politique_eau/chrono/chrono.shtml.

[32] Loi no 2002–276 du 27 février 2002 relative à la démocratie de proximité.

[33] A large staff at the Ministry of the Interior had been devoted to the management of public services under the model contract approach: Desmars interview, Sironneau and Riveau interview.

[34] Mescheriakoff interview. When Suez and Lyonnaise des Eaux merged in 1997, they declared an ambition 'to create a worldwide local public services group' (Ministry of Foreign Affairs 1997).

as well as mid-term renegotiations greater than ten years in length. They work from a model contract devised from experience of what issues cause problems on a routine basis, and from knowledge of the private companies' model contracts. For example, they encourage municipalities to include a clause that moderates price increases when company productivity declines.[35]

SP2000's role is an advisory and supportive one, and they regard it as 'important that we are not the state, we are not controlling or checking or punishing'.[36] Their work is usually catalysed by local government requests, but they make unilateral offers of assistance in cases when they hear of 'problems'. They have no direct contact with citizens or end-users. The organisation has a powerful stake in its independence: its publicity brochure stresses its unique combination of self-financing and legal limits on conflicts of interest, even to the point that they are banned from helping in definitional studies for water investments because these influence the costings of contractual offers.

SP2000 have helped achieve a number of successful outcomes. In approximately 10 per cent of the cases where they have assisted in negotiating fresh service delegations, the municipality in question has changed their choice of concessionaires. This is considerably more effective than the influence of water consumer consultative committees recorded above. They also play an important role in terms of reassuring municipalities of small companies' reputations, thus expanding the trust necessary for competition to flourish in a market otherwise dominated by four very large operators. They have negotiated initial price offers down by as much as 30 per cent, and claim that in the majority of cases they can negotiate considerable efficiency savings even within the confines of 'comfortable' delegations that have not yet expired. And in cases where there is no technical case for change, even detached legal advice on basic rights can help solve delicate political conflicts that might otherwise bar productive reform.[37]

Yet as important as the technical assistance role of SP2000 can be, they themselves concede that the factor of primary importance is leadership and political will at the local level. SP2000 carried out some work for the

[35] Julien Pointillart, an engineer for Service Public 2000, interviewed by Bronwen Morgan and Annabelle Littoz-Monet, Paris, 31 July 2004.

[36] Pointillart interview.

[37] Such as the case of the local town mayor, who had a powerful constituent affected by minor sewage leakages not amounting to a contractual breach, but which killed his valuable ducks: Pointillart interview.

municipal council in the Grenoble dispute, but the Greens, whose political organisational efforts were so central to the outcome of that dispute, felt that a local commission (La Gestion Déléguée) was considerably more effective in ensuring that it obtained correct data.[38] La Gestion Déléguée had been created in 1995 specifically in response to the localised conflict over delegation rather than under the framework of the 1992 national laws regarding the local consultative commission, once again illustrating the efficacy of institutions embedded in local political dynamics.

The domestic regulatory landscape of French water services provision that has been painted thus far is one that I would describe as 'political regulation'. What makes regulation *constructively* political is primarily vibrant local democratic politics that harnesses citizens' activism and legal mobilisation to the kinds of effects that Grenoble's Red–Green coalition achieved between 1995 and 2001. Commissions, consultancies and procedural statutory regulation are potentially important resources, but without local political energy and the Sapin Law, they are all too vulnerable to becoming dead letters. The Grenoble dispute shows the need for these monitoring bodies as well as their limits. The limits are stark, especially for rural areas and large cities negotiating with a very few and very well-resourced 'repeat players' from the private sector, in a context where strong central state guidance on the substance of contracts has been tardily replaced by procedural regulation.

### 2.3.2 Regulation: the external face of the French model

Fully understanding the regulatory landscape of French water services provision requires us to integrate an appreciation of the external face of French policy in this area. The main argument in this section is that French politicians and civil servants, French corporations and French professional associations have been pivotal influences on a variety of institutional initiatives shaping global water policy that have emerged since the 1980s. Together, these initiatives amount to what scholars have argued in different policy areas is a typically French response to globalisation: one that aspires to formulate and codify the 'rules of the game' (Gordon and Meunier 2001). In this case, the aspiration is towards a vision of 'managed liberalisation'.

France, it should be emphasised, is by no means the only player in the game. The UK, for example, also hosts one of the world's five largest private

---

[38] Comparat interview.

water service providers: Thames plc. The UK provides an interesting contrast to France, both domestically and externally. Domestically England's water services have long been far more centralised than those of France, for historical reasons relating to the linkage between water and sanitation problems and rapid industrialisation (Goubert 1989). Since the 1990s, the UK has also created an independent regulatory agency in water which has become a frequently diffused model overseas. Indeed, an implicit 'competition for the rules' between UK and French approaches as water service provision has become increasingly transnational, has arguably created, at national level in developing countries, a mixed model of delegated private management supervised by an independent regulator. The effects of such an approach will be explored in the Latin American case studies in Chapters 3 and 4. The focus of this chapter is not yet on the national regulatory space in developing countries, but on institution-building in a transnational space that is heavily inflected by French influence.

France's external role is embedded in the historical roots of the country's colonial history. Indeed, broader approaches to water resource management in France have always been influenced by experience in the colonies (Baron 2006). As one interviewee said:

> During the mid 1960s, most of my colleagues were coming back from French colonies, because there was no problem of water in France but there were water problems in the colonies. So I know this, that most of the institutions and the legislation that were implemented in the 60s in France were inspired by people who started their career 20 years before me, after World War II in North Africa, or black Africa, or Indochina where there were a lot of water problems because of the climatic conditions.[39]

In the post-World War II context, colonial ties have been supplemented by powerful World Bank influences on developing country water service policies. Catherine Baron (2006) distinguishes two stages since the 1980s: first a vision of universal access based on public investment and strong cross-subsidies. In the 1990s this was supplanted by a focus on public–private partnerships, decentralisation and market solutions to poverty. During this period, the external role of multinationals grew exponentially, as Figure 3 shows. This was a shift that was made possible by the rapid accumulation of power that the large water companies were able to achieve in the 1980s domestically, in the wake of decentralisation and the withdrawal from centralised contract modelling.

---

[39] Olivier interview.

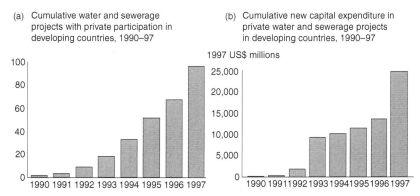

**Figure 3**   Increase in private sector investment in water services, 1990–7
Source: Silva, Tynan and Yilmaz (1998).

As discussed in the Introduction, since the early 2000s, the level of foreign investment by the transnational private sector has both dipped and shifted focus, moving away from Africa and Latin America to China, the US and Eastern Europe rather than Africa and Latin America.[40] But as the earlier discussion emphasised, this shift has not undercut the ongoing salience of the regulatory framework gradually being built at the transnational level. The emphasis by the World Bank and by the aid policies of wealthy Western countries continues to be on providing water services in a commercial framework, whether the operator is public or private. And the architecture of global water services policy continues to buttress that policy emphasis.

France makes consistent high-profile public commitments on the international stage to better water resources management, and aims to promote its model at the international level. The Environment Ministry has created a special sub-division devoted to water issues within the international affairs division that negotiates environment-related treaties. A 2003 report showed that more than a third of 'local actions' in France for improving access to water resources relate to developing countries and Eastern European countries (Guerquin *et al.* 2003). Since his retirement as president, Jacques Chirac has lobbied for the creation of a World Environment Organisation. France's ongoing role in shaping the flow of money and the composition of institutions in the global water policy field is summarised in Table 5.

The array of institutional activity summarised in Table 5 shows a fairly comprehensive attempt to shape the content of water-related policies in

---

[40] Laimé interview.

Table 5 *French-led institutional innovation in the field of global water policy*

| Date | Institution | French connections | Scope, aims and goals |
|---|---|---|---|
| 1984 | Programme Solidarité Eau (PS-Eau) | • Most member organisations are French or in ex-colonies<br>• Partially funded by French Ministry of Foreign Affairs | A network of French and foreign organisations that aims to improve access to water in rural and peri-urban areas of developing countries, by mediating partnerships between French and foreign local governments |
| 1993 | French Academy of Water | • An association under French law that brings together over 150 French and foreign water experts and civil society organisations<br>• Funded by French Environment Ministry | To promote public debate and awareness of water problems at the crossroads of science, ethics, management and politics |
| 1994 | International Network of Basin Organisations (INBO) | • International Water Office, based in Limoges, acts as the secretariat<br>• The six French water agencies are the founding members<br>• The French association for the study of irrigation and drainage (AFEID) has considerable input<br>• Partially funded by French Ministry of Foreign Affairs | 102 organisations in 42 countries, aiming to promoting integrated water resource management for catchment areas |
| 1996 | World Water Council | • Based in Marseilles, France<br>• French president, former CEO of provincial French water services operator | To promote awareness, build political commitment and trigger action on critical water issues at all levels |

| Year | Event/Organisation | Notes | Aim/Description |
|---|---|---|---|
| 1997 (repeated every three years) | First World Water Forum, Marrakech. Since then in The Hague (2000), Kyoto (2003), Mexico (2006) and Istanbul (2009) | • First WWF was in Marrakech, with strong postcolonial ties to France | To increase the importance of water on the political agenda; to deepen and concretise debate in this area and generate political commitment |
| 2002 | Camdessus Panel on Financing Infrastructure | • Chaired by the French former IMF president<br>• Strongly supported by the World Water Council | 20-member panel convened to address ways and means of attracting new financial resources to the water field |
| 2004 | Congress of United Cities and Local Government Organisation (UCLG) | • Founded by the World Water Council at a workshop held in Paris<br>• Mayor of Paris one of three founding presidents | Members from 127 countries, aiming to be the global voice of cities and the main local government partner of the United Nations |
| 2006 | French Institute for Delegated Management (IGD) | • French organisation with mainly local emphasis but recently developing initiatives directed at elected officials from small and medium-sized local authorities in the developing world | Business association promoting public–private partnerships as a means of delivering public services |

the global arena at a number of different levels. The breadth and density of initiative is particularly marked in comparison to the UK, where the NGO WaterAid, which emerged in 1981 in the wake of privatisation of the regional water companies to provide water to the poor in developing countries, is the only comparable institution to those that have grown up in France.

Functionally, France's influence covers a full range of activities, from a focus on intellectual frameworks and links with 'high politics' (the French Water Academy), training and organisational change (INBO and IGD), decentralised partnerships, education and service delivery (PS-Eau) and the provision of funding (the Camdessus Panel). Key interest groups are given a voice in the World Water Council (including international organisations, business actors and civil society) and UCLG (local government). The World Water Forum adds a highly prominent arena where the cumulative achievements of these groups and functional activities can be publicised. World Water Fora are similar in structure to large UN-sponsored meetings with Ministerial Conferences, but considerably more transnational rather than international. Activists[41] have long argued that there are close connections between corporate personalities in the water sector and the policy tenets promoted at the Fora, particularly in their early days. The First World Water Forum led to a suite of policy proposals – the World Water Vision (World Water Forum 2009) and an accompanying Framework for Action – which had much in common with the liberalised market-centred approach supported by international financial institutions such as the World Bank in the 1990s.

The activities described above, I would argue, developed an institutional space in the global policy arena where more specific concrete regulatory initiatives could be promoted. There are four of particular importance: contract modelling, international trade rules, bilateral investment treaties, and voluntary technical standards in the ISO. Together these create the vision of managed liberalisation by embedding contract (through contract modelling), market conditions (via international trade rules), property rights (via bilateral investment treaties), and self-regulatory standards (via the ISO standards) into the institutional space for addressing the problem of access to safe drinking water.

We saw in the earlier section that model contracts were for a long time central to the French strategy of providing universal access to water

---

[41] See the websites of the Corporate Europe Observatory (www.corporateeurope.org) and the World Development Movement (www.wdm.org.uk).

through delegated private sector provision. When delegated private management operates across borders, the contract is once again the central regulatory instrument of service provision. Several initiatives that can be grouped under 'contract modelling' have been trialled in the institutional space outlined above. The Camdessus Panel recommended a study that would develop best practice and model clauses in legal agreements for private sector participation in the water sector. The French Academy of Water worked with a UNESCO-sponsored project involving the UN, the World Bank and the EU to develop model legal contracts for the international context of water service provision. The Institute of Delegated Management has produced, in close association with UN-Habitat, a Declaration on the Right to Access Essential Services, which proposes an annex which would contain model water management principles of global applicability. These initiatives all aim to systematise the experience of French delegated service providers, feeding them into contractual specificity to standardise future delegations of water service management along similar lines.

Markets and property rights are complements to contract rights in a liberalised conception of water service delivery. France has, according to research by advocacy networks concerned about the spread of liberalised models, played a significant role in EU moves to add water service delivery to a broad agenda of opening up transnational markets for services. The European Union, in negotiations relating to the General Agreement on Trade in Services, requested seventy-two WTO member states to open up water delivery and waste water management to international competition in the negotiations beginning in 2000. The EU has also pressed for a reclassification of water services which would extend the coverage of the GATS agreement to fully include the provision of drinking water (Santiago 2003). Although the French government does not take an independent position in EU negotiations, NGOs and activists claim that the European Commission, which coordinates the EU's position in WTO talks, worked in close consultation with Vivendi, Suez and other major water companies when it finalised the EU liberalisation requests in May 2002. And in a move that mirrors the two-pronged approach of France domestically (closed water markets locally allied with strong attempts to expand internationally), the EU has taken a position that it will not make any further GATS commitments itself in public service sectors including water, but will instead preserve services of collective interest.

This concern to protect a unilateral conception of access to markets is buttressed by the protection of investors' property rights by means of bilateral investment treaties (BITS). BITS are controversial because they can potentially trump national and local regulatory protection, providing compensation for damage that investors suffer as a result of legislation, regulations, policies or practices of the state. In the context of a concession to invest in water services, an investor–state claim could challenge instances of state policy such as altering the required amount or duration of the investment, applicable operational requirements such as quality standards, or the level of authorised tariffs that an investor could charge and the methods of collection. At mid 2003, France had concluded sixty-five BITS, and was involved in several specific disputes as prosecutor.[42] As we shall see in future chapters, the other countries explored in this research are much more exposed than France to BITS-related legal actions, and the ostensibly neutral transnational regulatory structure of BITS in practice casts a powerful shadow over other countries' national regulatory arrangements.

The final aspect of the regulatory infrastructure of managed liberalisation has been the development of voluntary standards for the management of water and wastewater services within the ISO. Developed over six years, the final standards were published in 2007.[43] Although the ISO is a global organisation based in Geneva, the French state and other French actors were central to the origin and development of these particular standards. After President Chirac made a keynote speech regarding water at the 2002 Johannesburg Sustainable Development Summit, the French Environment Ministry supported a process taken forward by AFNOR, the state-approved French Standards Association, which wrote a business proposal for founding Technical Committee 224 (TC224) and later provided central secretariat services to the committee. According to civil servants in the Environment Ministry, the goal was to create systems appropriate to the context of developing countries but with room for gradual improvement via benchmarking to reach the standard of the developed countries.[44] The French delegation to TC224 included two French consumer associations as well as the water companies Vivendi and Suez. There was initial opposition both from developed countries such as Japan

---

[42] Calculated from ICSID (2009). This does not take into account other fora for investor–state arbitration such as the United Nations Commission on International Trade Law (UNCITRAL) and the International Chamber of Commerce, neither of which has an obligation to publish claims.

[43] ISO Water Management Standards ISO 24510, ISO 24511, and ISO 24512.

[44] Sironneau and Riveau interview.

and Germany (who were concerned that the French wanted to develop norms that would serve the interests of the French water companies) and from developing countries (who were afraid that the norms would be too strict for them to comply with).[45]

Over its six years of operation, TC224, with the assistance of PS-Eau, developed a number of mechanisms that supported wider developing country participation, including the recruitment of developing country representatives,[46] regional events held locally in developing countries, and an ad hoc group created to ensure the applicability of the standards to the global South. While the procedural aspects of the committee's work were opened up over time to both developing countries and to NGO observers, the substance remained contentious. In particular there were early vigorous debates over the degree to which the standards should integrate the notion of a human right to water, but the committee ultimately rejected this and proceeded down broadly consumerist lines in accommodating the concerns voiced by NGO observers on these issues.[47]

The ISO standards represent the 'managed' aspect of managed liberalisation. They regulate the substantive detail of economic activity rather than establishing the infrastructure for market activity, as the other activities described earlier do. And although the ISO standards are voluntary and would therefore operate as self-regulation if applied by water service providers, it is important to note the ISO's growing importance as a forum for developing 'trade-legal' standards.[48] As the discussion on legal trade and investment regimes above showed, such regimes often provide access

[45] Sironneau and Riveau interview.

[46] In 2005, seven of the twenty-five member country representatives were from developing countries (Argentina, Malaysia, Morocco, Nigeria, South Africa, Tunisia and Zimbabwe), and six of the eighteen observer representatives (Colombia, Cuba, Ecuador, Mexico, Turkey and Zambia).

[47] The committee recommended that language referring to 'human rights' should not be included in any normative section of the standard, but rather that 'customer expectations' should be the governing discourse. On the sensitive issue of cost, TC224's Drinking Water Standard acknowledges customer expectations that 'the service ... be fairly priced and that the relevant authority and/or responsible body ensure that affordability is not a barrier of access', but stresses that this standard 'depends on their needs and expectations and the ability of the institutions providing the water services to meet them' (ISO 2007).

[48] NGO work on water management standards catalysed the formation of an International NGO Network on ISO (INNI), established out of concern that the ISO's growing importance in this area could have a negative impact on the ability of developing county NGOs to advocate strengthened national standards, transparency and democratic decision-making: see INNI (2009).

to specific dispute resolution avenues that can be used to challenge at least some domestic regulatory decisions. Such challenges can be defended if domestic regulatory law meets a criterion of being the 'least trade-restrictive' regulatory option. One way that a national government can ensure that it meets such a criterion in advance is to mirror international standards that represent such a consensus. The ISO management water standards therefore have the potential to become the default 'trade-neutral' standards for the transnational provision of water services. At the same time, they are becoming embedded in French domestic policy, as illustrated by moves to integrate the ISO standards into the activities of the National Office for Water and the Aquatic Environment, which will collect and make publicly available data from France's 36,000 local water service providers on a range of performance indicators (Guérin-Schneider and Nakhla 2010).

These four components of the external regulatory infrastructure of managed liberalisation reflect a more transactional regulatory framework than the internal regulatory face of French water service delivery policy. They explicitly structure a market-based institutional space for private sector delivery of water services. By contrast, internal French policy now limits itself to procedural constraints on a substantively unregulated market. Carving out a structured market beyond national borders, in other words, requires a more proactive approach to the regulatory dimension of water services policy than it does domestically. But, politically, the approaches leave considerable discretion to both operators and governments on substantive contentious issues such as pricing and consumer participation. Political conflict over these issues manifests itself in rights-inflected dimensions of the problem of access to basic drinking water, which the next part of the chapter discusses.

## 2.4    Rights

### 2.4.1    Rights: the internal face of the French model

In France, oppositional rights-inflected activities in relation to domestic French water services policy have usually been grounded in conceptions of the French tradition of 'le service public', rather than expressed as explicit rights claims. They have centred on local mobilisation, mainly through consumer associations, who have lobbied, litigated and carried out direct action. The fragmentation of such activities reflects the decentralised structure of water service delivery in France. Although a limited degree of collaboration between consumer associations has gradually built up, the main outcomes have been two-fold. On the one hand, significant changes in the structure of production for water service delivery have happened in specific and limited instances, Grenoble being one, where oppositional conflict has aligned itself with extended political campaigns and direct electoral politics. On the other hand, the persistent regulation of conflict patterns, however fragmented, has over a decade or so resulted in increasing government recognition and implementation of a social safety net approach to water and social exclusion. In what follows, I elaborate on these strategies and outcomes in more detail, charting general patterns but illustrating them with specific reference to the Grenoble dispute.

The strategies of lobbying, litigating and direct action were common to many of the conflicts over water service delivery in urban settings in France during the 1980s and 1990s. France has thousands of small, local consumer associations, and those that have developed water-specific identities have remained on the whole local and fragmented. The Grenoble dispute provides a good example of the form and activities of such associations. In 1994, an organisation called Eau Secours was formed for the purposes of lobbying for the return of water services to municipal control and the correction of distorted pricing strategies that were used by Suez during its contractual tenure. Between 1994 and 2001, Eau Secours carried out protests and leafleting, focusing in part on broad critiques of the private delegation. In particular they concentrated on the way that tariffs had incorporated retrospective increases unrelated to volume consumed, and on the way the private operator used to recoup an 'entry fee' paid to the city when the contract began. Eau Secours supported this with a limited amount of direct action, and a sustained degree of litigation. A small number of citizens (some 50–100) boycotted payment but the strategy did not expand once Suez emphasised the potential illegality of the activists' boycotts.[49] This reflects the general pattern in France: payment boycotts have been persistent but mild, often taking the form of partially withholding a water payment and placing that money in a trust fund or with a lawyer while litigating the tariffs' legality.

Litigation has been a more pervasive tactic to supplement political lobbying and campaigning than direct action. During the late 1980s and through the 1990s, there was an increasing tendency for consumer organisations and citizen groups to take municipalities to court over public services, as interviewees emphasised: 'The only regulation we

[49] Comparat interview.

have is via users' court actions';[50] 'The water sector is really a prime example where case law has shaped the functioning of the water services.'[51] The prevalence of such lawsuits led municipalities to employ lawyers specifically to handle such conflicts on an ongoing basis.[52] The Environment Ministry estimates that 3 or 4 per cent of delegated service contracts have been challenged in court by municipalities and citizen groups.[53]

The French Constitutional Court has developed general constitutional principles, distilled from the preamble to the Declaration of the Rights of Man, which include principles of equality of treatment and transparency that have expanded the discretion of local administrative tribunals in relation to their capacity to adjudicate disputes between citizens and private operators. In this way, the scope and applicability of constitutional public law principles can filter down to the relationship between the citizen and private law delegates of public power – something difficult to achieve in a civil law system that normally preserves public law principles only for the relationship between the private law delegate and the municipality.

The sequence of litigation that occurred in the Grenoble dispute was a complex one, and critically interspersed with political strategies and actions. The Carignon criminal case was just the beginning. First, it was necessary to return to the administrative courts to re-launch a previously failed challenge to the decision to delegate. In 1997 this succeeded, when the Conseil d'État took judicial notice of the corruption facts from Carignon's trial, and annulled the city of Grenoble's decision to delegate its water services to Suez. But this decision only applied to the *municipal* decision to delegate services: it left the private contract legally in place. Meanwhile political pressure had continued: after the Red–Green coalition gained a majority in 1995, a new mayor was installed who had promised to cancel the contract. After election, he reneged on this promise and instead created a public–private partnership between the city and Suez, the structure of which leaned heavily in favour of Suez. Moreover a subsidiary owned 100 per cent by Suez still exercised the legal authority to exploit water.[54]

A local grassroots NGO, the Association Démocratie et Écologie Solidarité (ADES), through its leader Vincent Comparat, successfully

50   Laimé interview.
51   Sironneau and Riveau interview.       52   Mescheriakoff interview.
53   Sironneau and Riveau interview.       54   Comparat interview.

challenged this contract modification in an administrative tribunal, arguing that it was a sufficiently major modification to require a public and competitive re-tender under the Sapin Law. In August 1998 a judge declared the council's creation of the public–private partnership illegal on those grounds.[55] But litigation was only part of the story: the Greens also held many press conferences, marches and demonstrations and produced many leaflets, sometimes with the Socialists and unions, but mostly energised by their own members.[56] And the consumers' committee that the new mayor had created in 1996 just after the creation of the public–private partnership became, unusually in France, very energised and active. Citizen pressure continued, and finally, in 2000, the mayor relented and cancelled the contract in order to win Green support for his 2001 campaign.

Since the Grenoble dispute, competition law has also influenced the French water policy framework. Holding that the private water companies on occasion have abused their dominant market position, the French courts in 1998 required Suez to release its wholesale price for water in the context of a competitive tender,[57] and in 2002 blocked joint ventures by Suez and Vivendi.[58] But interviewees also widely acknowledged that competition within the water services delivery market in France, particularly from beyond France, is extremely weak, with one commenting that the first municipality to give the UK company Thames a contract within France would be committing 'political suicide'.[59]

Both litigation and direct action remain local and fragmented. There is no national consumer association for water: rather, small, local

---

[55] Tribunal administratif de Grenoble (1ère chambre) jugement du 07 août 1998 n° 962133, 964778, 964779, 964780, 98481, 98482 Monsieur Bernard et autres. As a public law decision, the court annulled the council decision to delegate, but the (private law) contract remained valid. It took continued political pressure until 2000 for the local government to finally terminate the contract.

[56] Unions had originally objected to the delegation but their support fell off in the 1990s as it emerged that the large private water companies had funded the national unions, who then pressured local unions not to make waves: Avrillier interview.

[57] Cour d'appel de Paris du 29 juin 1998 (BOCCRF du 16 juillet 1998), summarised at: www10.finances.gouv.fr/fonds_documentaire/dgccrf/04_dossiers/concurrence/juris_cassation/1998/29ca2906.htm.

[58] Conseil de la concurrence Décision n° 02-D-44 du 11 juillet 2002, available at: www.lexinter.net/JPTXT2/mise_en_commun_des_moyens_pour_repondre_a_des_appels_a_la_concurrence.htm.

[59] Pointillart interview, supported by Sironneau and Riveau interview, as well as Mangermont and Desmars interviews: all stressed the failure of Thames to make any dent in either the French or the Italian markets for water service delivery.

organisations respond to local price rises.[60] It is difficult even when litigating to create structures that support 'class actions' or 'test cases' in ways that would help to catalyse broader collective action. For example, the Federal Union of Consumers joined the criminal litigation in the Grenoble dispute from the outset, but it took them four years of appeals *after* Carignon was found guilty to successfully gain recognition of their standing. In 1999 the court finally declared that the consumers' association had suffered a collective injury that was distinct from both individual consumer loss and social harm to the public as a whole. At the political lobbying level, there was, however, some development towards broader representation and collaboration on a national level, albeit with limitations. Some twenty consumer associations (not water-specific) had long had a recognition agreement with the consumer branch in the Ministry of Economy and Finance, but internal divisions and differences between the groups limited their capacity to collaborate on national policy issues.[61] Eau Secours managed to achieve recognition in 2001, after Grenoble's water supplies returned to municipal control. It also helped catalyse the formation of a National Network of Associations of Water Consumers – a federation of over 200 organisations that lobby for municipal control of water services and share strategies and jurisprudence, partly online but also through regular conferences entitled 'Aquarevolt'.

The strategies described above over time influenced national policy in increasingly systemic ways, with two major outcomes. First, as I have already observed, the cluster of litigation cases in the late 1980s and early 1990s, together with highly publicised corruption cases such as the one against Carignon in Grenoble, were understood by local interviewees to have led directly to the procedural legislative regulation discussed in the previous section.[62] Second, entitlements emerged over this period that effectively created a 'social safety net' dimension to French water services policy. Although these entitlements are initially framed in terms of rights, their actual legal embodiment is more indicative of a social safety net that catches those in need post hoc than an entitlement built into the structure of water service delivery from the outset. Cross-subsidies for the poor at municipal level are blocked due to lack of legal authority (Smets 2007), and unlike with other utilities, there is no social tariff for water. Citizens

---

[60] Desmars interview.    [61] Desmars interview.
[62] Personal communication with Jean-François Davignon, University of Grenoble, Faculty of Law, 17 September 2004.

who have difficulty paying their bill[63] can apply to a social fund, financed by taxes, for income assistance with essentials. This possibility arose as a result of a sequence of activities between 1996 and 2000 that alternated between two responses: broad declarations recognising a 'minimal right to water' for those in economically vulnerable situations on the one hand, and the drafting of specific interdepartmental circulars guaranteeing specific assistance with access to water, gas and electricity for those in need on the other hand.[64]

By 2001 these initiatives had culminated in the enactment by the French government of a statutory guarantee of a right to access affordable drinking water.[65] However, the language of rights at this general level did not alter the structure of concrete legal entitlements, which continued to be fashioned as a post hoc and residual social safety net. Moreover, the concrete situation of those who are disconnected[66] still depends on discretionary patterns of local politics and locally embedded court actions. As Henri Smets argues (2007: 8):

> when French courts have to decide on a water disconnection case for non-payment, they usually order the reinstatement of supply in order to protect health and human dignity. As court proceedings are slow and costly, NGOs prefer putting pressure on mayors with a view to reinstating water without delay or cost. Officials as well as utility managers dislike publicity concerning disconnections of poor households because they know that the public would not support such drastic measures. In many municipalities, mayors have decided not to disconnect poor people any more, nor to allow water utilities to do it but will rarely admit it publicly so as not

[63] 1.6 million out of 62 million French citizens spend more than 3 per cent of their income on water, and the poorest families in France can spend as much as 5.5 per cent (Smets 2007: 4, 226).

[64] The sequence began with a Social Charter, drawn up on 6 November 1996, between the Professional Association of Private Water Companies (SPDE), the Federation of Municipal Syndicates (whose members provide water and waste services on a syndicated basis across several municipalities), the Association of Mayors and the Minister for Employment and Solidarity. It was followed in 1997 by an 'interdepartmental circular', in 2000 by a national convention on water solidarity, and later in 2000 by a further circular guaranteeing assistance whether or not a particular private distributor had signed the 2000 convention (French Department of Health 2000). Since gas and electricity in France are both state-owned this safeguard is explicitly applicable to water.

[65] Loi sur l'eau et les milieux aquatiques n° 2006–1772 du 30 décembre 2006, LEMA, Article 1: 'within laws, regulations and established rights, the use of water is for all and every physical person has the right of access to drinking water for nutrition and hygiene at an affordable price', discussed in Smets (2007).

[66] According to official statistics, 20,000 disconnections of poor people per year are taking place, of which 2,000 last more than 24 hours (Smets 2007: 8, 226).

to encourage non-payment of water bills. In some municipalities such as Saint-Denis, the mayor has [issued] a decree to forbid water disconnection of poor people. In Paris, disconnection has to be authorized by the Mayor.

In short, overall, rights-inflected activities at the domestic level in France mirror the experience of activists who have sought to change structural aspects of the production of water services towards a more participatory model – that is, they only succeed in limited instances, where they are aligned with extended political campaigns and direct electoral politics. At the level of general policy, the internal face of rights-inflected activities has reached an uneasy accommodation, one that mostly amends managed liberalisation at the margins, but at times provides a more fundamental challenge to the model.

### 2.4.2    Rights: the external face of the French model

When we shift to the external face of rights-inflected activities in the French context, a much more vivid sense of tensions and cleavages emerges. Absent a national legislative and policy context within which to forge uneasy consensus, the different groups advocate sharply different views. Government, and NGOs with close ties to government, continue the social safety net approach of the internal face of French policy. More radical activist NGOs, working in a network that extends well beyond France, hold a vision of rights that allies much more strongly with the public participatory model that will be fleshed out in more detail in the next chapter. And the large French water companies, while supporting the language of a right to water, envision its implementation in ways that maximise managerial discretion over the process of securing access, confining the 'right' only to the outcome of eventual access.

The French government supports efforts to address access to basic drinking water in other, particularly poorer, countries. This work is also supported conceptually and programmatically by French NGOs such as the French Water Academy and PS-Eau, both of which have strong ties to government funding from the Environment Ministry and the Foreign Affairs Ministry. The French Department of Health is coordinating international work on solidarity and equitable access to water and sanitation services under the framework of the Protocol on Water and Health, a legal framework recently in force which guarantees, for countries primarily in Eastern and Central Europe, 'equitable access to water, adequate in terms both of quantity and of quality ... for all members of the population, especially those who suffer a disadvantage or social exclusion' (UNECE 1992).[67] The approach taken here echoes that of domestic policy, using the language of solidarity in the provision of public services rather than rights, and centring on targeted individual assistance and cross-subsidies.

The French government also passed the Oudin Law in 2005[68] which legally permits French water service providers (local authorities, companies and river basin agencies) to use a proportion (maximum 1 per cent) of citizens' water payments to fund projects that improve access to water in developing countries. Prior to the Oudin Law, this practice had contravened the legal scope of the use of tax funds under French law. By the end of 2006, this project of cross-national solidarity had led to donations of 8.4 million euros.[69] Full use of Oudin Law contributions at the ceiling of 1 per cent would generate an amount comparable to the French national development aid budget for water projects. However, at present this seems unlikely to occur, since research has shown that officials nervous about keeping the price of water down do not give high political salience to cross-national solidarity, and citizens fear that successful projects would either be taken over by the government or exploited for profit by private firms (Langevin 2008).

These approaches construct the notion of a right to access water as attention to the distributive and equity issues in the outcomes of a managed liberalisation approach to water service delivery. Other NGOs and citizen organisations in France, however, take a more radical approach, insisting on tying the concept of a right to water to participatory models of public production that are very different from the 'French' model. The details of this model will emerge in the next chapter, but the presence of French elements in the network of actors and groups supporting it demonstrates the fact that models of service delivery are never monolithic or static – and nor is there any neat fit between national interests and particular constructions of solutions to the problem of access to basic drinking water. Indeed the outcome of the Grenoble dispute shows that alternative models can have traction even within France. Clearing space for this possibility, both within and beyond France, is the goal of a French nonprofit organisation entitled the Association for a Global Water Contract (ACME). Created in October 2001 by Ricardo Perera and Mario Suares, it

---

[67] See Article 5 for quoted text.

[68] Oudin Law, January 2005, concerning decentralised cooperation.

[69] This is 7 per cent of the maximum that could be raised legally. Ten authorities with existing projects saw a substantial increase in funding, and ten further authorities began new projects (Langevin 2008).

works with another association founded by Danielle Mitterrand – France Libertés – to create an international network of similar associations. The two associations visited Argentina, Brazil and Uruguay to promote public management of water services, and the concept of water as a public good and a right in the wake of failed private concession contracts there such as the ones discussed in Chapter 4.[70]

These networks make solidarity-based proposals, structurally not unlike those of the French government: for example, a suggestion that 1 per cent of the nations' military budgets should be mandatorily set aside to create a fund for decentralised cooperative projects that will improve access to basic drinking water.[71] The focus is on working with local councillors and local populations across national boundaries, a strategy that mirrors the structure of internal French trajectories such as the Grenoble dispute. The French associations that promote them consciously distinguish these strategies from strategies that confrontationally lobby powerful elites at the international level, which they link[72] with a coalition of activists[73] that also challenges strongly managed liberalisation, and about whom we will learn more in the next chapter.

Finally, the French water industry has non-commercial initiatives in the international arena that are structured as responses to calls for a right to water, and their corporate promotional materials, particularly those of Suez, also support the language of the right to water. In the mid 1990s, Suez and Vivendi both created operational units (WaterForce and Aquassistance respectively) that provide pro bono or subsidised assistance to water projects in the developing world. Aquassistance is an autonomous non-profit organisation, funded by Suez's Division of Humanitarian Action[74] with about 500 individual members, all of whom work for Suez. Aquassistance puts together technical assistance in response to requests from developing country associations, using recycled equipment and volunteer labour from both their members and the beneficiary community. They have an annual budget of half a million euros, supplemented by outside aid, in particular from some of the French river basin agencies under the Oudin Law discussed.

---

[70] Jean-Luc Touly, activist and ex-employee of Veolia, interviewed by Bronwen Morgan, Paris, 22 September 2004.
[71] Touly interview.    [72] Touly interview.
[73] Public Citizen (USA), Council of Canadians, Transnational Institute (Netherlands), Corporate Observatory (Belgium).
[74] The autonomy is formal only: the Director of Aquassistance is also Head of the Division of Humanitarian Action in Suez.

From Suez' point of view, the primary benefit of its 'social' arm is internal:

> it's more for internal cohesion; from a human resources point of view it's very important. When there is a meeting with the union, they always ask me what is happening with Aquassistance ... the association is important to them even if they don't themselves do a project ... Even for people who are not members of the association they know that there is this possibility, and that they can do it. They like that it is there ... what seems most important to me is that when you work in a big structure in France sometimes you just forget what you are doing really, which is bringing water – or bringing service – to the people because you are just a part of this big system that you don't see too much. But when you work on a small project like this you see it at the beginning and you see it at the end and you have water and you have all the children happy, you know, and women are singing and you just want to go back again.[75]

Suez viewed this as an entirely separate enterprise from its commercial activities, and Aquassistance consequently does not work in countries where Suez has or may have a commercial presence. However, since 1997 Suez has also taken a more 'social' approach to its commercial contracts, under pressure from both the World Bank and the polemics around water that this book documents.[76] They established a steering committee to give overall direction for pro-poor policy, and an annual meeting to exchange experiences in 'alternative methods of provision'. As with their social activities, though, Suez would insist that this is a set of activities entirely within the purview of managerial discretion. While supportive of the notion of a 'right to water', Suez and Vivendi both insist that they sell *service*, not water, and do so through competitively tendered contracts and concessions. In this view, any legal duties flowing from a right to water attach to government and not to private companies, and transnational corporate support for the right to water is primarily useful for increasing and legitimising market access in developing countries (Russell 2009).

## 2.5   Conclusion

This chapter has linked the emergence of a governance model for urban water services delivery that I have labelled 'managed liberalisation' to the

---

[75] Lisette Provencher, Secretary General of Aquassistance, interviewed by Bronwen Morgan and Annabelle Littoz-Monet, Paris, 31 July 2004.
[76] Denis Desille, Department of Potable Water, PS-Eau, interviewed by Bronwen Morgan and Annabelle Littoz-Monet, Paris, 30 July 2004.

Table 6 *The managed liberalisation model of water service delivery*

| Internal face of regulation | External face of regulation |
| --- | --- |
| • Contracts | • Contracts |
| • Procedural regulation of tenders | • Markets (GATS) |
| • Litigation | • Property (BITS) |
| • Consultancy assistance (SP2000) | • Self-regulatory standards (ISO) |
| **Internal face of rights** | **External face of rights** |
| • Litigation | • Oudin Law |
| • Social safety net legislative measures | • Corporate social responsibility |
| • Direct action | programmes |
| • Political electoral change | |

specificities of French traditions of public administration and water policy management. Long-standing historical experience with using the private sector to deliver urban water services, combined with a tradition of viewing the creation of a market economy as a state project, has meant that the French government has long welded together political control and private sector delivery in ways that have proved capable of powerful transnational diffusion. Table 6 summarises the elements of that model, which I will elaborate.

As the top half of Table 6 illustrates, both domestically and internationally, the core of managed liberalisation is a regulatory framework that centres on market, property and contract rights, with quality and standards enforced by private consultancies (domestically) or professional self-regulation (internationally), or the possibility of dispute resolution to enforce those rights (whether in courts domestically or in arbitration tribunals internationally). Political influence is a part of this framework, however, whether by means of model contracts issued by the central government or the statutory regulation of tendering processes (domestically), or though state lobbying on the structure and content of trade and investment agreements (internationally). Private sector participation as a state project, whether one that assists in controlling local municipalities domestically, or in projecting French commercial and state power internationally, is presented as an effective means of securing 'le service public' in a context of scarce resources and the high costs of capital infrastructure.

Tying this back to Chapter 1, the core of managed liberalisation is broadly consistent with the 'naming and blaming' ethos of the Washington

Consensus discussed in the Introduction, although fears of arbitrary political discretion domestically centre on municipal government, whereas, internationally, fingers tend to be pointed at the arbitrary political discretion of (other, usually developing country) state governments. This difference is echoed in the dual faces of monitoring and enforcement choices: domestically, disputes in the managed liberalisation model are handled mainly by state fiat and at the margins by local litigation, whereas internationally there is a much stronger emphasis on private litigation fora, or (as the next chapter will illustrate) independent regulatory agencies, something France has resolutely avoided domestically.

But the model is not solely concerned with the efficient commodification of urban water services: as the bottom half of Table 6 summarises, both domestically and internationally, efforts to institutionalise some redistributive elements to water services policy, as well as recognition of the social responsibility incurred in satisfying such a basic need, have occurred, both within France and in the 'foreign policy' face of the approach advocated by France internationally. However, here there is a rather more striking difference between the internal and external faces of French water services policy, one which arguably illustrates two different pathways for 'rulemaking, monitoring and enforcement' that can follow on from 'naming, blaming and claiming' that access to water is a fundamental basic *social need*.

Domestically, litigation and direct action have, in some instances combining with political electoral change, led to both national social safety net legislative measures, and, as the Grenoble case study together with other local struggles in France illustrate, political space for an alternative approach. This alternative approach veers between traditional state ownership and something closer to the public participatory model envisaged by the more radical segments of French activists. Domestically, however, it does reflect some commitment to combining cohesive political community with the building of a market economy. By contrast, the external 'rulemaking, monitoring and enforcement' dimension of managed liberalisation treats the social and redistributive dimensions of urban water services policy as residual or voluntaristic aspects of the overall model, to be addressed by financial aid contributions or corporate social responsibility.

This is, of course, a highly contested approach, even within the policy landscape of French-centred models for governing access to water. But within France contestation of managed liberalisation does seem to occupy some legitimate space in the overall policy framework. By contrast, externally the diffusion of managed liberalisation has led activists to articulate a model that is presented as an entirely distinct alternative, one that actively interrogates the centrality of contract, market and property that defines managed liberalisation. In Bolivia this strand of activism has succeeded in winning political leadership of the country, making it the ideal context to explore the contours of this competing model for governing access to urban water services.

3

# 'Another world is possible': Bolivia and the emergence of a participatory public provision model for access to urban water services

## 3.1    Introduction

This chapter tells the story of how a model of public participatory governance emerged from the actions of the Bolivian state and Bolivian actors as a response to the problem of access to water in the 1990s. As in the last chapter, it is told as an institutional story of changes over time in rights and regulation, illuminated by the contours of a particular dispute in Cochabamba involving the withdrawal of a large multinational company in the wake of serious and violent unrest. The dispute ignited long-simmering opposition by social movement activists to the gradual introduction within Bolivia of a managed liberalisation model of water service delivery policy. From the conflict emerged a public participatory model that combined pre-existing approaches to water resource use, particularly by rural and indigenous groups, with specific demands for social control and distributive equity. This model secured what seemed, in April 2000, to be a decisive victory, when the Bolivian state cancelled the concession contract with the multinational water company and enacted new water laws with substantial amendments proposed by social movement activists. And indeed the Cochabamba dispute is frequently characterised as 'a victory of human rights over corporate rights', an outcome that retains an iconic emblematic power in the broader global narrative on the politics of access to water.

The chapter will relate, in effect, two lines of narrative regarding this victory. On the one hand, it is true that the Cochabamba dispute has energised a distinctly alternative approach to global water services policy, one that I have labelled a public participatory model. At the same time, it is also true that institutionalising this model at a micro level in Bolivia, in the period since the Cochabamba water war, has met with considerable challenges. I argue that the co-existence of these seemingly incompatible outcomes is rooted in the fact that two different conceptions of access to water existed within the coalition of social movement activists fighting to promote the public participatory model. The first of these is access to water as a territorial question: here, lack of access to water is a visceral invasion of sovereignty, answerable by fostering regulatory pluralism – the co-existence of multiple alternative legal orders coterminous with particular community ways of life. The second conception is that of access to water as a service. The conception of access to water as a service is central to the managed liberalisation model presented in Chapter 2. But it is also salient to supporters of a public participatory model who frame lack of access to water as a question of unjust terms of exchange, answerable by the targeted calibrations of a unitary formal state legal order (for example, means-tested recipients of free basic water, time-limited licences for irrigation rights, employee shareholders in mixed public–private water companies). 'Water as territory' and 'water as service' were uneasy bedfellows in the struggle to articulate a public participatory model in the context of Bolivia. The friction between them opened up space for the rulemaking, monitoring and enforcement techniques of managed liberalisation to redefine the activists' agenda, at least at the micro level, while macro-level developments also reflected some of the contradictions and tensions between water as service and water as territory.

The Cochabamba dispute was rooted in the social movement formed by local and national activists who mobilised in opposition to the imposition of a managed liberalisation model, created by national–international coalitions who melded the approach to urban water services policy described in Chapter 2 into the conditionality frameworks of the international financial institutions. It is superficially easy to present this as a story of activists who 'name, blame and claim' in defence of a vision of 'water as life' against the depredations of the technocratic rules, monitoring and enforcement of the global template of managed liberalisation. But, as the chapter will explore, this is complicated when the 'shadow' triads of this beguiling picture of 'rights' versus 'regulation' are brought to the fore.

Thus, on the one hand, the conception of water as a service in a context of markets, contract and individual property rights is also animated by 'felt wrongs' that animate naming, blaming and claiming: wrongs that blame arbitrary political discretion, rent-seeking and a failure to recognise the commodity value of a scarce resource for failures of urban water services policy. On the other hand, the public participatory model had to face challenges of rulemaking, monitoring and enforcement that were considerable. The basic vision was clear enough, rooted in pre-existing traditions of local territorial control and regional developmentalism, and drawing on conceptions of water as territory: water as a dimension of physical sovereignty manifested by collective use – more of a commons than an object of individual property rights. The public participatory model also drew on the idea of water as a service, stressing concerns of social justice and distributive equity as necessarily tempering a focus on markets, contract and individual property rights. But, as we shall see, although these different dimensions successfully came together to secure the rejection of the managed liberalisation model in April 2000 (symbolised by the departure of the private transnational company and the transfer of the municipal company back to local political control), what happened next was more ambiguous. In essence, the ambitious legislative drafting project to encode the activists' vision of water territory became hybridised, and arguably severely diluted, by the monitoring and enforcement dimensions of managed liberalisation. At the same time, the hopes for 'social control' of the remunicipalised company largely failed, in part because of a lacuna in the rulemaking, monitoring and enforcement systems, in part because of pressures from the hybrid regime of broader water rights. In short, appreciating the two-faced nature of the triads helps understand the structural challenges at the level of political economy to the establishment of a genuinely distinctive model of governance for urban water services delivery, particularly in a deeply interconnected world of transnational coalitions and actors.

The chapter narrates this story in four stages. After a brief outline of the dispute context, I then describe the period leading up to the departure of the multinational company from Cochabamba, where a sharp dichotomy between managed liberalisation and public participatory approaches was indeed visible. The third and fourth sections, by means of a careful exploration of the patterns of rights and regulation that emerged after the 'water war' of April 2000, show that there was no simple victory of the vision of public participatory regional development. Rather, tensions between the models persisted at both micro and macro levels. In concluding, I explore two rather different trajectories of universalisation emerging from the Bolivian conflict. The first is the notion of the human right to water, embodied in the frequent claim that Cochabamba represents 'a victory for human rights against corporate rights'. This is most frequently made by a transnational coalition of social movement activists and NGOs with strong ties to the North. The second trajectory, pursued by the Bolivian state, is a regional strategy known as the Bolivarian Alternative for the Peoples of Latin America (ALBA) that has more affinity with 'water as territory'.

## 3.2    The Cochabamba dispute

Cochabamba is Bolivia's third-largest city, set in the western highlands in a context of increasing water stress resulting from substantial migration into the city in the wake of closing tin mines. In September 1999 the Bolivian government awarded a forty-year concession contract to hand over the operations of Cochabamba's municipal water company (SEMAPA) to Aguas de Tunari, a multinational consortium that was owned by International Water, a joint enterprise of United Utilities (UK) and the San Francisco-based construction giant, Bechtel. An executive presidential decree authorised exclusive negotiation with Aguas de Tunari, and legislative authorisation only emerged after the award of the contract.

Both the terms of the concession contract and aspects of the legislative authorisation gave rise to significant opposition from social movement activists. The contract angered these groups because it authorised tariff increases of up to 35 per cent, indexed water tariffs to the US dollar, charged small farmers for using water for irrigation and guaranteed a minimum profit of 15–16 per cent. The legislative framework, known as Law 2029, passed hastily in the wake of the contract's award, sanctioned the allocation to Aguas de Tunari of exclusive monopoly power over both water *services* (drinking water and sanitation services to the residents of Cochabamba) and water *resources* (the generation of electricity, and irrigation water for the region's agricultural sector).[1]

The social unrest catalysed by these aspects of the contract and the legislative framework rapidly spread to involve farmers, women, students, urban consumers and professionals. Between September and December 1999 they mobilised, forming a coalition of groups known as La Coordinadora,[2] with two primary aims: revision of the contract and reform of Law 2029.

Between January and April 2000, however, the conflict escalated. State institutions lost control of the agenda. The regulatory agency for water hosted a public hearing on tariffs that required mandatory

---

[1] Specifically, the concession contract included power over a large dam project known as Misicuni, which it was hoped would provide energy and irrigation for the Cochabamba region for many decades. The Misicuni project was rejected by the World Bank as not financially sustainable, but the Cochabamba municipal government and local elites strongly supported it.

[2] La Coordinadora Por la Defensa del Agua y la Vida (Coalition for the Defence of Water and Life).

pre-registration: when only fourteen people pre-registered, they had to suspend the hearing when they realised it was likely to catalyse a large social mobilisation that they could not control. Significant tariff rises, averaging 35 per cent but in some cases as much as 200 per cent, took place in January 2000 despite central political promises to limit them (in contravention of the contract). Direct action, backed up by direct political negotiations between La Coordinadora and the central government became the primary mode of managing the issue in January and February. When the transnational identity of the private water company finally came to light in March 2000 (the first time the contract was made accessible to civil society), it pushed the tensions to breaking point. The resulting violence, including repressive action by the police and loss of lives, forced the government to accede to the demands of the social movement activists in April 2000. By this point, their aims had taken on a more radical form than originally envisioned: outright cancellation of the contract, a new water law, and replacement of the transnational private company's control of SEMAPA, the Cochabamba water company, by 'social control' (an elected board that included civil society members). All three of these aims were achieved in April 2000, and it is this result that has become iconic, written about all over the world (Finnegan 2002; Olivera and Lewis 2004; Shiva 2002; Spronk 2007) and celebrated as a victory of human rights over corporate rights.

### 3.3    A clash of models

#### 3.3.1    The public participatory model

In the Cochabamba dispute, the period leading up to and including the moment of initial victory in April 2000 did portray a dichotomous clash between two very different models of water management. The public participatory model, although rooted in pre-existing approaches and traditions, emerged as an explicit model out of the conflict over the introduction of a version of the managed liberalisation described in Chapter 2. As we have already seen in Chapter 2, the managed liberalisation model intertwines different strands of rights and regulation, and I will present the public participatory model in the same way. But I would emphasise that using rights and regulation as perspectives for understanding the public participatory model of water services management in Bolivia is intended merely as an analytical tool for translating the worldviews of the actors involved. 'Regulation' and 'rights' were

Table 7 *Rights and regulation in the public participatory approach, pre-April 2000*

| Rights | Regulation |
| --- | --- |
| • Uses and customs<br>• Rights-inflected direct action Focused both on the commons (collective democratisation of property rights) and on socio-economic rights to consume affordably | • National Water Council blending planning and regulation – participatory drafting<br>• Social control of company and participatory management |

not categories used in local accounts of the events in Bolivia: rather, the actors involved relied on conceptualisations embedded in their own local historical, political and cultural worldviews. As we shall see in the next part, however, after the dispute's initial victory, rights and regulation became much more explicitly part of the mapping of policy changes. This happened both as part of the formal institutionalisation of the social movement activists' demands, and as a result of the ongoing influence of the managed liberalisation model. In order to understand the continuities and complex hybrids of the later stage, it is helpful to frame the earlier conflict in terms of rights and regulation too.

The social movement activists had two core wings – urban and rural – and although both articulated strong demands for participatory involvement and control over the basic necessity of water, the urban wing was catalysed by access and affordability issues, whereas the rural wing was more concerned with territorial integrity and particularly with preserving traditional rights, referred to as 'usos y costumbres' (uses and customs). As the protests crystallised into more sustained action, social movement activists shifted to more institutional goals: the rural wing wanted a National Water Council that would protect traditional 'uses and customs', and the urban wing focused more on social control of the renationalised water company, implemented via civil society participation on an elected board. This could be understood as a process of rights-claiming that over time focused on the regulatory implications of institutionalising the rights claimed. Table 7 sums this up.

The deep incompatibility between worldviews that underpinned the Cochabamba conflict, and the 'clash of models' can be understood as intimately tied to different conceptions of property rights. I have alluded to this in the opening part of the chapter, in relation to the notion of 'water as territory'. Two important groups of actors held this worldview particularly strongly: the irrigators' association,[3] and peri-urban communities who had migrated to the edge of Cochabamba city. Mostly in the South Zone of Cochabamba, these peri-urban dwellers were not on the city network under the public company SEMAPA, and had built independent communal water systems operated by residents (Zibechi 2009). Both of these groups faced expropriation of their collective property rights by virtue of the infrastructure they had already invested in prior to the signing of the forty-year concession contract. But there was also a deeper challenge: Law 2029 extended the jurisdiction of the local water company over water resources it had not governed before. This power directly clashed with indigenous, long-embedded norms protecting certain patterns of water resource allocation for farmers, referred to as traditional 'uses and customs'.

Although Bolivia has had a constitutional commitment to legal pluralism since 1985, the collective property rights of the rural and peri-urban social movement activists were recognised mainly de facto by the absence of state interference. There was no statutory entitlement to particular property rights: rather, the activists infused their understanding of their relationship to land in ways that were rooted more in a visceral sense of territorial integrity and control over basic necessities. Social movement activists, particularly in rural and peri-urban areas, spoke of water as life, water as a right and water as 'mother earth', without distinguishing between them. All these facets were mutually embedded in traditional 'uses and customs'. Interestingly, the activists turned more to the language of rights once they discovered that foreign multinationals were involved in the concession, arguing then: 'We defend our rights, our investment which we have invested out of necessity.'[4] But in the first few months of mobilisation, when all that was known was that the private sector was taking over SEMAPA operations, the focus of outrage was more a sense of exclusion, an invasion of a collective sense of self.

---

[3] The irrigators' association was known as the Federación Departamental Cochabambina de Regantes (FEDECOR).

[4] Damian Alvarez, taxi-driver from the south zone of Cochabamba, interviewed by Susan Buell, Cochabamba, 13 May 2004.

The urban wing of the social movement activists' coalition,[5] made up mainly of middle-class professional and intellectuals such engineers, economists and lawyers, had less of an explicit focus on 'water as territory'. Their principal focus was to challenge the tariff structures laid down by the contract.[6] This was rooted more in the notion of 'water as service', but in emphasising the social justice dimension of access to this service, their demands resonated with the demands for inclusion and the recognition of collective identity of the rural wing. Moreover, once tariff rises were actually implemented in January 2000, the resulting serious urban unrest mobilised more groups: workers, neighbourhood mothers, coca leaf growers and students. Although these groups also focused on access and affordability – aspects of water as a service – they viewed them as core aspects of basic necessities, exclusion from which affected a collective sense of identity:

> Yes, I believe [the cancellation of the contract] was a victory for our dignity, because now even if we had to pay double what Aguas del Tunari were going to charge ... we are managing it ourselves. They are not stealing from us, or confiscating our natural resources and there is social control ... if the community feels ownership for the system then we would all ensure that there are no irregular situations. That's what we call social control. We would control everything.[7]

As the quotation shows, for the urban wing of the social movement activists, social justice in relation to water as a service demanded 'social control' of the main institutions controlling water. As a broad principle, this had much in common with the demands of the rural wing that viewed water as territory, and it was only later, in the detail of implementation, that tensions emerged. At this stage, however, conceptions of social control were a common thread in the overall vision of public participatory management. And on 10 April 2000, those who had fought on the streets for a conception of water that mutually embedded and blurred conceptions of rights, life and common property, formally took charge of Cochabamba's water services.

---

5  The most important organisation was the urban-based Committee for the Defence of Water and Family Economy, formed in May 1999.

6  Father Luis Sanchez, community leader and board member of SEMAPA (Cochabamba Municipal Water Company), interviewed by Carolina Fairstein, Cochabamba, 1 and 2 March 2004; Carmen Peredo, lawyer for the Federation of Irrigators, interviewed by Carolina Fairstein, Cochabamba, 26 February 2004.

7  Raul Salvatierra, community leader and board member of SEMAPA, interviewed by Susan Buell, Cochabamba, 13 May 2004.

### 3.3.2 Managed liberalisation in Bolivia

In taking charge, the social movement activists directly rejected the model of managed liberalisation that had come to dominate water service delivery policy in Bolivia throughout the 1990s. Since 1985, under the combined influence of a new President (Gamarra 1995; Healy and Paulson 2000)[8] and a series of World Bank loans (Nickson and Vargas 2002), Bolivia had adopted a raft of liberalising structural adjustment policies in different sectors. Access to water, with an emphasis on the social goals involved, became a strong focus of this approach by the early 1990s, when Bolivia introduced a national plan to expand water coverage in urban areas.[9] The legal framework for Bolivia's National Water Plan in the 1990s mandated the provision of universal access to networked in-house tap water on a national basis, to be delivered by arm's-length operators and regulated by independent agencies. The framework is analysed in more detail below, but the conception of water at the heart of the model of managed liberalisation was unambiguously one of 'water as service': water as a resource to be harnessed and subsequently provided to users as a service. The comparative institutional structure to facilitate this is familiar from Chapter 2, centred on contract, property and markets and tempered by social safety net rights. Its instantiation in the empirical context of Bolivia is summarised in Table 8, in comparative perspective with that of the public participatory model.

The legal infrastructure was created in three phases. In the first phase (1992–4), the Department of Basic Water and Sanitation passed substantive regulations that established in-house networked water as the primary policy goal.[10] These regulations also gave providers of networked water important property rights over water supplies through exclusive jurisdiction and cut-off powers.[11] In the second phase (1994–7), the

---

[8] The Movimiento Nacionalista Revolucionario (MNR) in Bolivia introduced the party's New Economic Plan in the mid 1980s, a policy that embraced neoliberal orthodoxy (closure of state mines, devaluation of the currency, removal of price controls and public subsidies, curtailment of public expenditure in such areas as health and education, major tax reforms, and trade legislation to promote exports).

[9] 1992–2000 Dirección Nacional de Saneamiento Básico (National Plan for Water and Sanitation) also known as 'Programa de Agua Para Todos'.

[10] Ministerial Resolution No. 510: National Regulations for Water and Sanitation Service in Urban Areas (1992).

[11] These defined in-house water and sewerage services (as opposed to public standpipes, tanker truck delivery and latrines) as the only acceptable long-term water and sanitation solution for urban areas. The regulations also permitted utilities to cut off service to any

Table 8 *Rights and regulation in the two models compared, pre-April 2000*

|  | Public participatory model pre-April 2000 | Managed liberalisation model pre-April 2000 |
|---|---|---|
| Regulation | • National Water Council blending planning and regulation – participatory drafting<br>• Social control of company and participatory management (state as new social movement | • Contracts – exclusivity<br>• Law 2029 – property rights over water resources<br>• Market-enhancing regulation – competitive tender processes for contracts, supervised by regulatory agency |
| Rights | • Uses and customs<br>• Rights-inflected direct action<br>Focused both on the commons (collective democratisation of property rights) and on socio-economic rights to consume affordably | • International investor protection of property rights – strategically acquired by incorporation of subsidiary in the Netherlands<br>• Social safety net – regulatory agency monitors price control, consumer defence and fair competition |

government developed a detailed legislative structure for utilities as a whole, with a 'super-regulator' overseeing a range of sectoral regulators in gas, electricity, telecommunications and water.[12] In the third phase (1997–9), a specific water services regulator[13] was established, and the transnational private sector became involved in urban water provision: first in 1997, when a subsidiary of the large French water multinational Suez secured a long-term concession contract to deliver water services to La Paz, the capital city; and two years later in Cochabamba with Bechtel's subsidiary.

households that did not pay their water and sewerage bills within two months, and gave utilities significant control over private water sources in their concession areas (Article 63). All individuals and entities using a private water source (such as a groundwater well) were required to receive permission from the water utility, who could charge the users of such sources on a volumetric basis.

[12] 1994 Law No. 1600, 28 October 1994 framework of all regulators (Sistema de Regulacion Sectorial – SIRESE).

[13] The Spanish acronym is SISAB; in English, the Superintendent of Basic Sanitation.

In theory, these reforms put in place a balanced model of managed liberalisation: urban water services would be provided by specialist operators via competitive market tenders for long-term concession contracts (echoing the French approach), with an independent regulatory agency balancing the competing demands of equity for consumers, legal security for investors, and efficiency of service delivery (echoing the UK approach). But the practical reality in the Cochabamba context fell short of this ideal vision. The competitive market tender was replaced by a process of unilateral contracting-out in an atmosphere of executive secrecy, with the concession awarded to Aguas de Tunari after a presidential decree[14] authorised a period of exclusive negotiation with that company alone. And the emphasis of regulation quickly shifted to a primary focus on providing security for property rights to alleviate the concerns of both the transnational financial backers and the multinational companies contracting to provide the water services. More specifically, after the Cochabamba contract was signed, two strategic legal manoeuvres took place that deepened the threat of managed liberalisation for the social movement activists. The first related to the expansion of central regulatory authority over water resources, and the second to Bolivia's commitment to international investment treaty protection regimes.

The expansion of central regulatory authority over water resources (both 'macro' and 'micro' cycles) had long been a bone of contention for social movement activists, particularly rural irrigators, who feared it would dilute or eliminate existing rights accrued under traditional 'uses and customs'. As a result of opposition in the early 1990s, the basic regulatory framework for water had initially applied only to drinking water services (the 'micro' cycle). But in September 1999 this was altered by means of Law 2029, which created a legal framework for private sector participation via concessions. An obscure 'transition' clause in the law allowed SEMAPA to regulate and allocate not only water for drinking water services, but also water *resources* more generally (agricultural, irrigation, industrial and mining).[15] As we shall see later in the chapter, Law 2029's

---

[14] Decree 25133 (21 August 1998): 'we authorise the participation of the private sector in the provision of water to Cochabamba city and the Misicuni project'.

[15] The law in question was Ley de Servicios de Agua Potable y Alcantarillado Sanitario (1999). The clause gave SISAB power to allocate and revoke concessions and authorisations over hydrological resources until such time as a separate regulator is created under the Framework Regulatory System of Renewable Natural Resources (SIRENARE). To date there is still no regulator under SIRENARE.

general template approach (which centred on specifying the allocation of entitlements to water in the form of 'concessions') was incompatible in a number of ways with the common property regime underlying 'uses and customs'. But it facilitated contractual agreements based on the allocation of private property rights: indeed, according to SEMAPA's director at the time, the transnational private company Bechtel had insisted upon the clause as essential for the legal security of their Bolivian subsidiary (Maldonado 2004). In short, concessions over general water resources were core to the managed liberalisation model, but anathema to the social movement activists.

The second deepening of the managed liberalisation model was rooted in Bolivia's commitment to international investment treaty protection regimes. These made it possible for Bechtel to take advantage of multiple levels of protection of property rights. In December 1999, three months after signing the concession contract, and in the face of rising social turmoil over its implementation, Bechtel relocated the corporate headquarters of their Bolivian subsidiary, Aguas de Tunari, to the Netherlands, so that they would be protected by a bilateral investment treaty between the Netherlands and Bolivia (there was no such treaty between the US and Bolivia). Such treaties typically provide stronger protection for investors' property rights than would be provided by the local (in this case Bolivian) laws. Bechtel used a complex structure of indirect ownership in the Netherlands subsidiary in order to avoid the necessity of getting approval from the Bolivian regulatory agency for this move.[16] In other words, even though the regulatory agency's design and role was already strongly embedded in a model of managed liberalisation in a context of considerable transnational involvement, foreign investors were still wary of submitting to its jurisdiction. Instead, they preferred – and were legally entitled – to take advantage of an entirely supranational layer of property rights protection in a regime of international arbitration tribunals located at the World Bank.[17]

The above points show how extensively transnational private water companies could influence the Bolivian water policy environment at

---

[16]  As pointed out in the dissenting judgement of a case in which the Bolivian government unsuccessfully challenged this legal manoeuvre: Declaration of Jose Luis Alberro-Semerena, para. 16, *Aguas del Tunari* v. *Republic of Bolivia*, ICSID Case No. ARB/02/3, Decision on Respondent's Objection to Jurisdiction, 21 October 2005.

[17]  The bilateral treaty between Bolivia and the Netherlands referred investor–state disputes to the International Centre for the Settlement of Investment Disputes (ICSID), located at the World Bank.

both the contractual and the legislative level, but there were broader ways in which national and international actors were interpenetrated in the Bolivian policymaking process. The three phases of legislative reform throughout the 1990s were shaped and supported by transnational flows of expertise and money. The Inter-American Development Bank was the most significant transnational influence: it provided money and staff for both the Bolivian government unit that drafted the legislative framework, and the water regulatory agency.[18] The World Bank issued loans to strengthen the institutional capacity of specific municipal water service operators (including SEMAPA) in order to make them more attractive for private investors.[19] Gesellschaft für Technische Zusammenarb (GTZ), the technical assistance arm of the German development bank, played a major role in writing Law 2029,[20] a crucial element of the legal security provided for transnational investors in the managed liberalisation model. Although these financial institutions all exercise ostensibly indirect influence only, their influence was often extremely powerful, and the interpenetration of national and international was occasionally more stark (as exemplified in 2002 by the Inter-American Development Bank being accepted as a member of the Bolivian professional association of water companies).[21]

The Cochabamba dispute, then, created a powerful clash between two quite different models of water service delivery. On the one hand was a managed liberalisation model, created by national–international

---

[18] Silvia Arzabe, Planning Support Officer for SISAB, interviewed by Carolina Fairstein, La Paz, 27 April 2004. See also the 1996 loan of US$70 million aimed at promoting private sector participation, developing the regulatory framework, and strengthening local companies, all towards the general goal of 'improving the hygiene and health status of the Bolivian urban population'. Urban Basic Sanitation Program and Private Sector Participation in the Sanitation Sector, Project 987/SF-BO and ATN/MT-5442-BO, available at the website of the local execution agency, Fondo Nacional de Desarrollo Regional, www.fndr.gov.bo.

[19] SEMAPA in La Paz received US$490,000; SEMAPA in Cochabamba received US$1.25 million; SAGUAPAC in Santa Cruz received US$1.45 million: Carmen Ledo and Carlos Crespo, 'Case Study Cochabamba: Draft Report Outline', on file with author.

[20] Interview with René Orellana, sociologist, Centre for Judicial and Social Investigation, Cochabamba, appointed Minister for Water in April 2008, interviewed by Carolina Fairstein, Cochabamba, 2 and 3 March 2004; Fritz (2006).

[21] SEMAPA annual report 2002–3 (SEMAPA 2003). As the report clarifies, ANESAPA, the Bolivian trade association for water operators, began as a public sector trade organisation in 1982, expanded to allow private and cooperative companies as members in 1997 (the year Suez's contract in La Paz began), and in 2002 expanded to include 'national and international institutions, NGOs or natural persons with legal relations with the water sector'.

coalitions modelling an approach rooted in France and the UK that melded with conditionality frameworks of the international financial institutions. This model institutionalised a conception of water as a service in a context of markets, contract and individual property rights. On the other hand, local and national activists formed a social movement that mobilised in opposition to this model. This opposition made explicit an alternative model rooted in pre-existing traditions of local territorial control, regional developmentalism and a vision of public participatory management. The model drew on conceptions of water as territory: water as a dimension of physical sovereignty manifested by collective use – more of a commons than an object of individual property rights. The public participatory model also drew on the idea of water as a service, stressing concerns of social justice and distributive equity as necessarily tempering a focus on markets, contract and individual property rights. These different dimensions came together to secure the rejection of the managed liberalisation model in April 2000. The departure of the private transnational company and the transfer of the municipal company back to local political control symbolised this rejection. What Bolivia adopted instead in the period following the water war, which the next section explores, significantly blurred the bright line between the two models.

### 3.4    Micro-level outcomes of the public participatory model

With the departure of Aguas de Tunari and its transnational private owner from Cochabamba, the public participatory model entered a new phase – one of implementing the social movement activists' vision at the micro level of legal detail and operational implementation. In essence this involved the emergence of regulatory dimensions that institutionalised the rights claims made by the direct action of the social movement activists. These regulatory frameworks aimed to institutionalise an understanding of collective democratisation of property rights at the heart of water services management. There were two main micro-level processes. One concerned the restructuring of SEMAPA, Cochabamba's municipal water company, which had returned, as a result of the water war, to control of water service delivery. The other was a process of participatory legislative drafting that amended the regulatory framework for the water policy sector.

The participatory legislative drafting exercise, which continued from 2000 to 2004, successfully institutionalised into formal law the norms embedded in 'uses and customs' around water allocation. Despite the significant victory of this legal articulation of new rights, the process did not develop a sufficiently robust regulatory dimension to displace the influence of the concession-based structure of managed liberalisation. That structure continued to cast a powerful shadow over the new entitlements, partly through the indirect means of conditions attached to financial loans, and partly through strategic legal manoeuvres.

Institutionalising 'social control' in SEMAPA proved even more challenging: the process was significantly undermined by both the ongoing power of the managed liberalisation model, and the self-seeking interests that distorted the vision of participatory management. Significant failure, at least in the medium term, has been conceded by even those closest to the social movement activism.

The micro-level outcomes of the Cochabamba water war thus blurred the stark dichotomy between managed liberalisation and public participatory approaches. This happened because the tensions between 'water as service' and 'water as territory' within the social movement coalition were manifested in various ways: they rendered SEMAPA vulnerable to self-seeking interests that distorted participatory management; they provided opportunities for the ongoing power and influence of those who supported a managed liberalisation model (particularly international financial institutions and transnational private investors); and they underpinned the challenges of formally institutionalising tacit customs.

Perhaps paradoxically, however, none of this has prevented Bolivia, at a macro-political level of high politics, from charting a visibly alternative policy path from that of managed liberalisation. Whether this path will produce significantly different outcomes on the ground is, as the troubled events occurring at the micro level suggest, an open question. I will return to these events at the end of the chapter.

### 3.4.1 Social control of SEMAPA: the Achilles heel of the public participatory model?

On the day that the concession contract with Aguas de Tunari was cancelled, 10 April 2000, the mayor of Cochabamba and the coalition of social movement activists, La Coordinadora, signed an agreement, based on a suggestion by the government, to institute a transitory board with members from the municipal government, civil society and the unions (Maldonado 2004). Three elected members of civil society thus became part of the structure of SEMAPA. This meant that activists now had the responsibility to clearly delineate the operational consequences of the new conceptions of rights, life and common property they had fought for on the streets. This was an unexpected outcome from the perspective of the activists. Nor, as the next five years made clear, was it an outcome that successfully built upon the energies and achievements of the social movement activists. As one commentator observed: 'In Bolivia, the [social] movements have a great capacity for conflict, for fighting. The work of controlling a public institution is a different kind of work. It's not a game ... nobody has been trained to do it in Bolivia, not only in the water sector.'[22]

There were several challenges. There was internal conflict between those willing to work with political parties, particularly the mayor who had originally facilitated the transnational concession contract, and those who vociferously rejected 'politics'. Campaign literature for the social movements made vividly clear that while 'politics' represented an obstacle to social change, the solution was not technical expertise, but rather more extensive direct participation by those affected. Self-dealing was another severe problem: 'jobs for the boys' and dubious uses of expenses plagued SEMAPA after the water war as much as before, with one civil society representative quoted as saying that the company was 'still a space for robbing money' (Shultz 2008). Finally, paralysis or apathy undermined the social control of SEMAPA. Early on, transnational partnerships offered technical assistance to SEMAPA (for example, the international public sector union Public Services International), but the company lacked the technical capacity to take proper advantage of these opportunities[23] and the momentum was lost. Further, mobilising the energy to elect the civil society members of SEMAPA's board of directors turned out to be extremely difficult: in the first elections just a year after the water war, fewer than 4 per cent of eligible voters cast a vote (Shultz 2008).

Supplementing these internal failures were pressures from the external legal framework that will be clarified in the next section, but which placed the company at the intersection of a clash of models. As one commentator said:

> SEMAPA is now in a very difficult situation, because it is a public system, controlled by public entities, like the municipality, with social participation. There were elections last week. But at the same time, they are being

---

[22] Jim Shultz, executive director of the Democracy Centre, interviewed by Carolina Fairstein, Cochabamba, 27 February 2004.
[23] Shultz interview.

forced to operate like a private company to reinvest, reinvest and pay their loans.[24]

There was, at a deeper level, a basic incommensurability between the motivating energy and focus of the social movement activists and the tasks involved in running SEMAPA. The activists, whether focused on water as service or water as territory, were concerned with collective identity and social justice, and on participatory democratic processes as the means to address these issues. As one of their supporters commented: 'They understood that this was not just a fight for water, but a nation's fight for the rights of the poor against the interests of the multinationals and Bolivia's elite. The people understand when the time has come to fight.'[25]

But for the day-to-day mundanities of running SEMAPA, it was necessary to care about the fight as a fight for water, and to care about water more than about its representativeness of broader political currents. And this was the lacuna that undermined the public participatory model: the lack of interest in the day-to-day mundanities and operational issues at the coalface of service delivery. This was not a consequence of apathy or constraints on technical efficacy, but more a consequence of the alienating effects of functional specialisation and large-scale modernist bureaucratic organisation. For example, the Association of Community Water Systems of the Southern Zone, a federation of hundreds of water committees run on a cooperative basis by general assemblies, had enormous participatory energy at the very same time and in the very same areas of Cochabamba as those from which the low turn-out for SEMAPA elections emanated. Or, as the next section will show, the network of organisations involved in legislative reform of water laws had considerable legal and technical acumen as well as participatory energy devoted to concrete institution-building. But this participatory energy and legal–technical acumen was mobilised when the issue of water was integrated into the broader social and material context of people's lives – when it was under their control *as part of their livelihood* – the conceptual essence of both 'water as territory' and the social justice dimension of 'water as service'. When water became a specialised modernist object of sector-specific corporate governance, a technical vision of 'water as service', the activists' coalition had little to contribute beyond process. This was the Achilles heel of public participatory governance.

[24] Rocio Bustamente, lawyer, San Simon University Agronomy Faculty, interviewed by Susan Buell, Cochabamba, 15 May 2004.
[25] Shultz interview.

### 3.4.2 Legislative drafting and the transformation of Law 2029 by Laws 2066/2084

A very different narrative can be told about the outcome of the water war in relation to broader legislative frameworks of water rights, particularly those relating to rural irrigators. Here, 'water as territory' gained a direct legal foothold, and in the clearest victory for a public participatory model of governance, the norms embedded in 'uses and customs' around water allocation were formally institutionalised and protected in law. In addition, social justice and democratic process dimensions of 'water as service' at a regulatory level were secured. This was achieved by a remarkable process of participatory legislative drafting that took place between 1998 and 2004, using the energy of the water war to create detailed concrete counter-proposals to the managed liberalisation model epitomised in Law 2029.

The process linked a network of Bolivian civil society groups, research organisations and NGOs,[26] Bolivian state officials,[27] and transnational financial and research support.[28] In the wake of the water war, the government was weak, and the Bolivian network had deep roots in a process of mobilising indigenous rights since the 1980s. Indigenous and peasant groups had been working on different elaborations of the legal dimensions of water rights for many years, hoping to flesh out in detail the recognition by the 1993 Bolivian constitution of some indigenous customary rights over natural resources, rights which had hitherto remained abstract and general.[29] As a result of this, indigenous and peasant groups were in a position to take immediate advantage of the political opportunities created by the water war in ways that SEMAPA had conspicuously not been.

---

[26] Comité de Gestión Integral del Agua en Bolivia – Committee for Integrated Water Management in Bolivia (CGIAB).

[27] Via an Inter-Institutional Water Council (CONIAG) with representatives from five different ministries (Agriculture, Sustainable Development, Economics, Housing and Basic Services), as well as five civil society representatives (from peasants, irrigators, indigenous people, the private sector and academia).

[28] The Inter-American Development Bank funded the early stages of the participatory legislative drafting processes; in the later stages funding came from a Canadian development research organisation and the Swiss government's Development Department. Moreover, international NGOs involved in sustainable development and food security issues fund many of the water-related NGOs operating in Bolivia: Juan Carlos Alurralde, engineer, interviewed by Carolina Fairstein, Cochabamba, 29 April 2004.

[29] Bustamente interview.

Table 9 *Comparison of the legal basis for regulatory authority in Laws 2029 and 2066*

|  | Legal basis of regulatory authority over water allocation and use | | |
| --- | --- | --- | --- |
| Law 2029 | Concession | Licence | |
| Law 2066/2878 | Concession | Licence | Register |

A new law – Law 2066 – was proposed on the same day that a negotiated end to the violence and conflict occurred: 11 April 2000. Law 2066 put into place the basic building blocks of a system that institutionalised the goals of the social movement activists. Over the next four years, the Bolivian network (with assistance from a Canadian development research organisation) carried out extensive and costly technical empirical work that compared the effects of the social movement activists' proposals to those favoured by the government, and concluded that the former were more equitable and efficient.[30] A fuller elaboration of their proposals was passed in October 2004 as Law 2878.[31] In describing what these laws achieved, I will refer to them in compendium form as Law 2066/2878.

The essence of the innovation of Law 2066/2878 was to create a new type of right over water use known as a register,[32] and to amend the category of 'licence' that already existed under Law 2029 (see Table 9).

Registers were identity-based water rights, issued to indigenous and peasant communities, peasant associations and farmers' unions,

[30] Researchers used a water simulation model developed by the Danish Hydraulic Institute to build a computerised replica of Bolivian water systems, taking into account seasonal changes. They fed the model with existing cartographical information and data on water, precipitation and climate. A Geographic Information System (GIS) was used to map water rights. A database of existing customary (or traditional) water rights was also developed through lot-by-lot field work and surveys and liaison with members of irrigators' groups and farmers. The information was used to project which approach to water management would be most efficient: the one favoured by the government or the one indigenous communities believed would be best. The latter was shown to be more efficient and more equitable. See IDDC (n.d.).

[31] Law 2066 relates to drinking water; Law 2878 to irrigation, farming and forestry.

[32] See Articles 49 and 50 of Law 2066. The laws also created a category of 'authorisation' which was meant to replace concessions in relation to water *resources* (as opposed to drinking water services (Crespo 2003: 251). However the detailed implications of an authorisation (which probably retained more political authority over water than a concession) depended on the enactment of a general water resources law. Since this has still not occurred, it will not be discussed further here.

according to their traditional 'uses and customs'.[33] They guaranteed water for multiple uses (human consumption, irrigation and cultivation) to these groups, and were issued to a community or collectivity rather than an individual. Importantly, they created legal protection which was both free of charge and lasted in perpetuity. This legal protection was explicitly embedded in the constitutional protection of the right of indigenous people to use natural resources.[34]

Licences under Law 2029 had been limited to 5 years: under Law 2066/2878 they now applied for 'the useful lifetime' of the service. Rather than protecting traditional 'uses and customs', the amended licence applied to groups which could not take advantage of the identity-based registry category. It was essentially a category for social (non-profit) organisations, either rural or urban. A typical licence holder might be a peri-urban water cooperative such as those belonging to the Association of Community Water Systems of the Southern Zone. Like the rural irrigators, these groups also nurtured collective property rights, and their activism focused on structural change of the political and economic system (Conant 2009) in ways that resonated with the idea of 'water as territory'.

Both registers and licences differed from concessions in a number of ways. They protected collective ownership by social groups for multiple uses, where concessions resembled individual property rights to use specified units of volume per unit of time (litres per second) for specific uses. Moreover, concessions exacted a regulatory tax from their holders,[35] were time-limited, and were accompanied by extensive powers of monitoring

---

[33] Article 49 of Law 2066 defines 'registry' as the administrative act through which the government certifies a water enterprise as one *belonging to/concerning* indigenous and original populations, indigenous and peasant communities, peasant associations or farmers' unions, provides water services, and is eligible to access to governmental programmes for the sector. Article 49 says that the services of potable water and sewerage belonging to such communities and managed according to uses and customs will be certified by a registry guaranteeing in that way security for their holders during the useful lifetime of the service. Articles 49 and 50 of Law 2066 guarantee water for human consumption, and this was extended by Article 21 of the 2004 Law 2878 to cover water used for irrigation and cultivation.

[34] See Article 50 of Law 2066 and Article 171 of the Bolivian constitution.

[35] In fact, some controversy persisted over whether water users holding licences or registers had to pay a regulatory tax to the water services regulator. The legislation is inconsistent: the definition of the regulatory tax in Law 2066 only refers to concession holders, but Article 16 says that the regulatory tax has to be paid by all service providers that are regulated by SISAB, the water regulatory agency. The discrepancy probably lies in the assumption that a new body would in due course be created to regulate registers and licences; but until this happened, SISAB was the default regulator.

and potential intervention by the water regulatory agency. And Law 2066/2878 removed the exclusivity provisions that had so angered the social movement activists. Under Law 2029, concessions granted companies the exclusive control of water resources in the concessionable zone. By contrast, Law 2066/2878 recognised the existing rights of water committees, neighbourhood collectives and cooperatives, giving them the option of remaining independent or agreeing to transfer their infrastructure and installations to a concessionary company in return for economic compensation.[36] These aspects of Law 2066/2878 created, in effect, a space for regulatory pluralism so that alternative legal orders coterminous with the indigenous communities' way of life could flourish. In this space, the rights created by registries and licences could maintain ways of using water that were intimately tied to land-use patterns and traditional social contexts.

Finally, several other changes were also secured by Law 2066/2878 which applied to concessions as well as to registers and licences. These changes focused on 'water as a service' more than on 'water as territory', but still brought the model closer to one of participatory public provision, with a particular emphasis on equity and process. Law 2066/2878 created significantly more citizen participation opportunities in relation to setting tariffs, requiring the involvement of municipal government and neighbourhood committees every five years (Article 57). It also provided greater procedural protection for those at risk of disconnection (Article 73), and altered the balance of factors to be weighed in tariff decisions (removing the stipulation that economic efficiency and financial sustainability should prevail over solidarity, redistribution, simplicity and transparency, and requiring subsidies for the lowest-consuming sectors: Article 58).

### 3.4.3 The managed liberalisation model persists: regulatory gaps, international arbitration and the 'GTZ model'[37]

Despite the significant victory of the legal articulation of new rights in Law 2066/2878, the managed liberalisation model continued to cast a powerful

---

[36] Compare Article 34 of Law 2029 with Article 34 of Law 2066. There is some ambiguity about *future* exclusivity: one interpretation of Article 34 in Law 2066 is that once existing systems have been transferred for compensation, exclusivity will once again prevail in the future.

[37] The name comes from the technical assistance arm of the German development bank that played a major role in creating and promoting it. See Fritz (2006).

shadow over the new entitlements. This occurred partly through financial conditionality and partly through pressures created by the availability of expensive transnational dispute resolution fora for foreign private investors. The ongoing power of these two factors depended at least in part on the fact that the public participatory model did not develop a sufficiently robust regulatory dimension to displace the influence of the concession-based structure of managed liberalisation. The regulatory gaps and the fears of international arbitration gave legitimacy to an emerging hybrid solution known as the 'GTZ model', which clawed back significant gains won by Law 2066/2878.

## Regulatory gaps

The Inter-American Development Bank, which remained a major funder of water service delivery projects after the water war, insisted on retaining the concession structure relationship between the regulator and water service operators, even though Law 2066/2878 had created alternative possibilities. The detailed regulations for implementing registers and licences could not be agreed upon for years. In part because of this legal gap, and in part because of pressure from international financial institutions, the water regulatory agency focused mainly on concessions:

> Three types of rights had been created after the [water war] – concessions, licenses and registers. So what [the regulator] started to do was to work with concessions, because there were ... regulations, which allowed it to work somehow in that field ... The only thing [it] has done is grant concessions and almost forced all the municipal systems in many parts of the country to opt for that type of right. I think that's terrible, because the only form of right conceived in the law is aimed at private companies or some kind of cooperative, for example. It is for profit-making schemes. But the majority of water systems are municipal or public and there is no profit element and many have serious management problems and need governmental support. From the time you are granted a concession that is not possible.[38]

This affected SEMAPA in Cochabamba directly. In the absence of detailed regulation to implement registers and licences, the bank successfully pre-empted negotiations between SEMAPA and the Bolivian legislative drafting network to grant SEMAPA a licence under Law 2066. As the social movement activists lamented:

---

[38] Bustamente interview.

It's true that SEMAPA's legal status has not been clear over the past two years and that has affected its financing. Because the funding institutions have said: 'SEMAPA, we can't give a loan to an institution that does not have a clear legal status because we need to know who is assuming the responsibility.' We have been struggling with knowing how to resolve this for a year.[39]

### International arbitration

Although financial institutions correctly insist that they do not themselves impose legal structures, but only disburse funding, the Bolivian national government was reluctant to challenge the conditions of funders. This is partly due to the powerful shadow cast by international dispute resolution processes. As previously discussed, when Bechtel's subsidiary secured the concession contract for Cochabamba water service delivery, it was based in the Cayman Islands, but soon afterwards Bechtel created a holding company in the Netherlands in order to take advantage of the protection of a bilateral investment treaty that channelled disputes between foreign investors and Bolivia to a World Bank-based international arbitration forum.[40] Attempts by Bolivia's lawyers to challenge the legality of this strategic move failed,[41] and Bechtel lodged a claim for US$50 million in this forum soon after its Cochabamba contracted was terminated.

Fears of a possible second arbitration dispute influenced the applicability of Law 2066/2878 to Suez, which held the concession contract in the capital city La Paz, and which was hostile to many elements of the new regime, such as the requirement to hold public hearings on tariffs.[42] The Bolivian government sheltered the La Paz concession from the legal effects of the new regulatory regime, arguing that because of the regulatory gaps, the 1997 concession contract would remain the only legally operative constraint on Suez, supplemented by political negotiations with the Ministry of Basic Services where necessary.[43]

### The 'GTZ' model: a Trojan horse for privatisation?

The regulatory gaps for implementing Law 2066/2878 combined with the political pressures on a government fearful of expensive international

---

[39] Shultz interview.

[40] ICSID – the International Centre for the Settlement of Investment Disputes.

[41] *Aguas del Tunari* v. *Republic of Bolivia*, ICSID Case No. ARB/02/3, Decision on Respondent's Objection to Jurisdiction, 21 October 2005, released in a Bolivian government paper in December 2005.

[42] Orellana interview.

[43] Roberto Bianchi, general director of Illimani Water, interviewed by Carolina Fairstein, La Paz, 29 April 2004.

arbitration to make the Bolivian state receptive to a hybrid compromise. Two years after protracted negotiations to pass the regulations implementing Law 2066 had stalled, another approach called 'the GTZ model' was abruptly introduced by presidential decree (Decree 26587). Focused on providing a model of corporate governance, rather than on specifying particular rights over water, the model proposed mixed public–private company structures for Bolivian water service provision. The social movement coalition felt that the mixed company option was modelled on managed liberalisation, and that it diluted or even extinguished the regulatory pluralism so hard fought for in Law 2066/2878. Three examples of this dilution can be given. First, mixed companies would be supra-municipal, aggregating large numbers of small local water provider systems into larger units in ways that many feared was a precursor to another wave of privatisation, as the following comment from a senior civil servant in the then Ministry of Basic Services vividly supports:

> We think the markets in Bolivia are too atomised, we think that first it is necessary to create economies of scale, rationalise the current companies, to try to make them prettier. Now they are like ugly girls, they are not appealing to a privatisation process.[44]

Second, mixed companies' jurisdiction was based on concessions, which would replace the alternative categories of register and the amended form of licence created by Law 2066/2878, eliminating the advantages discussed above to the holders of such rights. Third, the capital (pipes, facilities, land, etc.) was transferred to the company, rather than owned and controlled collectively by user communities, and the structure of mixed companies precluded the possibility of contracting with collective user associations instead of individual consumers. Finally, even though mixed companies could rightly claim a 'public' dimension (given that their shares were held jointly by the region's citizens, cooperatives and municipalities), the applicability of commercial law meant that private corporate partners could be involved, and shares could be sold. Thus, full privatisation in the future was not precluded.

## A blurring of models?

In the different ways discussed above, managed liberalisation at the transnational level undermined the new legal regime brought into force by Law

---

[44] Alberto Camacho, General Director of Basic Services, Ministry of Basic Services, interviewed by Carolina Fairstein, La Paz, 28 May 2004.

Table 10 *Post-April 2000 landscape*

| Managed liberalisation post-April 2000 | Public participatory post-April 2000 |
|---|---|
| • Contract cancelled *but* IADB pressure retains concessionary structure and thus formal property rights<br>• Law 2066 *but* Law 2084<br>• SISAB becomes marginalised<br>• ICSID initially still an issue in La Paz contract but is then eliminated in 2006<br>• ICSID legitimises venue transfer and rejects amicus curiae brief | • NWC created *but* deferred<br>• Social control of company arguably a failure due to *both* internal distortion of politics, and funding conditionality pressures that persist with managed liberalisation model (GTZ and IADB)<br>• Regional transnational diffusion – Bolivarian Alternative for the Peoples of America – and human right to water<br>• Uses and customs become legal rights in Law 2066 – parallel structure (registry/licence) to concession/authorisation |

2066/2878, which was the principal success of the water war. Table 10 summarises the ambiguities of the outcomes.

One NGO lawyer involved in the protests explained that the effort to legally formalise the pluralistic and tacit nature of 'uses and customs' was inherently limited: it could at most create what she called 'local law' – a sense of a project-based set of norms, tacitly understood within a small space, operating dynamically and without too much explicit discussion. As she observed, 'something which summarises much of [peoples'] cultural vision and is useful is difficult to capture in a law'.[45] Law 2066/2878 did indeed create an innovative structure of collective property rights, but did so by creating a *parallel* structure to that of concessions, which were at the heart of managed liberalisation. The persistence of concessions within the overall regime created tensions which could be exploited by still-powerful advocates of managed liberalisation.

The difficulties faced by activists in formally institutionalising at state level their existing ways of managing water have been chronicled more

---

[45] Bustamente interview.

widely in the Andean area by Boelens (2009), who has charted the legal, illegal and non-legal strategies used by community groups in localised water user collectives in the Andes, including Bolivia. Boelens notes that those working within the law have shifted focus recently, away from arguing for specific rules or regulations, and instead struggling for legally recognised power to define their *own* rules and regulations. They do this in order to resist functional incorporation into a market economy that effectively disciplines and negates the spirit of their own ways of managing water. This happens even when the stated intention of market economy policies includes attention to redistribution. As Boelens (2009: 314) argues, 'In Andean water policies, the equality argument is not applied to achieve more equal access, but to *deny difference* and contain diversity. It de-legitimizes the demands of various ethnic and societal groups to manage water affairs according to their own rights repertoires.'

As a result, it becomes more important to preserve the integrity of rules and norms that 'stay out of the way' of formal law. As Boelens argues:

> The dynamics and multiple manifestations of local water rights systems cannot be codified into blanket legal terms without jeopardizing their foundations. They refer to a broad range of diverse 'living' rights systems and cultures that constantly reorganize their rules precisely to maintain their identity, and their capacity to negotiate and solve problems ... *Outside* (or on the margins of) the law are most rules, norms and practices that water user collectives apply when building their own organizations and practising their own water rights. These norms and normative structures are neither accepted nor denied by the law. The less detailed and codified they are in legal terms, the better they elude bureaucratic control.
>
> (Boelens 2009: 317)

But when, as in this particular case study, conflict not only necessitates an articulation of the impulses to 'name, blame and claim' the rights that undergird traditional uses and customs, but also requires specific legal embodiment of those rights in concrete rules, monitoring and enforcement systems, then serious obstacles to the realisation of the original vision emerge. For, as Boelens again vividly expresses it, 'a modern ... policy and lawmaker ... *recognizes* legal pluralism ... He or she studies and embraces local water rights and people's living law in order, with this information, to incorporate these particular rules and rights and subtly squeeze them to death' (Boelens 2009: 326). This arguably encapsulates what happened at the micro level in Bolivia in the immediate wake of the Cochabamba water wars, as a result of complex coalitions of interdependent national and international actors.

On the one hand, the real, yet precarious, success of 'water as territory' in the domain of water resources legislation was underpinned by an uneasy tension between the lenders' property rights at the heart of managed liberalisation and the collective property rights at the heart of public participatory governance. The collective property rights persisted as 'living law' to an extent, but were over time 'subtly squeezed' by the lenders' property rights. On the other hand, there were even more severe challenges to institutionalising an alternative conception of 'water as service' in Cochabamba. These can be explained by the absence of any 'living law' in the public participatory vision relevant to the crucial corporate governance of water services as a specialised enterprise. But as the final section of the chapter will show, developments at the macro level are, oddly perhaps, more dramatic in posing alternatives to managed liberalisation.

## 3.5   Macro-level outcomes

Despite the mixed character of micro-level outcomes pertaining specifically to water policy within Bolivia, the Cochabamba dispute has great importance in a longer macro narrative both internally and externally. Internally, the water war in Cochabamba was part of the catalyst for the rise to prominence of Evo Morales, Bolivia's first indigenous president elected in January 2006.[46] As one interviewee said in 2004:[47]

> Really the system of neo-liberalism in their specific components is starting to crumble and Bolivia knows it. You can explain the political crisis [that culminated in the election of Evo Morales in 2006] ... as a recurrence of the water war. The water war was the first crack. The first earthquake that the model suffered, and now it's changing.

Two former water activists[48] have held Bolivia's first water-specific ministerial post since that election. Although struggles over the regulatory detail of the water laws are still unresolved, shifts in the macro structure have begun to accumulate since Morales' election. These shifts are embedded in transnational mobilisation in continued pursuit of alternatives to managed liberalisation – for externally the 'water war' in Cochabamba

---

[46] 'Morales rose to prominence in the international anti-globalization movement during the April 2000 "water war" against US corporate giant Bechtel, when he foiled plans to privatize the drinking water supply of his hometown of Cochabamba through organizing popular protests' (Saytanides 2003).

[47] Orellana interview.

[48] Abel Mamani, an activist from the capital city, and, since April 2008, René Orellana.

has acquired an iconic status whose meaning seems detachable from the complex concrete post-struggle outcomes. The shifts take two directions that are rather different politically. One focuses on the legal protection of a universal human right to water, the other on a regional cooperation initiative known as the Bolivarian Alternative for the Peoples of Latin America, or ALBA (the Spanish acronym).

### 3.5.1   Human right to water

The movement around the human right to water is extensively supported by and linked to Northern NGOs especially from the anglophone world. One wing of these NGOs[49] supports a radically participatory approach to the human right to water that sees it as synergising with the public participatory model of governance. Other NGOs, including those discussed in Chapter 2 such as PS-Eau and WaterAid,[50] also support the human right to water but see it not as an alternative model but rather as a way of softening the harsher distributive effects of managed liberalisation. Over time these different wings seem to be less distinct from each other: for example, in 2008 Maude Barlow (a Canadian activist and key supporter of the human right to water from a radical perspective) became a senior advisor on water issues to the United Nations General Assembly. Since the United Nations Committee on Economic, Social and Cultural Rights produced a General Comment on the Right to Water[51] in 2002, both transnational companies and the United Nations[52] also now support the human right to water. An international housing NGO, the Centre on Housing Rights and Eviction, has produced a *Manual on the Right to Water* to aid governments in reforming their water laws so as to comply with the human right to water (COHRE *et al.* 2007).

Whether all of this represents victory for the radical wing or a muting of its goals is as yet an open question. For Bolivia, endorsement of the

---

49  Transnational Institute, Food and Water Watch (formerly a division of Public Citizen), Corporate Observatory.

50  Mainstream environmental NGOs such as WWF and IUCN also belong to this wing, as well as Freshwater Action Network and WaterAid.

51  A General Comment lacks the legally binding status of a treaty or a General Resolution: it provides guidelines for States Parties on the interpretation of specific aspects of the human rights treaty of concern to the particular committee. Many argue it still has indirect legal force but in the case of the right to water this is controversial since the right is not explicitly enunciated in the general treaty guaranteeing economic, social and cultural rights. See Russell (2009).

52  Especially UN-HABITAT and the Council of Human Rights (OHCHR).

human right to water is a rejection of the managed liberalisation option, and yet is not a way of resolving the tensions discussed at the micro level. It is a rejection insofar as Bolivia has taken a publicly controversial stance on this issue at the World Water Forum. The Ministerial Conference at the 2009 Fifth World Water Forum in Istanbul declined, as they have done in previous fora, to recognise water as a human right, conceding only that it was a 'basic need' in the Ministerial Declaration. Led by Bolivia, Ecuador and Venezuela, twenty-four countries[53] including half of those in this study (South Africa, Chile and Bolivia) signed a counter-declaration that recognised access to water as a basic human right.[54] Further, Bolivia's new constitution, which was approved in January 2009 after several years of consultations, specifically recognises access to water as a fundamental human right (Article 20). And in the transnational sphere, the radical network of Northern NGOs that supports the human right to water succeeded by 2006 in persuading international financial institutions to support the strengthening of public water service operators via transnational North–South partnerships, instead of emphasising privatisation as the sole policy path for the global water policy field.

Yet the tensions over what this means operationally at the micro level are not resolved by this recognition. The same clause of the Bolivian constitution forbids concessions or privatisation in the water and sewage sector, but allows public companies, community companies and cooperatives *and mixed companies* to provide essential services. The addition of mixed companies to this clause was a crucial battle in the constitutional drafting process, echoing the conflict over the 'GTZ model' that emerged after the success of Law 2066/2878. The social movement coalition regarded the insertion of the reference to 'mixed companies' as a lost battle. Similarly, the policy of supporting public service operators in the transnational sphere was ultimately institutionalised by a Water Operators Partnership that includes both public and private enterprises.[55]

---

[53] Bangladesh, Benin, Bolivia, Chad, Chile, Cuba, Ecuador, Ethiopia, Guatemala, Honduras, Morocco, Namibia, Niger, Nigeria, Panama, Paraguay, Senegal, South Africa, Spain, Sri Lanka, Switzerland, Uruguay, United Arab Emirates and Venezuela.

[54] A subset of these countries also signed a further declaration mounting a sharp critique of the World Water Forum as a legitimate forum for debate on global water policy, given its hybrid private–public nature and the ties it has to the managed liberalisation model (Chapter 2).

[55] See UNSGAB (2006) and the Global Water Operators' Partnership Alliance (n.d.).

At the end of the day, as the current Minister for Water, then an activist and academic, observed in 2004: 'We use [the idea of] water as a human right in a general way, but our work is much more focused on regulations. The UN document [on water as a human right] is useful as a principle, let's say – the problem is converting it into reality.'[56] Just as, at the legislative level, a detailed regulatory dimension is essential to making rights into reality, so too at the constitutional level or in the transnational sphere, the 'devil is in the [regulatory] details'.

### 3.5.2    Bolivarian Alternative for the Peoples of Latin America (ALBA)

The other direction taken at the macro-political level by Bolivia has, like the human right to water, a transnational dimension, but is both much more regionally focused and more redolent of national sovereignty issues germane to 'water as territory'. ALBA aims to create an alternative institutional path, especially around natural resources and urban public services, for countries which have not benefited from market-enhancing regulation, free trade and privatisation. The principal focus so far has been on negotiating People's Trade Agreements with regional neighbours (Shultz and Draper 2008). These create socially oriented trade blocs that emphasise needs-based reciprocity as alternatives to free trade agreements that 'level the playing field' in accordance with market power.

The cooperation of Bolivia and other Latin American countries in relation to the counter-declaration on the human right to water is consistent with their cooperation in ALBA more broadly. The human right to water, however, resonates more easily with the notion of 'water as service': hence its stronger connections to Northern NGO networks. But ALBA would move more strongly towards a regional Southern alternative at the macro level, based on building new regional multilateral institutions that provide a structural alternative to the institutions of the Washington Consensus. The possibility of this happening can be seen in the conclusion of the chapter, which narrates the story of significant changes in the dynamics of international dispute resolution shaping the decision-making field for Bolivian water services policy.

As discussed above, the initial efforts of the Bolivian state to challenge the legality of the arbitration tribunal (which was ICSID) failed.[57] However, over the medium term, the macro-political shifts discussed

---

56  Interview with René Orellana.    57  See pp. 96 and 107.

above, particularly their incorporation of transnational counter-mobilisation, led to a different outcome. In March 2002 two US citizens living in Cochabamba[58] helped mobilise local NGOs and social movement actors[59] to establish an 'international citizens' campaign to intervene in the ICSID case' (Shultz 2006). The campaign built a coalition of actors embedded in the global movement for economic justice, which focused on two strategies: political lobbying (of Bechtel in the US and the Bolivian government) and socio-legal moves that explicitly drew on US legal experience to push the boundaries of the then-current legal framework for international arbitration.

The coalition developed and presented to ICSID an 'International Citizens Petition', drafted with the help of two US NGOs with experience in analogous claims in the context of the North American Free Trade Agreement, and signed by 300 organisations from forty-three countries. The petition was a legal document, patterned after the device of 'administrative petitions' used by citizen groups in the US to obtain action from state and national public agencies. It married solid policy and legal substance with broad international citizen action, containing a background summary of the history and issues in the case, a specific set of demands to ICSID that focused on opening up the process to public involvement, and the legal basis for those demands, from ICSID's own rules of conduct. Although no legal basis, at least in obligatory terms, then existed in international arbitration law for the participation of external groups in international arbitration, ICSID's own rules of conduct clearly gave ICSID the right and the opportunity to open up the process (e.g. to 'visit any place connected with the dispute or conduct inquiries there').[60] The coalition viewed their strategy as a democratic device to focus on actions that the tribunal could take if it wanted to and to create a visible, forceful public pressure campaign on the tribunal to take those actions.

ICSID denied the petition. However, Morales' election changed the political landscape. Abel Mamani, his first Water Minister (originally a leader of water protests in the capital city) mounted a constitutional court challenge against the constitutionality of treaties referring disputes

---

[58] Tom Kruse, Centro de Estudios para el Desarrollo Laboral y Agrario, interviewed by Carolina Fairstein, Cochabamba, 29 April 2004; Shultz interview.
[59] La Coordinadora, FEDECOR, Acción Andina, Fundación Solon and the Bolivian Forum on Environment and Development.
[60] ICSID Arbitration Rule 37: see www.sice.oas.org/dispute/comarb/icsid/icsid2b.asp.

to ICSID.[61] On 19 January 2006 Aguas de Tunari and Bolivia settled the ICSID case for a nominal 2 bolivianos (US$0.25) (Medalla 2006; Shultz 2006). In May 2007, Bolivia withdrew from ICSID, the first country to take such a step. And as we shall see in the next chapter, similar pressures to open up ICSID processes to more transparency and broader participation in Argentina succeeded,[62] and have since spread.[63]

The ICSID narrative thus illustrates a country reclaiming its sovereign autonomy in relation to foreign investors, aided by a process of transnational mobilisation which fought for transparency and participation by vulnerable groups affected by foreign investment. For a moment in the complex landscape of global water service policy, water as territory and water as service worked together to create a glimpse of an alternative to managed liberalisation – another world was, momentarily, possible. For the most part, however, complexity and tension reigned at the micro level, and challenged the apparent shifts at the macro level. The 'naming and blaming' that animated the challenge to managed liberalisation was drawn back into the 'rulemaking, monitoring and enforcement' of that same model when it articulated its claims at the micro level, at considerable cost to the energy and efficacy of its original vision.

To conclude, the Cochabamba dispute was an arresting exemplar of conflicts over access to water – one that created a significant opportunity for an alternative to managed liberalisation to emerge in the broader global field of water services policy. Far more than the other case studies in this book, the terms of conflict concerned property rights in the structure of production, rather than rights to access the fruits of production. The results posed a particularly stark challenge to managed liberalisation, pushing not to ameliorate the effects of managed liberalisation but to propose an alternative basic structure based more on the collective democratisation of property rights. But that alternative vision appeared more vividly in moments of resistance than in the more routinised phase of institutionalising the gains of the social movement

---

[61] He presented formal accusations of wrongdoing against two of the former directors of the regulatory agency for water alleging that the contract they signed with Aisa (Suez), still ongoing when Morales came to power, was in violation of the constitution and against the interest of the state. See Medalla (2006).

[62] See Chapter 4.

[63] In 2005 the process was followed in a case involving foreign water services investment by the UK company Biwater in Tanzania: *Biwater* v. *Tanzania*, Case No. ARB/05/22, Procedural Order No. 5.

activists. In this phase, tensions between conceptions of 'water as service' and 'water as territory' fractured the activists' coalitions, as well as playing into ongoing conflict between the two models themselves. The micro-level story in Bolivia should remind us that although 'another world is possible', institutionally it will most likely use complex hybrids of rights and regulation that constitute similar building blocks to the world of managed liberalisation.

# Regulatory arbitrage and popcorn politics: contrasting disputing pathways in Argentina and Chile

## 4.1 Introduction

In the 1990s transnational flows of money and investment, which as we saw in the last chapter were influential in Bolivia, created common trajectories of institutional change across many other countries too, particularly in Latin America. In global terms, Latin American countries experienced the greatest level of foreign involvement in water services in the 1990s, signing 106 of 223 cross-border water services contracts between 1990 and 2002 (ECLAC 2002; Kirkpatrick and Parker 2004). Suez, Vivendi and Thames all invested significantly in Chile and Argentina during this period. Suez, which as noted in Chapter 3 had held a long-term concession contract in La Paz, Bolivia, bought the regional water company providing water to Santiago, Chile, and secured long-term concessions in Argentina in Buenos Aires, Santa Fe and Córdoba. Thames bought three regional water companies in the south of Chile. Vivendi had a stake in the Buenos Aires concession and also secured a long-term concession in the province of Tucumán, Argentina. Disinvestment has since occurred in all the Argentinian concessions, and Thames Water has sold its Chilean holdings (Lobina and Hall 2007(a)), but the remaining Chilean acquisitions have remained in foreign hands.[1]

This shared experience of transnational investment in cross-border markets for the delivery of water services generated pressures for the adoption of a managed liberalisation approach to governance. This resulted in the common adoption of semi-independent regulatory agencies in the water sector in many countries, many of which shared basic formal similarities. Chile and Argentina provide a particularly interesting pair of

---

[1] Suez has exited from direct involvement in the Santiago water company, but remains the major shareholder of the ongoing majority shareholder, Agbar. The Ontario Teachers' Pension Fund also owns a considerable portion of the Santiago water company. See Lobina and Hall (2007(a)).

case studies to compare the 'rulemaking, monitoring and enforcement' patterns of this classic facet of managed liberalisation. Both countries adopted formally similar regulatory institutions in the water sector, yet the broader context of the politics of water services policy reforms in each was profoundly different.

Four contrasting features stand out. First, Chile established an agency at central government level, along with twelve centrally controlled regional public companies, while Argentina developed agencies at provincial level. Chile's rejection of the 1980s wave of decentralisation that was so popular elsewhere in Latin America, including Argentina, reflected the internalisation of the 'naming and blaming' ethos of the 'Chicago boys': economic technocrats holding powerful positions in government, many of whom were educated at the University of Chicago economics department. They argued that there was insufficient professional capacity at local government levels, and that the private sector would provide more reliable expertise as well as efficiency gains. Argentina's transferral of responsibility for delivery of water services to the provincial level in 1981 arguably bore out such fears. In the case study of Tucumán explored here, the provincial state water company experienced considerable difficulty in taking on these responsibilities, reflected in fifteen different changes of director between 1981 and 1996.

These institutional differences were accompanied by three further differences that led to a much greater magnification of the 'problem' of access to water in Argentina as opposed to Chile. In terms of policy context, access to water in Chile is far more widespread than in other developing countries. In 1930, the Chilean central government made the provision of water and sewage services (WSS) a developmental priority, and unusually high coverage was achieved as early as the 1970s (Chechilnitzky 2003), with 91 per cent having access to safe water by 1998 in comparison with only 71 per cent in Argentina (UNDP 2000). Moreover Argentina experienced a serious economic crisis in 2000, while Chile remained stable, depoliticised and investment-friendly during the period studied. Finally, in terms of political culture, there is a relatively low level of civil society activism in Chile, particularly around issues of socio-economic policy (Foweraker 2001; Houtzager and Kurtz 2000), while Argentina has a long tradition of robust popular activism, symbolised by the *piqueteros* with their mass blockades of public roads to demonstrate opposition.

Bolivia, as explored in Chapter 3, represented the strongest articulation of a public participatory model of governance for access to water in this research, and, as we saw, the salience of 'water as territory' to the emergence of this model was important. The Chilean–Argentinian comparison takes further the cleavages *within* a conception of 'water as service', cleavages that produced significantly different outcomes in the two countries, despite the broadly similar assumptions embedded in the managed liberalisation underpinning the introduction of a semi-independent regulatory agency in both. In Chile, managed liberalisation became relatively well internalised and stable. Chile's regulatory agency acquired technical competence and, within a relatively narrow remit, political salience. In Argentina a hybrid case emerged: managed liberalisation failed, but in regulatory terms, no stable political alternative emerged. The provincial regulatory agency in Tucumán became highly politicised. Despite its lack of technical competence, it played a salient role at an interesting intersection of party politics, popular direct action and small claims lawsuits.

In essence, this pair of case studies demonstrates contrasting contexts in which ordinary citizen–consumers experienced the introduction of managed liberalisation as a felt injury. Differences in institutional choices, political culture and policy context created a situation that catalysed significantly more 'naming and blaming', and consequently more oppositional activism, in Argentina than in Chile. While the Chilean case was not uncontested, two quite different disputing pathways emerged from the significant cross-national differences in the effects of creating a semi-independent regulatory agency. The Chilean pathway focused on regulatory arbitrage, while the Argentinian pathway exhibited what I call 'popcorn politics': an explosive interaction between the rules, monitoring and enforcement practices of managed liberalisation and the naming, claiming and blaming ethos of public participatory governance.

## 4.2   Regulatory agencies in comparative contrast: Chile and Argentina

### 4.2.1   Structure and genesis

In comparing the structure and genesis of the two agencies, what is most striking is that Chile's regulatory agency was to a much greater extent a product of domestic political dynamics, while in Argentina regulatory agencies were imposed on the provinces by a federal government itself strongly influenced by the recommendations of international agencies and transnational regulatory policy advisors. Overall, we will see that the Chilean case shows how domestic internalisation of the managed liberalisation model over a long period, combined with retaining central control, resulted in a more politically salient, stable regulatory agency. The Argentinian case shows that exposure to international arbitration, together with opportunist populist use of loan conditionality, resulted in rushed reforms that created agencies with inadequate expertise for their new role, particularly in the context of decentralisation.

Chile created a regulatory agency in the water services sector[2] that was much closer than Argentina's to the 'ideal' supported by international financial institutions and a strong epistemic community. The water services sector in Chile was dominated by a technocratically oriented regulatory agency, a centralised executive commitment to efficiency goals, and a highly bureaucratic subsidy system that neutralised the political resonance of affordability issues. The regulatory agency was established in 1989 along with a suite of reforms that corporatised the regional water companies. This occurred nine years *before* full privatisation in 1998, creating space for regulatory expertise and independence to accrue before the more controversial step to privatisation was taken. Of course, the 1989 corporatisation of water service delivery in Chile was by no means uncontroversial, and some argue that privatisation would have occurred much more quickly had Pinochet's dictatorship regime not been defeated in 1990. But the process still differs starkly from Argentina, where Tucumán's water services operator was abruptly transformed into a regulatory agency[3] in 1995, halving its workforce in the process. The Tucumán regulator was established more or less through central fiat, *after* a legislative framework for privatisation had been passed. This was an almost direct reversal of the timing in Chile, and reflected an opportunistic and hasty response to the entry of the foreign private sector. The Tucumán regulatory body only came into formal operation several months after the French water company Vivendi secured a thirty-year concession contract in 1995.[4]

---

[2] Known as SISS (the Superintendency of Sanitation Services). Chile's water resources (i.e. the 'macro' water cycle) are regulated by the general water department (DGA), a unit of the Ministry of Public Works which oversees a complex system of tradable water rights established in 1981.

[3] ERSACT (Ente Regulador del Servicio de Agua y Cloadas de Tucumán).

[4] The contract was signed with the Argentine affiliate company Aguas del Aconquija, controlled in substance by Vivendi despite its separate legal personality. The parent company was actually known as Compagnie Générale des Eaux (CGE) at the time of entering into the concession, and more recently as Veolia, but is more popularly recognised as Vivendi, the name used in this text. Furthermore, as noted in 4.4, Vivendi Universal, the still-existing media company, is the beneficiary of the ICSID compensation award, and not Veolia Environnement, the now separate water division. See Lobina and Hall (2007(a)).

The different motivations for involving the foreign private sector in the two cases exacerbated resulting differences in staffing, expertise and politicisation of the regulatory agency. In Argentina, President Menem's sweeping neoliberal reforms were a highly politicised, economy-wide linchpin of his political project, and were linked more to systemic efforts to centralise executive power via the top-down imposition of market reforms than to any sector-specific needs or goals (Walker 2006). Menem imposed privatisation projects, often by executive decree without legislative debate, in a wide range of sectors, of which urban water services was only one. Moreover, private sector involvement in the Tucumán water services sector occurred when very substantial numbers of citizens lacked access to water and had done so for decades under the remit of troubled public water operators. In such a context, the rushed introduction of a regulatory agency was highly contentious and politically sensitive.

In Chile, basic access to water services had already been achieved, and the catalyst was both more sectorally specific and more technical: the need to raise private finance to build waste treatment plants (Chechilnitzky 2003).[5] This is not to say that private sector involvement was apolitical: rather, the technical needs of the sector resonated well with domestic preferences for economic export-oriented goals as well as transnational pressures from the US–Chile free trade agreement. There were both legal and political pressures to meet international standards in wastewater treatment in order to facilitate fruit exports, highlighted by what one interviewee referred to as the 'incident of the poisonous grape', when contamination of grapes exported for wine-making to the US had caused considerable domestic consternation about Chile's reputation in the international trade arena.[6] Combined with considerable lobbying from domestic construction companies,[7] this range of domestic political, legal and technical pressures led to the centre-left Frei government passing a legislative framework for privatisation in 1995. This was by no means uncontested: indeed, in 1998 the centre-left Lagos government that succeeded Frei's altered the legal framework from one of full asset privatisation to a system of long-term concessions. This was done in response

---

[5] The percentage of treated wastewater almost doubled between 1998 and 2005. Treated wastewater levels were 42 per cent in 2003 but were on target to reach 81 per cent by the end of 2005.

[6] Eugenio Celedon Snr, retired senior civil servant, interviewed by Bronwen Morgan and Carolina Fairstein, Santiago, Chile, 14 January 2004.

[7] Loreta Silva, Chilean Chamber of Commerce, interviewed by Bronwen Morgan and Carolina Fairstein, Santiago, 24 January 2004.

to a general public backlash against privatisation, including an unofficial plebiscite conducted in the southern city of Concepción where a huge majority of the city's population rejected (unsuccessfully) the purchase of its regional water company by UK-based Thames Water.[8] Yet, strikingly, almost no interviewee in Chile thought this shift in legal framework had any powerful political or even practical implications, particularly concerning the regulatory agency. And in stark contrast to the very openly politicised process that took place in Argentina, in Chile, major decisions were made in the interstices of technical and obscure legislation. The 1998 legislation to allow privatisation was passed with a ceiling on ownership[9] that was quietly removed a few months later in a little-noticed tax bill.[10] A few years later, by means of another little-noticed tax bill, full asset sales of four of the five companies originally privatised in the late 1990s were permitted to proceed.[11]

The much greater political sensitivity and contention surrounding the introduction of the regulatory agency in Tucumán compared to Chile had two marked effects. First, it undermined staffing and expertise in Tucumán, where the transformation from operating water services to regulating them was institutionally superficial. Tucumán's regulatory agency was effectively carved out of the original municipal operating company at the time that privatisation occurred. That company, which employed 2,400 staff in 1990, transferred 700 staff to the new concessionaire, laid off some and kept 900 employees, mainly hydrological and chemical engineers, lawyers and accountants (Crenzel 2003). But employees were given little additional training or preparation for their entirely new role of regulating rather than operating.[12] The management council of the regulatory agency was appointed by the executive with legislative approval, rendering it subject to relatively close political control. By contrast, in Chile, the regulatory agency had a technical and controlling mandate from its inception, supported by detailed legislation drafted

[8]  Celedon Snr interview.
[9]  General Law for Sanitation Services (Law 19,549, 1995 bill) of 5 February 1998.
[10]  Article 5 of Law 19,888 of 14 July 1998 (a general tax law) abolished any ceiling on the sale of shares in water companies.
[11]  A bill to 'establish the funding needed to ensure the priority social objectives of the government': Law 19,888 of August 2003, Article 5. Emos, the Santiago company and the most politically sensitive, was not included.
[12]  Daniel Arancibia, former president of the regulatory body ERSACT (Ente Regulador del Servicio de Agua y Cloadas de Tucumán) and director of the former state-run water company, interviewed by Carolina Fairstein, Tucumán, Argentina, 1 July 2004.

quite literally by economists.[13] It was staffed by a stable collection of 140 well-qualified professionals and technicians, including engineers, lawyers, scientists and economists, all of whom were trained from the outset to control and monitor rather than to operate (although many also had engineering backgrounds that helped them to understand the technical imperatives of operating).

Second, in Chile, social issues were kept firmly separate from the regulatory agency, while in Tucumán social issues dogged the regulatory agency from the start. Chilean social policy in the utility sector centred on affordability delivered across a number of policy domains (water, electricity, gas, housing) by means of a complex subsidy scheme administered by municipal governments. The staff in the regulatory agency for water consequently did not develop any expertise in this area. Instead, regulatory staff focused mainly on issues such as tariff-setting, accounting processes for investment obligations, procurement processes and mergers. In approaching these issues, technical economic expertise was very much to the fore. For example, to set tariffs, the regulator and the company each produced an estimate based on hypothetical models of a perfectly efficient company, using complex formulae laid down by the legislative framework. They then negotiated for fifteen days, and if no consensus was reached, the final decision was made by an expert panel of three, typically chaired by a Ph.D.-qualified economist along with nominees from the relevant company and the regulatory agency.[14]

By contrast, in Tucumán, the regulator was confronted from very early on with the social issues raised by tariff-setting in ways that were densely intermingled with the technical issues. For example, as we shall see below in more detailed discussion of the disputing pathway that developed in Argentina, consumer activism culminating in water payment boycotts was closely linked to objections to the way in which Vivendi's subsidiary included certain taxes in its tariff structure. The consumer activism led to the regulator making a ruling on this tariff structure that took account of the affordability concerns driving the bill payment boycott. In addition, pressure from consumer activism led to constant legislator enquiries to the regulator regarding the fine detail of micro measurements underlying the service goals of the concession contract,[15] enquiries which were

---

[13] Silva interview.

[14] The expert panel decisions have never been judicially reviewed, though heated technical debates regarding the parameters of the models have persisted and been clarified over time by legislative revision.

[15] Arancibia interview.

led by attempts to pass a series of bills in the legislature to create 'social tariffs' for those who could not afford the pricing structure under the new concession contract. The regulatory agency in Tucumán ultimately became so immersed in direct political conflict that its board of directors was temporarily removed, in a procedure akin to the administration of a failing company,[16] and during the suspension of its board, the legislature took over the job of drafting a new regulatory framework with which to renegotiate the concession contract with Vivendi's subsidiary. As we shall see below, this failed to quell the rising disputing dynamics.

Overall, regulatory politics in Chilean water services mirrored broader macro characteristics of Chile's economy, which gives priority to market incentives across many sectors of social policy, yet remains markedly unfriendly to ordinary consumers: a kind of openly clientelistic version of neoliberal reforms. The space for articulating claims of fairness, equity or human rights was severely constricted, whereas in Tucumán, Argentina, regulatory politics became almost overwhelmed by claims of fairness, equity and rights. These contrasting dynamics are evident in a closer exploration of how regulatory politics in the two case studies intersected with consumer demands .

### 4.2.2    *Consumers, rights and activists compared*

It is striking that in both Chile and Argentina opposition to private sector participation in the delivery of urban water services was often articulated through consumer identities. Although we saw in Chapter 2 that some of the activism in France took the form of consumerist demands, this was a relatively minor aspect of the overall emphasis on local public participation, and the Bolivian case study showed a marked absence of consumerist-embedded opposition. It may seem surprising that a basically economic identity is mobilised in opposition to a process of commodification, but as Matthew Hilton (2009) has recently documented in fascinating detail, the consumer movement is a global one, and its trajectory in the global South during the 1980s and 1990s in particular has been very different from the form it has taken in the industrialised world. While the core goals of the consumer movement in the developed industrial countries have emphasised choice, quality, safety and individual welfare, those emanating from the global South have focused far more on basic needs,

---

[16] Tucumán legislators Graneros and Ramos, interviewed by Carolina Fairstein, Tucumán, 3 July 2004.

access, participation and collective welfare – a difference embedded in the raw fact that without access to basic needs, the capacity to choose high-quality and safe products is hollow.

What emerged in the Chilean and Argentinian consumer-embedded activism around water services is a striking contrast *within* the global South that rather mirrors Hilton's distinction between North/South consumer activism. Chilean consumer opposition was funnelled (though not without contestation) into a diluted form of the consumer demands typical of the industrialised North, while in Argentina, consumer activism was almost entirely animated by strong demands for access to basic needs and full participation. The contrast could be seen as two different ways to 'name, blame and claim' in the face of felt injuries, with the Chilean approach more resonant with the discourse of managed liberalisation and the formal introduction of quasi-independent regulatory agencies than the Argentinian.

Both, in contrast to Bolivia, fleshed out contestation over the terms of 'water as service' rather than engaging with the conception of 'water as territory' that in Bolivia led in a very different direction from consumer-embedded activism. As we shall see, the two created contrasting ways to participate in policymaking (with Argentina giving much more prominence to confrontational direct action), and as a result created two very different disputing pathways.

## 4.3    Two disputing pathways

In Argentina, serious disputes over private sector participation in urban water services arose in many parts of the country, including Buenos Aires, Córdoba, Santa Fe and Tucumán, this last being the site of the dispute which was at the centre of the detailed research case study. By contrast, in Chile, although private sector participation was certainly contested, no particular dispute ever emerged in substantial formal legal terms between ordinary citizens and the private water service operators: formal legal disputing energy was rather channelled into interactions between the regulator and the private companies.

### 4.3.1    *Argentina: background*

The dispute between Vivendi's subsidiary and the people of Tucumán centred on the method for measuring water consumption, the level of tariffs to customers, the timing and percentage of any increase in tariffs, the remedy for non-payment of tariffs, Vivendi's right to pass through to customers certain taxes, and the quality of the water delivered. When in the summer of 1995 manganese contamination turned the water orange-brown, consumer anger boiled over into a series of actions leading to mass payment boycotts in 1996. These boycotts played a substantial role in undermining the economic viability of the concession contract, leading to its very premature termination in 1997. The consumers formed two main associations with different histories and aims. One[17] was an umbrella organisation for consumers in many different cities as well as in rural areas, focusing only on water, and supportive of direct action, street protests and an oppositional stance, or on large-scale structural reforms such as re-municipalisation. The other[18] was based only in the provincial capital and focused on essential services more broadly, highlighting in-depth study, negotiations with legislators and focused reforms such as a social tariff.

Both groups formed as a direct response to the entry of the foreign private sector, a catalyst which also influenced their self-designation as consumer associations. Their stance rejected any notion that consumers were individualised, apolitical agents: rather, they viewed collective organisation as consumers as the appropriate form for playing a dual role that bridged direct and 'unruly' action of a more overtly political nature with more formal legal modes of participation. This dual role combined collective social protest via payment boycotts, street marches and demonstrations, on the one hand, with more traditional policy lobbying and acting as a conduit for ensuring legal protection of the boycotting consumers, on the other.

This dual role enabled Tucumán consumer associations to enact in an almost dialectical way a public participatory model of governance. Their focus on collective social protest pitted them against the state even while their function as a conduit for legal protection brought them directly into dialogue with the regulatory agency. That they could do both simultaneously was in part because since 1994 the Argentinian legal system had recognised the right for affected individuals and organisations to resort to the judiciary for the protection of *collective and diffuse rights* by the promotion of a special writ, the 'collective *amparo*' (Article 43 of the National

---

[17] ADEUCOT (Asociación en Defensa de los Usuarios y Consumidores de Tucumán, i.e. Association in Defence of Users and Consumers of Tucumán).

[18] DUDAS (Defensa de los Usuarios de Agua y Servicios, i.e. Defence of Users of Water and Utilities).

Constitution). Over time, the use of this writ has enabled judges to require the political branches to consider policy responses for large collectivities in ways that amplify the political ramifications of legal decisions far beyond specific individuals, in the process bridging collective protest and the policymaking process.

By maintaining both aspects of this dual front, the consumer activists were able to demand reforms of the policy framework that were in tune with a public participatory model of governance. In other words, the 'naming, claiming and blaming' energy of a basic needs vision of consumerism led to particular rulemaking, monitoring and enforcement demands that had both procedural and substantive dimensions. In procedural terms, the activists proposed public hearings in tariff-setting procedures, and the appointment of a consumer representative to the governing board of the regulator. From a substantive angle, they sought a ban on disconnection and a social tariff structure. While not all of these proposals found formal endorsement, the disputing pathway described below led to a number of sponsored bills by legislators who were lobbied by the consumer associations. The regulatory politics that emerged was a kind of 'popcorn' incrementalism, a phrase intended to convey the cumulative but unplanned impact of the various strategies employed by consumer associations.

### 4.3.2    Chile: background

In stark contrast to the Tucumán setting, there was a marked absence of space in Chile for the incorporation of 'everyday citizen' demands. Direct action during the 1990s was remarkably muted, and public media coverage of water provision issues focused overwhelmingly on making the country safe for foreign investors. There was certainly contestation. Some came from individual legislators who took up the cause of constituency members.[19] Citizen groups also mobilised from time to time, albeit weakly. But although Chilean regulatory culture promoted an image of a legalistic conception of the public interest underpinning regulatory dynamics, it was in practice a public interest that filtered out the general public. The legal device of *recurso de proteccion* (effectively the ability to obtain an injunction) did not facilitate collective consumer action: it was

---

[19]  See motions filed by Chilean House of Representatives member Patricio Walker, or the Christian Democratic (DC) deputy Antonella Sciaraffia and senate candidate Fernando Flores: *La Estrella de Iquique*, detailed in Foerster (2002).

used mainly by the water service companies against the regulator, not least because it had to be filed within fifteen days of any harm occurring and thus favoured 'repeat players'.

Nor did Chile have administrative courts where individuals could challenge abusive and illegal action. Consumer law provided only highly individualised forms of action, focusing on choice, safety and quality. Conscious of the limitations of this, consumer associations in Chile had battled for almost six years to amend consumer protection legislation to provide a mild form of class action. In 2004 they finally succeeded, but public services were expressly excluded from its remit (Engel 2005).[20] The rationale given was a technical-legal argument that the regulatory framework of utilities law overrode in its specificity the more general provisions of consumer protection.[21] Yet utilities law provided *less* protection to consumers than the general consumer law would have done. The politically sensitive issue of infrastructure provision with high capital costs was, in a political culture of paradoxically pro-market bureaucratic authoritarianism, in many ways 'off-limits' to the ordinary citizen–consumer as far as the legal framework of rules, monitoring and enforcement was concerned. Draft amendments to facilitate consumer involvement in the tariff process and monetary compensation for service breaches were blocked by central government.[22] In light of this it is perhaps not surprising that in 2005 the World Economic Forum gave Chile first place for macroeconomic handling in a global survey, but only fifty-third place for consumer responsiveness (Engel 2005).

Of course, it is not that politically contested aspects of lay-offs and tariff rises, or the undue influence of private operators, did not exist in Chile. Rather, they seemed not to spark the same kind of political mobilisation as in Argentina. One interviewee from the Central Labour Union in Chile said – with some regret – that 'in Argentina, when the lights go off, the people burn tyres on the roadways and build barricades, while in Chile they simply go down to the supermarket and buy candles'.[23] Even when consumers did collectively mobilise, they rarely found the government in any way responsive: as one foreign private provider commented, for

---

[20] Engel also notes that only three collective actions were lodged in the law's first year of validity.

[21] Alberto Urregado, director of SERNAC (Servicio Nationale de Consumers), interviewed by Bronwen Morgan and Carolina Fairstein, Santiago, 28 January 2004.

[22] Silva interview.

[23] Miguel Soto, Central Workers' Union, interviewed by Bronwen Morgan and Carolina Fairstein, Santiago, 27 January 2004.

groups like this, 'it's like talking to a brick wall, everyone knows that'.[24] The very different ways in which consumer mobilisation around 'water as a service' evolved in Argentina and Chile created a striking contrast in the disputing pathways that evolved in relation to the regulatory agency in the two countries. In Chile, the primary disputing energy focused on relationships between the water companies and the regulator, while in Tucumán the 'amparo' writ facilitated a sprawling disputing trajectory that played out between individual consumers, the Ombudsman, the regulator, the provincial legislature, the federal government and international arbitrators.

### 4.3.3   Regulatory arbitrage in Chile

While the consumer activism in Chile energised a certain amount of legislative activity around draft bills to ameliorate conditions on the ground for consumers (around, for example, disconnection practices or the ability to dig wells on private grounds), none of the draft bills ever succeeded due to the executive centralism prevailing in the political culture. Instead, what disputing energy there was found much more expression in the relations between the regulatory agency and the companies providing water services. During the 1990s, when the water companies were corporatised in form but publicly owned, relationships between the regulatory agencies and the water companies were ones of negotiation and fairly cordial bargaining. The shift to privatisation in 1998 inaugurated a more adversarial relationship between operators and regulator. In the wake of the rapid privatisation (1998–2001) of five of Chile's thirteen regional companies, fines imposed by the regulator increased by 69 per cent between 2000 and 2001 (Foerster 2002). An analysis of data from the internal records of the regulatory agency on its adjudicatory decisions together with judicial appeals (1995–2005, see Table 11) shows the distribution of those increased fines across types of company.

The data shows that the privatised companies dominate the statistics of above-average fines levied, the highest rates of large fines, and the highest appeal rates against fines. One interesting exception to the general pattern is Essbio, the regional company owned by UK-based Thames Water (previously RWE-Thames). Essbio attracted the highest fines from the regulatory agency but had a relatively low rate of appealing those fines.

---

[24]  Jose Manuel de Castro and Camila Manzano, Casal (Biwater), interviewed by Bronwen Morgan and Carolina Fairstein, Santiago, 27 January 2004.

Table 11 *Analysis of cases brought to Chilean water regulator SISS, 1995–2005*

| Company | No. of fines | Percentage of total | Appealed or not | Percentage appealed | Fines = or > 300 UTM | Average fine (UTM) |
|---|---|---|---|---|---|---|
| Essar | 5 | 3 | 0 | 0 | 0 | 9 |
| Esmag | 2 | 1 | 0 | 0 | 0 | 55.5 |
| Essan | 3 | 2 | 0 | 0 | 0 | 85.67 |
| **Essel (owned by RWE-Thames)** | **23** | **16** | **2** | **9** | **10** | **243.43** |
| Essam | 10 | 7 | 1 | 10 | 1 | 259.8 |
| Essat | 12 | 8 | 2 | 17 | 2 | 260.33 |
| **Essbio (owned by RWE-Thames)** | **23** | **16** | **5** | **22** | **8** | **488.91** |
| Essco | 7 | 5 | 2 | 29 | 2 | 137.14 |
| Emmssa | 3 | 2 | 1 | 33 | 0 | 48.67 |
| **Essal (owned by Iberdrola)** | **13** | **9** | **6** | **46** | **3** | **217.15** |
| Emssat | 6 | 4 | 3 | 50 | 0 | 48.33 |
| **Emos/Aguas Andinas (owned by Suez)** | **21** | **15** | **11** | **52** | **3** | **137.14** |
| **Esval (owned by Anglian Water)** | **13** | **9** | **8** | **62** | **5** | **446.85** |
| Total | 144 | 100% | 31% | 33.10% | 23.61% | 202.92 |

Table 11 (*cont.*)

Notes:

| | |
|---|---|
| Average fine | 202.92 UTM |
| Above-average fines | **Essbio**, **Esval**, Essat, Essam, **Essel**, Emmssa (descending order) |
| Average appeal rate | 31% |
| Those with highest appeal rates | **Esval**, **Emos**, **Essal** (descending order, all > 1,000 UTM) |
| Highest rate of big fines | **Essbio**, **Essel**, **Esval**, **Essal**, Essat, **Emos**, Essam (descending order) |
| Highest fines per se | **Essbio**, **Esval**, Essam, Essat |
| Big fines as percentage of total fines | **Essbio** + **Esval** + Essam + Essat = 10,968/total fines 36,487 = 30.06% |

Privatised companies are in **bold** type, UTM = multiplier unit for fine levels
Compiled from analysis of internal SISS records

Relatedly, Essel, also owned by Thames, also tended not to lodge appeals at a high rate. Essbio attracted more political controversy than any other water company in Chile: it was the location of the city-wide citizens' initiative referendum mentioned above that roundly rejected the privatisation of the regional water company. Although the referendum result was just as roundly ignored by the government, Thames may well have considered the political costs of appealing greater than the likelihood of success.

The actions summarised above constituted the primary formal legal disputing activity in Chile around the provision of urban water services. There were also very important judicial disputes emerging around water resource rights: although mostly beyond the scope of the focus taken here, the foreign private providers in the big cities did have large stakes in the outcomes of these debates, and were vigorously litigating to defend their position,[25] albeit against a different governmental department from the water services regulatory agency. This pattern of disputing was, almost without exception, initiated by the regulator or the company rather than consumers, and focused mainly on defining the limits of property rights between regulator and operator. In other words, the patterns typified the regulatory politics of managed liberalisation, where the rights and entitlements of 'end-users' are bracketed in favour of a focus on the allocation of rights and responsibilities between the state and the service provider. Moreover, although the regulator usually prevailed upon appeal, and although at least some of these instances should have indirectly benefited consumers, they rarely did so, since (as discussed above) the Chilean water sector lacked any legal device for indemnifying consumers. In short, rulemaking, monitoring and enforcement of managed liberalisation in Chile was unresponsive to the naming, blaming and claiming of disaffected citizens, even when it was articulated in the relatively narrow terms of a consumerism of choice and quality.

### 4.3.4  Popcorn politics in Argentina

While Chilean water politics focused on regulatory arbitrage, the disputing patterns in Argentina cumulatively exploded to draw in a very wide range of political, institutional and citizen interests in a 'popcorn politics' that bounced back and forth between polarised alternatives. As mentioned above, in the summer of 1996 in Tucumán, many thousands of users ceased paying their water bills, citing orange-brown water and

---

[25] Castro and Manzano interview.

illegitimately imposed water taxes as the reason. With these ordinary citizens represented in political lobbying efforts by the consumer associations described earlier, the bridging of direct protest and traditional reform channels was greatly facilitated by the role played by the Ombudsman, who was able to use the collective *amparo* process in an intriguing manner that parlayed individual consumer action into the collective articulation of basic needs with a real political impact. The Ombudsman's action linked disparate activities by consumers, the regulator and the legislature, all of which were focused on integrating redistributive policies protective of the least well-off (such as social tariffs and a prohibition on disconnections) into the regulatory framework governing the foreign private provider.

The first step taken by the Tucumán Ombudsman was to help create a legal shield that extended and protected the most efficacious of the consumers' protest activities: their boycotting of bill payments which had significant effects on the ongoing political and economic viability of the concession contract. The Ombudsman advised boycotting consumers on how to lodge a formal administrative dispute with Vivendi's subsidiary, giving precise guidance on how to draft a 'dispute letter' alleging that services had been deficiently rendered due to inferior water quality and incorrectly calculated tariffs.[26] Long queues of people formed outside the Ombudsman's Office asking for the form of the letter for them to use. The Ombudsman also gave collective legitimacy to these individual disputes by issuing a series of official resolutions that highlighted the details of why the invoicing was incorrect, drawing also on a public auditors' report to the same effect.

The effects of this strategy involved the regulatory agency in the growing dispute. Vivendi's subsidiary did not respond to the dispute letters received within fifteen days, triggering a legal provision that bounced the dispute to the regulator. The regulator essentially supported the position taken by the Ombudsman, issuing two resolutions that discounted consumers' bills: first, by the amount of disputed taxes that Vivendi's subsidiary was passing through on the bill, and, second, by the amount paid for water during the periods that turbid, orange-brown water was provided.[27]

Although only about 10 per cent of payment boycotters filed the appropriate paperwork, this still amounted to some thousands of people.

---

[26] Resolutions No. 66 and No. 67 of 1996: Tucumán Audit Office Report 015, on file with author.

[27] Resolution No. 212 and No. 213 of ERSACT, the regulatory agency for water services in Tucumán.

Vivendi's subsidiary did not challenge the decrees of the Ombudsman or those of the regulator in local courts, and issued amended invoices to disputing customers. However, the company continued to voice its disagreement with the approach of the Ombudsman and the regulatory agency, eventually complaining that the Tucumán government was frustrating the contract through a 'concerted public attack ... which included a series of inflammatory statements and other acts encouraging customers not to pay their bills'.[28]

Repeated attempts to renegotiate the concession contract between the government and the company failed, at least in part because of multiple amendments to the renegotiated framework secured by a hostile legislature which was fighting to support social tariffs and the prohibition of disconnection. In September 1997, three years into the thirty-year concession, Vivendi's contract was terminated, and in October 1998 Tucumán province took back the delivery of water services into public hands. Once this occurred, the French parent company immediately filed a suit against the boycotters to recover the unpaid charges in accordance with the *original* invoices, in defiance of the legal implications of the resolutions made by the Ombudsman and the regulator that legitimated the amended invoices (which its subsidiary company had earlier ignored). The Ombudsman's Office took two unprecedented steps in response to the lawsuits against the boycotters, justifying their approach on the basis that the private company was by then no longer in a legal relationship providing water services for the province. First, the Ombudsman's Office offered individual legal assistance to consumers at no cost, having failed to secure such assistance from the local bar association.[29] Second, the Office tried to lodge a collective *amparo* lawsuit in the courts on behalf of the boycotters, but this was rejected in multiple consecutive fora by a series of different judges. A more detailed account of the responses of local lawyers and judges in relation to these two moves makes increasingly clear how politically sensitive the matter was.

The individual legal assistance given to consumers by the Ombudsman's Office did not have any precedent, and was arguably

[28] Paragraph 30 of *Compañia de Aguas del Aconquija, S.A. & Compagnie Générale des Eaux v. Argentine Republic*, Award, ICSID Case No. ARB/97/3 (12 November 2000), 40 ILM 426, also available (with subseqent decisions on the same case) at: www.worldbank.org/icsid/cases/awards.htm#award15.

[29] Maria Bossio, Ombudsman, interviewed by Carolina Fairstein, Tucumán, 10 August 2004.

formally outside their authority to provide.[30] Consumers who could afford a lawyer were given a precedent defence to take to a lawyer as a first step; those who could not afford legal assistance were simply helped directly. This was done with some discomfort as a direct response to need and the reluctance of local lawyers to respond to that need. As the Ombudsman said:

> First, I went to talk [to the local bar association] and I told them: why don't you give a commission to young lawyers, pro bono work by the bar association? We will give you all the material for you to reply but you handle the proceeding. They didn't say yes or no. They didn't say anything. So, we had to do it ourselves. And as I told you, this means the Ombudsman in an unprecedented action became a free consultant on the water issue for [Vivendi's subsidiary]. And that generated great concern, a lot of work. Well, somehow we provided a service that was not being offered and no one, no private lawyer would do it because it took five days to study this whole privatisation issue, the invoicing, if it was correct or not.[31]

What followed was an even more striking sequence of multiple evasion, this time by judicial authorities. The Ombudsman made two attempts[32] to file a collective *amparo* that would have had the effect of defending the boycotting consumers from the back-payment lawsuits as a class, meaning that instead of each citizen having to file detailed defence papers, the Ombudsman could do so on behalf of all of them. As the Ombudsman said herself: 'Well, what happened? Justice acted terribly, because this was sent everywhere and nobody wanted to take it.' The first judge rejected the case on the grounds of conflict of interest because 'looking through his personal belongings' he found an unpaid water invoice. The second judge pleaded incapacity to hear a collective injunction lawsuit in his residual jurisdiction. The third judge argued that his jurisdiction did not extend to the issues of contractual documentation raised by the injunction proceedings. The fourth judge suggested it belonged in the administrative courts' jurisdiction, but the fifth judge, in the administrative jurisdiction, thought the reverse. This returned the matter, after eighteen months, to the first judge. The then Attorney-General's comment seems well

---

[30] Bossio interview.
[31] Bossio interview.
[32] The first attempt was rejected on procedural grounds and the second attempt tried to achieve the same effect through a kind of 'backdoor' route: in essence by seeking a declaration rather than an injunction: Bossio interview.

justified: 'they passed the ball from one to the other and nobody wanted to receive us'.[33]

The sequence of judicial evasion described above contrasts with the fact that the courts heard many individual claims against non-payers (those who had not issued dispute letters) and frequently issued sentences convicting them, suggesting that they were concerned above all not to make any kind of systemic intervention into this politically explosive issue. Media coverage of the issue, which was critical of the refusal to engage, had no effect[34] and the executive was equally unwilling to engage: a lawsuit filed by the Provincial Attorney-General against Vivendi for breach of contract was later withdrawn when a change of government occurred and never re-filed, despite the promises of three consecutive Attorneys-General.[35] The legislature, however, took up the cause of the boycotting activists in another strikingly curious sequence. The legislature passed a series of laws, every six months, suspending the enforcement of any sentences handed down by judges for specific individuals. Such laws were unconstitutional (because they offended separation-of-powers principles), but because it took at least six months for courts to hand down a finding of unconstitutionality, iterative enactments of such laws succeeded in creating a perpetual zone of defence for boycotters who had not lodged a dispute letter,[36] however much it offended constitutional and political propriety between branches of government. Those consumers who had lodged a dispute letter appeared to use it successfully to stave off legal action for non-payment, even after the Ombudsman's legal action stalled.[37] As one of the consumer association leaders said:

> [Vivendi's subsidiary] demanded that thousands of people pay the debt. Among these people, around five thousand go to DUDAS and tell us: 'They are asking us to pay, what do we do?' So we told them: 'Here you have the official reply. Go and tell them that you do not owe what they are demanding. I owe a different sum of money according to several legal arguments, a decree, the Government auditor's report, the Ombudsman's Office and the others ... and therefore my debt is lower and I owe half of it.

---

[33] Maria Pedicone de Valls, Provincial Attorney-General of Tucumán, interviewed by Carolina Fairstein, Tucumán, 11 August 2004.

[34] Bossio interview.

[35] Bossio interview; Pedicone de Valls interview; Jose Domieu and Jorge Abdala, president and vice-president of ADEUCOT consumer association, interviewed by Carolina Fairstein, Tucumán, 22 August 2004.

[36] Graneros and Ramos interview.

[37] Interview with Jiminez Lascano, DUDAS consumers' association, interviewed by Carolina Fairstein, Tucumán, 24 August 2004.

Do the adjustments and I will pay.' None of the people who presented that note have ever been sued by [Vivendi's subsidiary].[38]

## 4.4    Transnational dimensions

### 4.4.1    Argentina

When Vivendi's subsidiary left Tucumán, the parent company in France filed a US$334 million dispute at ICSID at the World Bank in Washington.[39] This became one of the longest-running international arbitrations in ICSID's history (Khumprakob 2004), ending in 2007 with an award of $US105 million in favour of Vivendi.[40] Although it is difficult to substantiate directly, it is very likely that the shadow of the international power dynamics was an important determinant of the way that the Tucumán disputing pathway evolved, especially the looming possibility of the ICSID arbitration. The issue had created significant problems at the federal level: indeed, the federal government undertook a diplomatic mission to resolve the dispute informally, sending former President Menem to France to negotiate there, and pressuring provincial officials in Tucumán both publicly in the press and privately. The Minister of the Economy at the time even threatened a federal–provincial lawsuit for the damage caused to Argentina's image in the eyes of foreign investors. Anxious about the potential impact, the federal government helped prepare a new agreement between Vivendi and Tucumán province with a Working Group of the Provincial Attorney-General, a union representative and the CEO of Vivendi.[41]

Although this agreement ultimately failed, these pressures influenced the local dispute resolution dynamics, however subtly. A key focus of the broader regulatory dynamics was the legislation that the legislature was trying to pass that would have mandated 'social tariffs' in an attempt to temper the effects of tariff rises under the concession. The mix described above of party-political moves, popular action on the streets, and defence strategies against small claims lawsuits had kept pushing forwards this

---

[38] Lascano interview.

[39] *Compañia de Aguas del Aconquija, S.A. & Compagnie Générale des Eaux v. Argentine Republic.*

[40] Oddly, the award was made in favour of Vivendi Universal, the original parent company, and not Veolia Environnement, the now separate water division. See Lobina and Hall (2007(a)).

[41] Pedicone de Valls interview.

focus. But tension caused by transnational pressures altered the political dynamics. Before the ICSID claim was filed, the Tucumán provincial government preferred to continue with political negotiations. Once the ICSID machinery was invoked there was a distinct sense that this constrained the domestic substantive and procedural possibilities, even if the precise mechanisms of intervention were disputed or indirect. The provincial government placed the regulatory agency into a state akin to receivership and appointed an alternative auditor to oversee the concession on the grounds that the company felt persecuted by the regulatory agency.[42] There were also vociferous – albeit disputed[43] – claims that the World Bank inserted a condition around that time on a large health and education loan that required conflicts with public service concessions to be eliminated or resolved. But as the conclusion will summarise, Argentina's 'popcorn politics' has continued, both in terms of further ICSID claims in the water sector since the Tucumán claim that reinforce managed liberalisation,[44] and in terms of attempts to claw back some aspects of the public participatory model both transnationally and domestically.

### 4.4.2 Chile

By contrast with Argentina, international arbitration was not a powerful feature of the regulatory space in Chilean water politics. One interpretation of this, consistent with the 'ideal' mode of managed liberalisation, is that international investors respect the combination of the formal independence and substantive expertise of the regulator as sufficient to provide the political stability they need and seek. But an equally plausible reason for this comfort could be the political support

---

[42] Arancibia interview.

[43] Interviewees gave conflicting reports but a 13 August 1998 report in the local newspaper La Gaceta quoted Governor Bussi as saying that US$55 million from the World Bank could not be disbursed until the federal government had taken over the concession, allowing Vivendi to leave.

[44] Suez lodged three cases on 17 July 2003 relating to its concessions in Buenos Aires, Santa Fe and Córdoba: *Aguas Provinciales de Santa Fe, S.A., Suez, Sociedad General de Aguas de Barcelona, S.A. and Interagua Servicios Integrales de Agua, S.A. v. Argentine Republic* (Case No. ARB/03/17); *Aguas Cordobesas, S.A., Suez, and Sociedad General de Aguas de Barcelona, S.A. v. Argentine Republic* (Case No. ARB/03/18); and *Aguas Argentinas, S.A., Suez, Sociedad General de Aguas de Barcelona, S.A. and Vivendi Universal, S.A. v. Argentine Republic* (Case No. ARB/03/19), a joint venture with Agbar, a Spanish company, and Vivendi.

enjoyed by international investors. The international private sector directly provides the majority of Chile's citizens with water services. The policy environment is sensitive to perceptions of 'investment climate' held by these investors, and this undoubtedly shapes the regulatory dynamics.[45] The legal framework for privatisation was drafted by a small team in a closed, technocratic environment, with the assistance of the World Bank. The core tariff-setting process was written into the statute by an economist in highly technical terms that even included clauses containing algebraic formulae.[46]

Moreover, Chile is arguably a rulemaker in regional terms, at least in respect of the managed liberalisation model. It has extensive links to regional and global standard-setting associations, such as the InterAmerican Association of Engineers (AIDIS). Santiago also hosts the Latin American branches of both the UN Economic and Social Commission and Consumers International, which puts Chile at the centre of international networks of actors who develop the social and consumer dimensions of water policy. All this means foreign investors may well have found negotiations with government sufficient for their protection. Since, as we have seen, the government was relatively unresponsive to the demands of ordinary consumers that might derail regulatory expectations in the way that occurred in Argentina, the naming, blaming and claiming energy that comes from ordinary citizens need not be incorporated into the rulemaking, monitoring and enforcement regime of water services delivery.

## 4.5   Conclusion

### 4.5.1   Chile

The Chilean case study is an interesting example of a managed liberalisation approach to water services policy being established in a developing country as a primary consequence of internal domestic politics rather than imposed externally. Both the genesis and the ongoing dynamics of the resulting regulatory regime were still, however, embedded in transnational relations, whether at a broad general level (such as such the influence of the 'Chicago boys'), or in ways more specifically germane to the

---

[45] Some interviewees made off-the-record comments regarding the subtle but powerful (investor-friendly) influence of the Ministry of the Economy over the Chilean water regulatory agency.

[46] Silva interview.

history of water services policy (such as in the 'poisonous grapes' incident and the influence of international trade issues on pressures to upgrade water treatment standards). But these transnational dimensions exerted less direct influence on domestic institutional design than in the cases of either Argentina or Bolivia. And arguably the greater domestic control accounts for the greater institutional stability and better outcomes in relation to access to water that Chile has undoubtedly secured.

However, this institutional stability and these impressive outcomes came at a cost to the development of any participatory dimension to the governance model for urban water services. A political culture of pro-market bureaucratic authoritarianism made the legal framework of rules, monitoring and enforcement highly inaccessible to the ordinary citizen–consumer. Day-to-day regulatory dynamics in Chile were dominated by a legalised power struggle between government and private companies, from which ordinary consumers were largely excluded. The focus of the emergent disputing pathway on regulatory arbitrage and the failure of the consumer law framework to penetrate utilities management illustrate this marginalisation. There were energies of 'naming, blaming and claiming', as illustrated by the polarised public political debate over the privatisation process, but they failed to alter the direction of the policy trajectory. Party-political dynamics influenced the managed liberalisation model at the margins but their effectiveness was severely limited by the strong centralisation of executive power in Chilean constitutional structure.

### 4.5.2    Argentina

In Argentina, the legacy of the intersection of national and international developments was ambiguous. In the short term, effects on participation opportunities were disappointing. No right to public hearings was obtained, and a promised consumer representative on the regulator's board of directors never came to fruition. But substantive gains were made, including legislative prohibition of water cut-offs to those using less than the basic minimum. The Tucumán water services were fully renationalised, in corporatised form, by the federal government in 2004, after a little over five years' limping along under provincial control. Although the public federal company has struggled to improve water services, the forms of civil society involvement that were catalysed initially by private sector involvement persisted into the renewed era of public service operation. After renationalisation civil society continued to promote many legislative proposals, particularly relating to tariff structures, disconnection and the recovery of unpaid bills, both before and after the return of water services into public hands.

At the *transnational* level, interesting outcomes developed over the medium term that link this case study to the activist currents around ICSID and the human right to water noted at the end of Chapter 3 in the context of the Bolivian case study. A series of consumer group mobilisations occurred in the various locations of private sector water services contracts across Argentina, several involving coalitions with international NGOs. Two of these provide a neat contrast between campaigns that focus on the rulemaking, monitoring and enforcement aspects of managed liberalisation, on the one hand, or that try, on the other hand, to flesh out a rulemaking, monitoring and enforcement regime more closely tied to the UN General Comment 15 on the human right to water.

In the first, in a claim arising from the concession for Buenos Aires water services, a coalition of local and international NGOs[47] succeeded on 19 May 2005 in convincing an ICSID tribunal for the first time that it had the power to accept amicus curiae briefs from civil society organisations, even in the face of objections from parties. The petition supporting this request focused explicitly on 'transparency and public participation'.[48] While this is a significant opening, there are important limits too. The tribunal declined to decide the issue of whether it would allow access to documents of private parties, and stressed that it would only accept amicus submissions from persons who could establish to the tribunal's satisfaction that they had the expertise, experience and independence to be of assistance in the case. However, the tribunal also acknowledged the diffuse and extended public interest dimensions of water services as the catalyst for allowing amicus participation, even cautiously endorsing the notion that these are human rights issues. The push for expanding transparency and participation rights for non-parties in investor–state arbitration has continued to date, bolstered by a significant recognition of similar rights in a not dissimilar struggle over

---

[47] Composed of two local legal NGOs: Centro de Estudios Legales y Sociales (CELS) and La Associación Civil por la Igualdad y la Justicia (ACIJ); two local consumer/public services NGOs: Consumidores Libres Cooperativa Ltda. de Provisión de Servicios de Acción Comunitaria and Unión de Usuarios y Consumidores; and an international environmental NGO: Centre for International Environmental Law (CIEL).

[48] Presented on 28 January 2005 in relation to the ICSID arbitration of the Buenos Aires concession. Although the defendant here was Suez and not Vivendi and the specifics of the concession differed from the Tucumán concession, the key arguments presented in the petition were entirely general.

private sector participation in water service delivery in Tanzania.[49] This would seem to presage a shift towards public participatory governance, but recent commentary notes that long-term reform efforts to promote efficiency in investor–state protection have equal if not stronger traction in the field, with the capacity to reverse the shift back towards managed liberalisation (Nottage and Miles 2009).

At best, this line of development suggests an uneasy hybrid between a locally embedded public participatory model and managed liberalisation at the interface with transnational actors. For even though the ICSID process amendment is a victory for participation, it is a form of participation that still sidesteps democratically elected governments, and does nothing to expand their policy space. The US$105 million awarded to Vivendi for compensation arguably suggests that the opportunity to lodge a brief in ICSID hearings is at best a marginal amendment to the overriding dominance of managed liberalisation. From this perspective, Bolivia's decision to withdraw from the ICSID convention, pursuing instead an alternative institutional path through the Bolivarian Alternative for the Peoples of Latin America (discussed in Chapter 3) seems to have more potential to embed a properly alternative model.

The resonance of Chapter 3 and the Bolivian case study re-emerges in relation to the second trajectory of development in the broader Argentinian picture. In another provincial city, Córdoba, Suez had, like Vivendi, acquired a thirty-year concession in 1997 for water and waste-water services. But unlike Vivendi in Tucumán, in this case the local challenge avoided direct intersection with the ICSID process. Instead, protest was channelled into a lawsuit by a public interest legal advocacy organisation *against the local and provincial governments*,[50] arguing successfully that the contamination of river water by untreated sewage infringed a human right to safe drinking water that is implicit in the right to health.[51] By focusing the challenge on the domestic state, a different kind of international influence from that of ICSID could be invoked: that of UN General Comment 15 on the human right to water. Consistently with the approach of General Comment 15, the plaintiffs argued that the

---

[49] *Biwater* v. *Tanzania*, Case No. ARB/05/22, Procedural Order No. 5.

[50] Although Córdoba's water and wastewater services were managed by the Suez subsidiary, the municipal government retained responsibility for residential connections and the provincial government for a somewhat uncertain scope of infrastructure responsibilities.

[51] *CEDHA* v. *Provincial State and Municipality of Córdoba*. The court also held that the government had failed in its obligation to provide a healthy environment.

state is the guarantor of human rights, irrespective of the internal organisational structure it might choose to adopt. The court's recognition of the
human right to safe drinking water via the right to health explicitly cited
General Comment 15.[52] In the wake of the decision, the Córdoba municipality presented a US$7.75 million 'integral sewage plan' for expanded
investment in sewage infrastructure, and construction work connecting
homes to the expanded networks. The Municipal Executive also declared
that 'the Executive will not authorize new sewage connections until [the
municipality] improves the capacity of the sewage plant',[53] leading construction lobbies of real estate agents and engineers to pressure the executive to expand capacity even faster.

In a mirror effect, a poor neighbourhood in Buenos Aires recently
invoked its right to water with the assistance of an international and a
local NGO,[54] combining political advocacy with litigation. Rather than
simply winning the right to submit a brief at the international level, the
community succeeded, after four years' campaigning, in getting itself
exceptionally added to the plans of the service provider to construct new
networks for piped water (Fairstein forthcoming). As this work shows,
the implications of the Bolivian chapter have further resonance here. The
NGO which leads this project has argued (Fairstein forthcoming) that
recognising the right to water as part of a legal framework for water service
delivery is insufficient. Rather, the more important challenge is to focus
on putting in place regulations and institutions to ensure participation in
decision-making processes, monitoring and the capacity to enforce fulfil-
ment of rights (Fairstein forthcoming) (i.e. rulemaking, monitoring and
enforcement) and even then, constant community advocacy is needed to
realise the right to water. It is significant, however, that General Comment
15 provided the appropriate baseline norms from which to develop the
regulatory dimension for the work in this case. Moreover, the community
advocacy and judicial litigation strategies used these norms, and *not* the
norms governing liberalised management, to argue for increased access.

In short, while outcomes such as opening opportunities to participate
in international arbitration are valuable, they are insufficient for fleshing

---

[52] The 7 April 1995 judgement of the Supreme Court of Argentina in the case of Horacio
David Giroldi (No. 32/93) requires local courts to take account of international interpret-
ative guidelines such as those contained in General Comments as a basis for interpreting
domestic laws.

[53] Resolution D-79/04, 26 October 2004.

[54] COHRE, the Geneva-based NGO that assisted in the drafting process of GC15, and the
Centre for Legal and Social Studies, Buenos Aires.

out a public participatory model of governance. What is needed, in the absence of an alternative macro-structural political economy, is a thicker elaboration of the regulatory dimensions of the human right to water that does not fall into the hybrid dependency on managed liberalisation that we saw illustrated in Bolivia in Chapter 3. As long as pronounced power imbalances persist, however, hybrid governance models will be a fragile resolution, as the next chapter on South Africa and New Zealand will show from a more decentralised and politicised perspective.

# Moonlight plumbers in comparative perspective: electoral v. constitutional politics of access to water in South Africa and New Zealand

## 5.1   Introduction

New Zealand and South Africa, may, at first sight, appear an incongruous pair of case studies for close juxtaposition. But they share a key feature distinguishing them from the previous pair of case studies (Argentina and Chile): neither country created an independent regulatory agency to supervise access to water. Relatedly, both countries delegate the provision of drinking water services to local municipalities. As we saw in Chapters 3 and 4, the design and intended practice (though not always the operational reality) of independent regulatory agencies tended to reflect the influence of the managed liberalisation model. These two case studies, then, both demonstrate an absence of centralised technocratic control over the provision of access to water, and, as such, a public participatory model of provision should have more space to develop.

The chapter argues that a tempered public participatory model subsists in both case studies, though not in any 'pure' form, at least partly because both countries experienced pressures to adopt a managed liberalisation model. South Africa has developed a well-known indigenous and progressive model of governance that is nonetheless constrained by other contradictory aspects of the country's broader political economy commitments. The South African model is also much more powerful on paper in policy and legislation than at the operational level of implementation. New Zealand has retained a model based on public provision, embedded in small-scale local government, but some restructuring in Auckland has nonetheless taken place along modified managed liberalisation lines.

Put like this, these case studies may seem to resemble milder versions of the outcome in Bolivia (Chapter 3). But the absence of a centralised regulatory agency, the related prominence of local government delivery, and the relatively narrower scope of foreign private sector participation distinguish them from Bolivia. At the heart of disputing in these two case studies was a tension between socio-economic rights on the one hand, and contract and market rights on the other, a tension underpinning the terms of exchange controlling access to water. Although this tension was central to the Bolivian case, it plays out here in a very different political context: one of predominantly municipal governance and relatively less transnational imposition of managed liberalisation. In Bolivia, the primary focus of the struggle was on property rights, articulated in mass direct action inspired by a conception of 'water as territory'. By contrast, the main tensions in these two case studies were between different aspects of 'water as service'.

A focus on 'water as service' was also a shared facet of the struggles chronicled in Chapter 4, in Argentina and Chile. But whereas the two Latin American cases focused on 'regulator versus consumer' conflicts, in both New Zealand and South Africa public debates over access to water, and in particular the repertoires of social protestors, prominently featured ideas of access to water as a fundamental socio-economic right, articulated in the context of local government politics. If the tension was seen in terms of consumerism at all, it was from a perspective that either rejected consumerism altogether, as in South Africa, or playfully manipulated the category of consumer for strategic purposes in certain instances, as in New Zealand. Perhaps relatedly, both countries had social protestors who withheld payment for water services as a means of protesting against wider issues related to water service policy.

The central distinctiveness of the two case studies explored in this chapter, therefore, is that they open up the question of whether – given the centrality of 'water as service' to the managed liberalisation model as depicted in Chapter 4 – socio-economic rights can inspire a conception of 'water as service' that is compatible with a public participatory model. The chapter argues that socio-economic rights *can* support a public participatory model if developed along dual tracks, with 'outsider' and 'insider' dimensions broadly associated with the two triads explored in Chapter 1. Outsider participatory strategies, embodied in direct action that enacts a 'naming, blaming and claiming' process, can energise democratic experimentalism. This is complemented by insider participatory strategies that engage with the detail of rulemaking, monitoring and enforcement and thereby foster institutional stability: socio-economic rights are a core example of an insider strategy in both case studies in this chapter.

But socio-economic rights are, as the case studies will illustrate, often disappointing in terms of their direct legal effects. When judicially elaborated, they often give rise to a right to a 'reasonable regulatory approach' which, on its own, translates into a constitutionalised administrative law rather than a discourse of substantive entitlements. However, *when deployed in a mutually interdependent manner with civil and political rights*, they can help to build a bridge between insider and outsider participatory politics. The combination pries open political spaces and energises and legitimises political organising, lobbying and participation. These activities can then interact with socio-economic rights to make them 'justiciable' in a much broader sense of the word than its purely technical meaning – rendering them *capable of being judged*, not only by courts, but also by political actors and structures that have the power to change the rules of the game.

Whether the rules of the game do eventually change depends partly on the balance of power in specific contexts, but also upon strategies that relink rights and regulation. The case studies illustrate two routes for effective bridge-building of this kind: electoral politics and constitutional litigation. As we shall see, South Africa has relied more on constitutional litigation, a route which has to date not resulted in significant rule changes in the face of pressure from managed liberalisation. While electoral politics in New Zealand did secure substantive rule changes protecting a public participatory model, it is also true that New Zealand was contextually under considerably less pressure to adopt managed liberalisation than South Africa. In short, the very different political economies of a wealthy OECD country and a middle-income developing country also play an important role in shaping outcomes here.

The chapter will illustrate the above argument in concrete terms by juxtaposing the two case studies from four angles. First, the basic narrative in each country is juxtaposed; second, the main aspects of the regulatory policy framework; third, the rights-based strategies at the core of the disputes; and, finally, strategies that link rights back to regulation are comparatively discussed.

## 5.2 Two stories

In both the case studies in this chapter, the commercialisation of public sector water service delivery was a central focus of social activists' concerns to a greater degree than the entry of the private sector. Activists focused on the terms of exchange over access to water rather than direct challenges to the governance structures of water service delivery. In particular, in both South Africa and New Zealand, boycotts of payments for water services were an important aspect of social activism. The process of withholding payment, although essentially a consumer act, is also usually an illegal act. This aspect of illegality means that rights claims become central to the legitimation and political impact of such actions. And such actions – strictly illegal but part of a wider rights-based campaign of activism by those participating – are at the heart of the two stories of conflict underpinning the case studies explored here.

In Durban, South Africa, in 2000, the municipal water company disconnected Christina Manqele from her water supply for failure to pay for consumption above the free basic limit provided to all citizens. The context was one in which thousands of people in South African townships had not paid their water bills, in some cases for many years, in a complex mix of the impact of poverty, the lingering effects of apartheid, and anger against the new democratic government. Christina was a 35-year-old washerwoman living below the poverty line and a single mother with seven children. At some point following the disconnection she was reconnected illegally to the water supply by what people in South African townships call 'moonlight plumbers'.

Later, her case was brought to court by public interest lawyers, who argued that the disconnection breached her right to access sufficient water, a fundamental constitutional right fleshed out by the Water Services Act 1997. Extensive evidence was brought by the water company about the fact that she had tampered with the network, which was defined as criminal activity by the legislative framework. Against this, her own lawyers brought evidence showing that the network was leaking very badly, causing water bills to be significantly out of proportion with the actual consumption levels of citizens. Christina Manqele lost the case because of a technical decision that more detailed government regulation was necessary before the court could enforce the statute. There was no reference in the final judgement to any of the evidence about her conduct or about the state of the network, but witnesses in the court room on the day of the trial argued that the judge's attitude was sharply altered by the evidence of her dealings with moonlight plumbers.[1]

Christina Manqele's story is one moment in a pattern of unruly rights-based activism that South Africa experienced on a mass scale both before and after the transition from apartheid in 1994. This activism influenced regulatory politics to adopt and retain aspects of a public participatory model in water services policy in 1994. At the heart of this model was a constitutional guarantee of the right to access 'sufficient water'. But

[1] Shanta Reddy, solicitor, interviewed by Bronwen Morgan, Durban, 17 September 2003.

the model was always one that experienced powerful tensions between its legal and constitutional dimensions and its financial and commercial dimensions. This tension has continued to play out in constitutional litigation which has been disappointing in strictly legal terms, but which, together with direct action shielded by civil and political rights, has continued to clear a space for ongoing debate about the direction of water services policy.

In Auckland, New Zealand, where six different municipal councils provided water services, a group of citizens came together to form the Auckland Water Pressure Group (WPG) in 1996. With a fluctuating membership of as many as 2,000 people, mainly from lower-working-class families, the group's primary aim was to prevent the corporatisation of the largest of the six into a public company known as Metrowater. They also lobbied against shifts from flat tariffs (based on property rates) to 'user-pay' tariffs (based on metered volume), and the disconnection policies of the various water companies. Sister groups in other districts of Auckland formed in their wake, and alliances developed with existing environmental community groups, all focused on protesting against similar structural changes. Soon after forming, around 500 activists refused to pay some or all of their bills. When disconnected, they reconnected themselves illegally to the system, like the 'moonlight plumbers' of South Africa, with whom they maintained a supportive dialogue over the internet. Some activists poured concrete over their water meters to prevent further disconnection. In some cases, when Metrowater responded by digging up the pipes linking their houses to the mainline road pipes, they parked a fire truck over the road housing the pipes.

In time, Metrowater brought a series of legal actions against the payment boycotters in the Disputes Tribunal, a forum for small claims resolution. The boycotters defended themselves by articulating socio-economic rights claims through a variety of traditional public law avenues in consumer, administrative and public health. While the claims were sufficiently plausible to win them time, they ultimately failed in legal terms. But they bought time – time that was vital to securing important political and legislative changes through routes other than the courts. The activists leveraged the pressure from their direct activism with political lobbying that exploited two other crucial features of the institutional environment: small political parties and autonomous, fragmented local government. As a result, they successfully won legislative amendments that constrained both the scope and extent of private sector participation in water services, as well as prohibiting the disconnection of citizens who did not pay their bills.[2]

These two stories illustrate in concrete two very different contextual developments of the relationship between 'naming, claiming and blaming' and 'rulemaking, monitoring and enforcement'. In the South African story, the former dominated, while disputing energy in New Zealand built stronger links between the two. As we shall see below, however, the regulatory framework in the global South exposed South Africa to much more powerful pressures to adopt managed liberalisation than existed in New Zealand.

## 5.3 Regulation in South Africa and New Zealand

### 5.3.1 Autonomous localism in New Zealand

During the 1980s New Zealand was an early and strong advocate of neo-liberalism, and took the lead in privatising many formerly state-owned functions and enterprises. But water has been markedly different. Water in New Zealand is a responsibility of regional and local government which has strong autonomy, both traditionally and in terms of financial capacity. Each local municipality has had the discretion to make separate governance arrangements for the delivery of water. In Auckland, a single supplier delivers bulk water to six different municipal governments that cover the city's jurisdiction. Pressure to expand the role of the private sector in delivering water at both bulk and retail levels came from both local and foreign business interests. During the first half of the 1990s, two major reforms of the 1974 Local Government Act increased pressure on local governments to demonstrate value for money in all their activities and to explicitly justify decisions *not* to use the private sector in providing services to local communities. But few local governments extended this logic to water services. Public determination to establish water as a 'final frontier' of the marketisation policies of the 1980s helped contribute to the formation of the Alliance Party, a radical left party that won electoral success at regional government level in Auckland, on a platform of anti-privatisation. In the subsequent political battle between local and central government that followed, the Alliance Party succeeded in passing legislation that explicitly prohibited the privatisation of the bulk water supplier

---

[2] Local Government Act 2002 (NZ), sections 130–7 and section 193(1).

for Auckland.[3] The bulk supplier was corporatised, but the Alliance Party fought to include social clauses that restrained profit-making: a statutory duty to work in the best interests of those who live in Auckland, a duty to maintain prices at the minimum levels consistent with the effective condition of its business, and a prohibition on paying a dividend to the local municipality shareholders.

The battle then shifted to the 'retail' end of water delivery, where municipal government was directly providing services to citizens across six councils. In 1997, Papakura District Council – the smallest of the six – signed a thirty-year concession contract with the foreign private sector (a joint consortium of subsidiaries of Thames and Vivendi), and in the same year Auckland City Council corporatised its water services, creating Metrowater, a local authority trading enterprise fully owned by the local council but subject to company law governance structures. The activism of the WPG, however, derailed other councils' plans to corporatise. By 2002 it also secured legislative constraints on privatisation at the level of local government, supplementing the outcomes secured at regional level by the Alliance Party. The effect was to prohibit local governments from divesting themselves of water supply and wastewater services within their areas, except to another local government authority. Limited contracting-out of water services operations was permitted, but restricted to fifteen years, and councils were mandated to retain control over water pricing, water services management and the development of water policy at all times. While these restrictions did not prohibit all public–private partnerships outright, they did outlaw any future arrangement similar to the Papakura franchise, and significantly diluted the commercial scope and attractiveness of other contracting-out initiatives.[4] Finally, an additional unintentional, but equally important, legislative amendment was also secured: water disconnections were prohibited and water restrictions allowed only where it would not create unsanitary conditions.[5]

### 5.3.2    Tensions in South Africa

The South African regulatory framework for water service delivery instantiates deep internal tensions, the nature of which can be vividly captured by juxtaposing two texts. First is the 1997 White Paper on Water Policy,

---

[3] The Local Government Act 1974 as amended in 1998: the prohibition was achieved by blocking Watercare's six local authority shareholders from selling their shares.

[4] See Local Government Act 2002 (NZ), sections 130–7.

[5] See Local Government Act 2002 (NZ), section 193(1).

which began with a poetic invocation of the fundamental importance of water, seen in the context of the transition away from a brutal apartheid system:

> The dictionary describes water as colourless, tasteless and odourless – its most important property being its ability to dissolve other substances. We in South Africa do not see water that way. For us water is a basic human right, water is the origin of all things – the giver of life. We want the water of this country to flow out into a network – reaching every individual – saying: here is this water, for you. Take it; cherish it as affirming your human dignity; nourish your humanity. With water we will wash away the past, we will from now on ever be bounded by the blessing of water. (Department of Water Affairs and Forestry of South Africa 1997: 1)

Yet just before this policy paper was drafted, the South African government made a decision to follow a policy of full cost-recovery for major users of water.[6] A speech given a few months later by the then mayor of Johannesburg captured the jarring economic and transnational pressures that constrained the vision of the 1997 policy paper:

> Transformation has a price. Our country has been liberated into an era governed by the fundamental principles of non-racism, non-sexism and justice for all. But please understand the particular conditions of government which require resources to give people the basic services which are their fundamental right as citizens of this country ... Businessmen from the US are used to fast services. It takes us six months to find out who owns a piece of land. There are danger signals when our councillors and administrators do not meet the investors' aspirations. Some administrator tells the investor to go to such a room and there they find a woman painting their nails. This is the way to rule ourselves out of international global competition.[7]

While there will always be tension between policy aspirations and the detail of implementation, this speech echoes a deeper conflict embedded in South African water service policy: that between a public participatory model and the influence of managed liberalisation. The basic outline of South African water services policy was one more in spirit with the public participatory model. The first democratic government explicitly chose

---

[6] A cabinet decision taken in February 1996, fleshing out aspects of the 1994 White Paper on Water and Sanitation (which was a narrower document than the 1997 White Paper on Water Policy: see p. 22 of the latter) (Department of Water Affairs and Forestry of South Africa 1994; 1997).

[7] Tokyo Sexwale, mayor of Gauteng Province, September 1996, in a speech launching a new phase of the Masakhane campaign, aimed at improving payment rates for public services.

not to create an independent regulatory agency to oversee the delivery of water services, maintaining direct political control at least over the framework for provision, even if not always over service delivery itself. The framework focused on ensuring democratic input into decisions about water service delivery,[8] stated a legislative preference for public provision and gave the national government a residual power to cap profits from water services.[9] Moreover, the important power to collect bills and to disconnect consumers for failure to pay was reserved, at least initially, to local government.

From early on, however, managed liberalisation also exerted its sway, particularly in relation to the entry of the foreign transnational private sector into South Africa, which grew rapidly between 1995 and 2003 to cover about 15 per cent of the population. In 1997, private banks withdrew their financial support for a major concession contract as a result of concern over financial risks related to the powers of bill-collection and service disconnection. In the following years, the legislative framework shifted towards protecting transactional risk, clarifying that all water service providers (including private companies) could be directly involved in these functions (Kriel 2003), diluting the original statutory preference in favour of public provision,[10] and gradually increasing treasury control from the centre.[11]

The public participatory model, however, retained energy and salience. In part because of the conflicts narrated below, private sector participation levelled off from 2003 onwards, although public water service delivery continued to face strong pressures to commercialise its production model. Central to this was a policy of cost-recovery through tariffs reflecting the costs of service delivery. Important equity policies were also introduced to temper the impact of this: a Free Basic Water Policy

---

[8] Section 78 of the Municipal Systems Act 2000 requires local government to carry out public and labour consultation before entering into long-term delegation of water service delivery to the private sector.

[9] Water Services Act 1997, section 10(2)(b): a clause pressed for by labour unions who strongly resisted private sector involvement.

[10] Municipal Systems Act 2000 (SA), overriding not only the disputed interpretation of the 1997 Water Services Act but also a Framework Agreement for the Restructuring of Municipal Service Provision negotiated by the unions in 1997 that had tried to re-affirm a strong preference for public provision and create institutions to monitor this: delegate from South African Municipal Workers Union, interviewed by Bronwen Morgan, Pretoria, 6 October 2003.

[11] See the Municipal Financial Management Act 2003 (SA) and the creation of the Municipal Infrastructure Investment Unit.

in 2001, and a 'credit control code' animated by principles of due process and compassion in its 2003 Strategic Framework. These equity policies were, however, carefully confined to the arena of 'soft law' or 'mere policy', in contrast to the hard law amendments driven by imperatives of transactional risk described above. Arguably South Africa's passionate commitment to a human rights approach developed over time into a type of soft consumerism. As the following remarks of a senior municipal official indicate, managed liberalisation was the dominant narrative shaping the rulemaking, monitoring and enforcement dimensions of equity policies:

> You've got to be able [to] provide the free basic services, cut the damn thing off when the person's consumed that amount and be able to bill in a reliable way. [But] your credit control policy must include – as opposed to the hard-line 'forcing people' kind of approach – a customer relations function, a complaints centre, a mechanism of incentivising payment ... *It's all about creating new systems, new management capacity* and we're saying, really, that whilst you're doing that, pay attention to *the human consumer issue stuff* because if you don't do that you've got very little chance of success[12] (emphases added).

As we shall see in the next section, the implicitly peripheral position of 'human consumer issue stuff' was powerfully challenged by a range of rights strategies, in both New Zealand and South Africa.

## 5.4    Rights in South Africa and New Zealand

This section narrates, in comparative perspective, the rights-based strategies used in South Africa and New Zealand to challenge the encroachment of managed liberalisation onto the subsisting public participatory model of water governance. I begin with direct action, which articulates emerging norms embedded in the everyday practices of marginalised citizens. In both countries, these norms were subsequently taken up in explicit rights claims of both socio-economic and civil–political natures.

### 5.4.1    Direct action

#### South Africa

The impact of social activism at the local level in South Africa on water services policy has been significant. Ken Conca has described the struggle of

---

[12] Senior official, Municipal Infrastructure Investment Unit, interviewed by Bronwen Morgan, Johannesburg, 6 October 2003.

the poor majority for social citizenship in the realm of clean water, electricity, public health and other survival and livelihood considerations as 'the most consequential form of social activism in South Africa today' (Conca 2005). The scale of direct activism in South Africa has historical roots in a struggle to open up opportunities for political participation and influence of the most basic kind. In peri-urban 'townships', mass non-payment for services had been a long-standing strategy of collective political action taken by township residents in protest against apartheid. With apartheid ended, even diluted cost-recovery principles applied under the influence of managed liberalisation raised tariffs very significantly from the low flat rate that was charged (but not paid) under apartheid. Township residents boycotted payment, and in relation to water employed a wide mixture of strategies to disrupt the policies of the government, including marches, protests, payment boycotts, illegal reconnections, political education and test case constitutional litigation. They were supported by umbrella coalitions of NGOs such as the South African Water Caucus. In addition, organised labour contributed, through strikes and direct action, to protests against the influence of managed liberalisation – though labour also had a wider role in the governing African National Congress (ANC) coalition – and through lobbying as described in the regulatory section.

Direct action strategies were shaped strongly by both local political dynamics and the social characteristics of different activist groups. For example, the Durban region of South Africa is a region with a complex political history that provides a rare counterweight, through Zulu tribal and Indian interests, to the dominance of the ANC in national politics. There was substantial social activism in the area against the commercialisation of water services (Durban Metro Water Services was a corporatised division of municipal government), but the local political dynamics varied according to the social characteristics of different groups. Table 12 shows this schematically, by linking focus group discussions in four different communities to a range of different strategies for influencing the water services regulatory framework.

As the table shows, groups in strongly ANC areas tended to restrict their strategies to either adversarial protest or cooperation with the process of commercialising water. It was only groups which had some non-ANC political support that were willing to extend their range of strategies towards potential political party-building. Such groups also used – with considerable ambivalence – litigation, as we shall see below.

Direct action strategies focused on protesting against the terms of service offered for access to water in ways that rejected individual consumer

Table 12 *Spectrum of reform strategies and linkages to different social groups*

|  | Collective | Individualistic |
|---|---|---|
| Adversarial | Test case litigation (1) | Legal defence |
|  | Marches, protests, illegal | (1) and to a lesser but |
|  | reconnections (1) (2) (3) | growing extent (2) |
| Cooperative | Marches, protests (1) (2) (3) | Customer Service |
|  | Political education, building social | Agents/Community |
|  | movements and potentially | Development Officers |
|  | political parties (1) (2) | (4) |

Key to group strategies
(1) Chatsworth focus group: moderate anti-globalisation. Previously Indian township, historically Democratic Alliance or Minority Front. Young organisers and older members; civics-type structures, significant reliance on legal strategies as well as mass direct action.
(2) Mpumalanga focus group: radical anti-globalisation. Previously black semi-rural township built on traditional Zulu land, historically Inkatha Freedom Party and tribal, but mixed ANC and Inkatha Freedom Party more recently. Young students, loosely organised, fluid, often violent activism.
(3) Ntuzuma focus group: social democratic welfare state (the 'Reconstruction and Development Programme' (RDP) constituency). Previously black township, strongly ANC. Mid–late thirties 'forgotten generation' with very little formal education. Primarily involved in community groups pursuing livelihood/survival activities, little direct political action; no reliance on legal strategies.
(4) Kwamashu focus group: 'The Great U-Turn' (the 'Growth, Employment and Redistribution' (GEAR) constituency). Previously black township, strongly ANC. Mid twenties in their first or second job; community development approach focusing on pragmatic service delivery problems.

agency. For example, citizens mobilised in what some called '10 rand marches', converging in large crowds on the offices of the water service provider with 10 rand notes in their hands to symbolise what they were willing to pay per month for water. By making this point collectively, as 'outsiders' with a community identity, the protestors were envisioning a transformation of the structural forces that led to a situation in which 10 rand is the maximum affordable amount an individual can pay. Theirs was a strategy that melded political agency and consumer responsibility, articulating an emergent norm that blurred civil and political rights with socio-economic rights claims. In this emergent form, direct action transcended some important tensions that exist between different kinds of rights-based claims once they take a more explicitly legal form. Such tensions will be explored in more detail when the South African story is taken up again below.

## New Zealand

New Zealand's activists were far more limited in number, but, in the very different context of a wealthy industrialised country, they also saw themselves as marginalised by the mainstream economy system and policymaking process. As described in Section 5.2, the activities of the Auckland WPG were at the centre of the protest activities. The WPG's direct action centred on refusing to pay water service bills either in full or in part. This was done in tandem with a written defence sent to the water company justifying the non-payment on the basis of a legal dispute. The 'letter of dispute' claimed that the pricing method used by the company strategy breached the New Zealand Consumer Guarantees Act. The nub of this defence was that a fixed charge from the bulk water supplier passed onto the customer as a volumetric fee (calculated at 75 per cent of the water used that month) was misleading, because this fee is in fact fixed, and not related to usage. The activists also argued that this breached aspects of the human right to water by burdening poorer (usually larger in number) households with disproportionate water expenses.[13] The production of numerous letters of dispute defending the boycotters became a major focus of meetings and collaboration, and also a significant source of administrative work for the social movement leaders.

Supplementing this strategy, the WPG carried out other forms of direct action also infused with a rhetorical public emphasis on human rights and environmental and social justice issues. Apart from boycotting bill payments, they staged rallies, postcard campaigns and street marches, and draped banners across their houses on which they accused named politicians of betraying the public interest by creating a corporate structure for the municipal water company. The beginning of the chapter has already recounted the 'moonlight plumber' strategies that escalated from illegal reconnections to concreting over water meters and blocking pipe access with a fire truck. The activists deliberately cultivated a kind of

---

[13] Para. 27 of General Comment No. 15, 2002, by the UN Committee on Economic, Social and Cultural Rights states: 'Equity demands that poorer households should not be disproportionately burdened with water expenses as compared to richer households.'

carnivalesque atmosphere to these actions, which helped to garner media attention. They also kept supportive ties, mainly through online dialogue, with the South African activists carrying out analogous activities, links which had a history in the strong ties of several of the activist leaders with anti-apartheid activism in New Zealand during the 1970s and 1980s.

### 5.4.2   Socio-economic rights

#### New Zealand

As we have seen from the above, direct action in New Zealand was tied both to a political articulation of access to water as a socio-economic human right and to linking this vision to formal legal entitlements. Since New Zealand lacks any direct formal legal protection of socio-economic human rights, the activists made strategic use of (some would say distorted) administrative law and consumer rights litigation. Somewhat paradoxically, these strategies stressed the activists' status as consumers of a commercial service, even while their direct action strategies vigorously rejected this commercial framework.

For example, one case argued that the old common law 'doctrine of prime necessity' applied to water, in particular the principle that monopoly suppliers of essential services must charge no more than a reasonable price. The High Court declared[14] that although this principle existed, it was displaced by the Commerce Act, which regulated prices, precluded private enforcement and restricted regulatory intervention solely to the 'lighthanded touch' of the Commerce Commission on the motion of the minister. As the Commerce Act said nothing specific about water, the judgement in effect confirmed the legitimacy of treating water delivery as a commercial service. This litigation was therefore, for the activists, a signal failure.

The attempt to invert commercial law against the commercialisation of water services was also core to the use of the Consumer Guarantee Act discussed above in relation to payment boycotts. This 'letter of dispute' was accepted by Metrowater as a legitimate defence for three years. It was also used proactively by the activists, who lodged dozens of small claims court actions based on the 'letter of dispute'. These claims were often successful, not due to the legal point made, but due to personal financial hardship that each individual was able to demonstrate. After

---

[14] *Metrowater* v. *Gladwin et al.*, High Court of New Zealand, 17 December 1999, unreported judgement of Salmon J.

several years of defending these claims individually in court, the activ-ists' leaders decided to increase the stakes and mounted a case based solely on the legal point, hoping to have an indirect class-action, 'test-case' effect. They lost this case, buttressing the dispiriting effect of liti-gating socio-economic rights. But the 'letter of dispute' created a legal buffer for the boycotters for three years: one that opened up the political space to influence rulemaking, monitoring and enforcement via elect-oral politics.

## South Africa

In South Africa, the potential for socio-economic rights litigation over access to water was, on paper, the polar opposite to the situation in New Zealand. Endowed with a fully fledged constitutional human right to access sufficient water, one might have expected legal strategies to be a powerful tool for ameliorating the impact of market-based water ser-vice delivery on poor consumers. But, taken together, the cases brought so far – including a prominent case heard by the Constitutional Court – have met with only limited success. Nonetheless, by focusing on three cases in sequence, it is possible to trace an increasingly self-conscious link between litigating socio-economic rights and leveraging non-legal political strategies, including those shielded and energised by civil and political rights. Such linkages preserve the possibility of building bridges between insider and outsider participatory politics that help to protect the erosion of the public participatory governance model.

The first of the three cases, *Manqele*, was summarised in the opening section of this chapter. The case failed to achieve reconnection for the plaintiff, who had not directly pleaded the constitutional obligation but had relied on the Water Services Act whose regulations specifying the minimum amount of water to which each citizen has a right had not yet been enacted.[15] A second case challenging disconnection brought soon afterwards, *Bon Vista*, was somewhat more successful, providing tem-porary relief by mandating that fair and equitable procedures, such as reasonable notice of intent to disconnect or provision of an opportunity to make representations, were required before disconnecting consumers from their water supply.[16] But disconnection for inability to pay was not itself outlawed.

---

[15]  *Manqele* v. *Durban Transitional Metropolitan Council* 2002 (6) SA 423.
[16]  *Residents of Bon Vista Mansions* v. *Southern Metropolitan Local Council* 2002 (6) BCLR 625.

The cumulative effect of these two cases was to provide important but purely procedural protection to 'responsible consumers' – citizens who pay what they can afford, and who refrain from civil disobedience in their broader demands to the political decision-makers. The litigation had no effect on the principal issue that motivated the social activists: the justice or appropriateness of a cost-recovery approach to the delivery of water services. It softened the impact of that policy approach, but in a way that provided a social safety net dimension to managed liberalisation, rather than according political voice within a public participatory model. The social movement activists felt ambiguous about the constrained legitimating effects of socio-economic rights litigation. On the one hand, the court provided a public forum for communicating competing norms that challenge the taken-for-granted practices of responsible consumerism. For example, in the *Manqele* case, the plaintiff was able to reconstruct criminal delinquency as responsible parenting:

> [Moonlight plumbers] are going around reconnecting everyone's water and electricity and all this, and she obviously is not going to say this in court, and she couldn't, you know, I mean let's be straight to the point – she has to live, she needs the water, the children who depend on her, she has a responsibility to ensure that they survive, so she has to see to it that the water's reconnected. And that is the model argument and the constitutional argument.[17]

This legitimation effect potentially went beyond personal and relational issues to reframe divisions around the broader political economy:

> There is this huge ideological project – the local press and the vast majority of academics are all saying 'there is one way of doing things, it's the way that competitive nations do things. We've all got to pull together, these [water activists] are messing it up for us, they're holding us back.' Now getting a court case can really help with the ideological stuff – it helps show these people are not criminal, they are not lazy, [their actions] are actually in line with the values of the new society that was founded.[18]

However, at the same time activists in both case studies were acutely conscious of the limits of litigating socio-economic rights. These limits were especially acute in relation to the identity-building potential of 'naming, blaming and claiming processes': they all too easily had a negative impact on fostering collective political agency. Consciousness of these limits was

---

[17] Reddy interview.
[18] Richard Pithouse, researcher, Centre for Civil Society, University of Natal-Durban, interviewed by Bronwen Morgan, Durban, 9 September 2003.

directly expressed by social movement activists in the city of Durban, who feared that relying on law, especially on socio-economic rights claims, could directly *undermine* political agency. They were particularly concerned about a then-emerging constitutional challenge that Johannesburg activists were planning at the time. This challenge evolved into the third and most important of the three cases: the *Lindiwe Mazibuko* litigation in the Constitutional Court.[19]

In July 2006, Mazibuko and four other residents of Phiri in Soweto, Johannesburg, filed a case challenging two aspects of local water services policy, and putting the constitutional right to access water at the centre of its argument. First, the Phiri residents argued that pre-paid meters, introduced into the township during a five-year management contract held by a subsidiary of Suez, France, were unconstitutional forms of 'self-disconnection' because they lacked the procedural protections required by the *Bon Vista* case. Second, they argued that the Free Basic Water Policy of 25 kilolitres per household per month was an insufficient supply and should be doubled to 50 kilolitres, on the basis of WHO recommendations and average household sizes of eight.

The case was initially strikingly successful, but this success was eroded at both levels of appeal. The lower court upheld both claims of the plaintiffs in 2007, leading to powerful claims of victory from the activists and celebration in linked networks worldwide. Two years later, that successful, but still unenforced, decision was diluted on appeal: the 50 kilolitre requirement was reduced to 42 kilolitres, and judges suspended the order that the pre-payment meters were unconstitutional for two years, explicitly in order to give the state time to explore ways to retain the pre-paid meters in a legal manner.[20] Finally, in 2009 the Constitutional Court removed the necessity for the state to do even that, holding that national legislation and the city's own by-laws authorised the city to introduce pre-paid water meters and that the cessation in water supply caused by a pre-paid meter stopping is better understood as a temporary suspension in water supply, not a discontinuation. The Constitutional Court also stated that the constitutional right of access to sufficient water does not require the state to provide every person with sufficient water upon demand, nor does it allow judges to specify a quantified standard determining the 'content' of the right. Instead, it requires the state to take reasonable legislative

---

[19]  *Lindiwe Mazibuko and Others* v. *City of Johannesburg and Others*, Case CCT 39/09 [2009] ZACC 28.

[20]  *City of Johannesburg and Others* v. *Lindiwe Mazibuko and Others*, Case 489/08 [2009] ZA SCA 20 (25 March 2009).

and other measures progressively to realise the achievement of the right of access to sufficient water within available resources. The Constitutional Court's decision was greeted with dismay by socio-economic rights activists, community organisations and a wide range of actors working on the right to water.[21]

In short, socio-economic rights, when judicially elaborated, gave rise in South Africa to a right to a 'reasonable regulatory approach'. This translated into a constitutionalised administrative law rather than a discourse of substantive entitlements. Although this could potentially shape the distributive implications of regulatory frameworks for the provision of water, the reluctance of the judiciary at the highest level to directly exercise such influence only magnifies the importance of more political pathways for linking rights and regulation.

### 5.4.3   Civil and political rights

#### South Africa

In contrast to the divisions over socio-economic rights strategies, South African social activists were united on the importance of *civil and political rights* as a crucial shield for preserving collective political agency. For the context of social protest against the collection of unpaid debt for water services here was profoundly polarised and harsh:

> It's ... brutal in Cape Town – I've seen with my own eyes in Khayalitsa a woman with 200R (US$20) debt [for water] having her goods removed – she had no electrical goods so they took her bed and clothes – it's completely blindly, fanatically, fundamentalist ideology – you send armoured vehicles and men with guns, that costs money, much more money, all the young men come out of their houses, there's a stand-off, people can end up in prison – I sound melodramatic but it's insane, the policy is insane.[22]

Following the events mentioned in this quotation, the Anti-Privatisation Forum in Cape Town called for assistance in setting up a legal defence fund that would provide cover for water warriors and all activists and community members engaged in active grassroots struggle against privatisation and neoliberal policies (e.g. evictions, forced removals, cut-offs, education and environmental struggles). Law here is a buffer, a tool for clearing a political space: 'The [Durban-based activist lawyers] have taken great care to use the law in ways that keep the space open for politics, in

---

[21]   See www.escr-net.org/caselaw/caselaw_show.htm?doc_id=1110326.
[22]   Pithouse interview.

the way that the Zapatistas talk about using their guns to keep the space open for civil society, for politics'[23]

The salience of civil and political rights, when used in tandem with direct mass action, was that they enabled disputing dynamics to shape political conflict over structural power, rather than mutating into technocratic debates over policy implementation details. In other words, the capacity for 'naming, blaming and claiming' to energise the building of collective political agency was retained. As we shall see later, however, this arguably came at the cost of effective linkage back to rulemaking, monitoring and enforcement.

## New Zealand

In New Zealand, in a much less economically polarised social context, the protestors also made strategic use of civil and political rights litigation to support the continuation of their more directly political activities. Their specific lawsuits were, like their socio-economic rights strategies, legally unsuccessful yet politically productive. For example, local government officials ordered protestors to remove banners they had draped across their houses, on which they accused named politicians of betraying the public interest by creating a corporate structure for Metrowater. The activists argued that this order breached their right to free speech under the New Zealand Bill of Rights Act 1990. Although they lost the case, the substantial publicity given the case and consequent political ramifications[24] led to a legislative amendment to clarify that the Human Rights Act does apply to local government.

In another example, the protestors asked the court to nullify a local election on the basis that electors had been induced to vote by a misrepresentation.[25] Candidates who had been elected on an anti-privatisation platform had later revealed their support for public–private partnerships in water services. The notion that they had misrepresented their position depending on equating 'privatisation' and 'public–private partnerships' (essentially long-term concession contracts of twenty or thirty years that delegate the technical and financial management of water service delivery

---

[23] Pithouse interview.
[24] The occupant of the house refused to comply and was charged with contempt of court. He continued to refuse to comply and was jailed for eighteen days. The Auckland City Council moved for a withdrawal of the contempt order in embarrassment at the publicity it was receiving on the issue.
[25] *Bright v. Mulholland* [2002] DCR 196.

to the private sector). After taking expert evidence from an economist, the judge rejected this equation, in revealing terms:

> Some might say that it is of the very nature of politics that candidates will promote their policies in a way [that] takes advantage of knowing that different interpretations might be put on the meaning of his or her words, unrestrained by any political equivalent of the 'misleading or deceptive conduct' provisions of the Fair Trading Act relating to commerce.[26]

Political choice, quite literally, was distinguished from consumer choice in a commercial context – and marked as less binding. Like the free speech case, this election case created space for a public debate over the specific forms of private sector involvement mooted in New Zealand's regulatory framework, a debate that led to substantive changes as the final section will show. And as in South Africa, while the activists' strategies of direct action had exposed them to some degree of public censure for undercutting norms of responsible consumer behaviour, their capacity to air their arguments in court (even while losing) legitimised their cause, and at the same time amplified the publicity they received regarding their civil disobedience. In New Zealand, however, it was the civil and political rights claims that generated a positive public reaction, while in South Africa, direct legitimating effects at the level of policy debate were more attached to the socio-economic rights claims. As we will see in the final section, this difference echoes different pathways linking rights claims back to regulatory frameworks in the two case studies: a more legalised constitutional litigation pathway characteristic of South Africa, and a more directly political electoral game typifying the New Zealand trajectory.

## 5.5 Rendering justiciability operable

Thus far, the case studies of New Zealand and South Africa suggest that protecting and enforcing access to water as a socio-economic right, whether directly by constitutional means or indirectly through public law, does not by itself translate into significant political change. Judicial enforcement of socio-economic rights with nothing else tends to secure, at most, purely procedural gains that are very politically vulnerable. Interdependent linkages with civil and political rights, however, can produce much better leverage, especially when combined with direct action. Civil and political rights clear a protected space for direct

---

[26] *Bright v. Mulholland*, para. 47.

action encompassing civil disobedience. When the direct action articulates emerging norms embedded in the everyday practices of marginalised citizens, it draws hitherto illegal actions into a space of potential legality. Litigating these actions in terms of socio-economic rights then gives them legal form in policy-relevant ways, helping to imagine them as operational dimensions of a new policy order in the future. Civil and political rights thus act as a crucial hinge that provides a foundation for the energy of naming, claiming and blaming to be productively linked to the institutional stability of rulemaking, monitoring and enforcement.

As we have seen in previous chapters, however, fostering productive links between direct action, civil and political rights and socio-economic rights is a necessary but insufficient means of securing secure lasting change in governance regimes. Governance with the potential to facilitate inclusive social change is based on productive linkages between rights *and regulation*. In short, imagining socio-economic rights as central facets of water services policy is only one step towards rendering the vision operable at an everyday policy level. Securing and embedding the desired social change involves directly engaging *both* of the two triads at the centre of Chapter 1's analytical framework. Indeed, one could fragment the triads into three stages of social change thus: imagining the change (naming and blaming), legitimising the change (claiming and making new rules), and routinising the change (monitoring and enforcing those rules).

Rights claims only address part of this six-fold process, primarily imagining the change and beginning the work of legitimating it. As we have seen, direct action, energised and protected by civil and political rights, does the task of 'naming, blaming and claiming' from an outsider perspective. Socio-economic rights 'name, blame and claim' from an insider perspective, using existing norms and entitlements to frame the process of imagining an altered order. The combination of outsider and insider influence is crucial for shifting the boundary between illegality and legality: a necessary foundation for the later work. That later work is an extended engagement with rulemaking, monitoring and enforcement: this is crucial for actually embedding the imagined change into a working policy order. Such engagement is what builds a productive bridge between rights claims and regulatory frameworks. The two case studies in this chapter point to two different routes for such a bridge: electoral politics and constitutional litigation.

### 5.5.1 Electoral politics

In New Zealand, social activists used the political space and debate created by their direct action and rights claims to focus on electoral change in order to create new 'rules of the game'. The electoral change route grew out of the way in which direct action and rights first imagined and then legitimated their demands for change. Although none of the court actions described earlier were successful in legal terms, the way in which they were combined with direct and often illegal action was significantly more successful – perhaps even *because* of the activists' frank disregard for the coherency and consistency of their strategies *in legal terms*. Most of their potentially successful legal arguments would at best have tempered the commercial provision of water at the edges. What they cared about was the ability to mobilise politicians to vote, asserting repeatedly, 'it's not the court of law that counts but the court of public opinion'.[27]

The cases legitimised, at least in part, the political cost of being perceived as unruly and irresponsible consumers. Three examples of legitimation effects can be given. First, one of the protestors (who had no legal qualifications) was asked to give a training session to the police on proportionate responses to social protest. Second, for three years Metrowater accepted the 'letter of dispute' as a legitimate basis for not disconnecting customers who refused payment. And, third, the election case fostered a public debate about popular versus technical meanings of the word 'privatisation' that created the political space for key politicians, who were being continually lobbied by the protestors, to secure crucial amendments to the Local Government Act 2003.

New Zealand had altered its political system to proportional representation in the early 1990s, which had opened up the possibility of relatively small numbers of voters successfully electing their candidates. By the late 1990s a new small party (the Alliance), backed by the activists at local level, had won seats at the national level and held the balance of power in coalition with the Green Party. After several years of the kinds of protest described earlier against water restructuring reforms, this Green–Alliance coalition was persuaded to secure some crucial amendments to the principal regulatory framework for water service delivery (which

[27] Penny Bright, Water Pressure Group, interviewed by Bronwen Morgan, Auckland, December 2003.

was embedded in the Local Government Act 2002). These amendments limited the involvement of the private sector in water service delivery.[28] They prohibited local governments from divesting themselves of water supply and wastewater services within their areas, except to another local government authority, restricted any contracting-out of water services operations to fifteen years, and mandated local government to at all times retain control over water pricing, water services management and the development of water policy.

Moreover, in the committee hearings on the bill, the Department of Health took the opening created by the Water Pressure Group to move an amendment prohibiting the disconnection of water. This gave the activists fresh leverage to access information under freedom of information legislation to create pressure for operational implementation of the new disconnection policy. They mobilised information from the six different municipal councils in the Auckland region, and as a result were able to illustrate important disparities between the policies of public and private providers in relation to disconnection. This provided ongoing fodder for their broader campaign of electing political representatives committed to a policy of reinvigorating public sector water supply. In this way, the New Zealand case study illustrates an electoral route to linking rights claims back to the regulatory framework.

### 5.5.2   Constitutional politics

The political context in South Africa was much less amenable to the pursuit of an electoral route by social movement activists. The dominance of the ANC, and its substantial legitimacy as the party representing the long years of struggle against apartheid, made channelling protest energy into the formation of potential political parties not only challenging but possibly even dangerous, according to the leader of the South African Anti-Privatisation Forum.[29] As we saw earlier, in the representation in Table 12 of varying local political dynamics according to the social characteristics of different groups, only Durban-based groups, which had some non-ANC political support, were willing to extend their range of strategies towards potential political party-building. Such groups also used some litigation but were, as discussed in the section on rights,

---

[28] See discussion at the end of Section 5.3.1.
[29] Trevor Ngwane, Anti-Privatisation Forum, interviewed by Bronwen Morgan, Johannesburg, 3 September 2003.

deeply ambivalent about this. Only the activists based in Johannesburg, where the ANC was entrenched as the main party, made a strong and explicit choice to follow a constitutional litigation route for embedding rights claims into operational policy. And as we saw above, the ultimately disappointing outcome of the *Mazibuko* case shows that while constitutional politics are capable of changing the rules of the game, they cannot do so in isolation, and as a strategy are subject to significant limits.

The basis of these limits lies in the nature of constitutional socio-economic rights as they are institutionalised in South Africa. South Africa's Apartheid Museum unfolds to the visitor a dramatic and harrowing story of political struggle that closes with a sparse, silent image: a wall bearing a large metal plaque with the rights of the 1996 constitution inscribed on it, stripped of the fine print, articulating fundamental entitlements of individual dignity and survival in unqualified terms of bright-line clarity and precision. Section 27, for example, reads simply:

**Health care, food, water and social security**
Everyone has the right to have access to health care services, sufficient food and water, and social security.

But compare this image to the actual text:

**Section 27: Health care, food, water and social security**
(1) Everyone has the right to have access to ... sufficient food and water.
...
(2) The state must take reasonable legislative and other measures, within its available resources, to achieve the progressive realisation of each of these rights.

This tells a much more qualified story: of a right that is, strictly speaking, not an entitlement to the thing itself, but a claim that obliges the government to 'take reasonable legislative and policy measures, within its available resources' in pursuit of its provision. The *Mazibuko* case carefully calibrated its accommodation of changed rules with a wide scope for 'reasonable' government response. This is at the heart of the limits of this strategy as a route for rendering rights claims operable.

In essence, when attempts by activists to harness the guarantees of constitutional human rights leave broader questions of collective representation and responsiveness to be determined by political institutions that increasingly adopt managed liberalisation, then rights fail to energise the public participatory model and instead buttress 'soft consumerism', a social safety net dimension of managed liberalisation. This leaves activists who seek to assert a collective political identity pushed to do so in oppositional and unruly forms that are both unrecognised and increasingly repressed by the formal political system.

## 5.6    Conclusion

Socio-economic rights, when judicially elaborated, give rise to a right to a 'reasonable regulatory approach', which translates into a constitutionalised administrative law rather than a discourse of substantive entitlements. Negotiations over the bounds of 'reasonable regulatory expectations' are shaped most importantly, therefore, by the evolution of regulatory policy in *non-judicial* organs of state. In both South Africa and New Zealand, this evolution has come under significant influence from the managed liberalisation model, but more intensely so in South Africa.

But it is also important to note the *limits* of conceiving of rights in terms of a dialogue with the state at all, whether judicial or non-judicial. For socio-economic rights claims are also, crucially, cries of contestation – modes of collective action that forge communities independent of state structures and sometimes in self-conscious rejection of them. As such, they can be energised only when interlinked with civil and political rights and the 'outsider' pressure of direct action. In New Zealand the combination of illegal protest and the use of courts enlarged the space for the political participation of ordinary citizens in policymaking. In South Africa, similar dynamics were observed but the impact was more tempered, and the activists expressed more self-conscious ambiguity about the legitimating impact of law.

Issues over access to water are politically emotive and at the same time generate highly technocratic issues of large-scale bureaucratic reorganisation. Is it inevitable that when political emotivism is channelled into, say, civil society negotiations with business and government, it becomes more technocratic and routinised? Yes. But is it also inevitable that it embeds managed liberalisation via moderate reforms that accept the larger framework of commercialised imperatives for water services even while hoping to temper their harshest effects on vulnerable consumers or the environment? Not necessarily. Developing 'insider' participatory democracy strategies accepts routinisation but still aspires to a public participatory model of governance. The challenge is to build participatory governance structures that can channel either electoral success or constitutional litigation successfully into an ongoing substantive dialogue with civil society about operational issues. Only in this way can naming, claiming and blaming develop a productive interdependency with rule-making, monitoring and enforcement, entwining rights and regulation to constructive effect.

# 6

## Law's work: legality and identity in transnational spaces

### 6.1 Introduction

The previous chapters located their narratives of struggles over access to water in national domestic settings. They focused on particular disputes in specific urban localities that brought together a wide range of organisations, actors and rules from different levels of governance. This made it possible to locate understandings of rights and regulation in these narratives as embedded in local political and institutional forces, as well as in the material specificity of particular urban settings. Thus, for example, although rights were important in both Bolivia and South Africa, the importance of social movement activists from rural areas in the Bolivian case study meant that conceptions of water as territory figured much more prominently than the South African township activism, which configured access to water as a basic service right.

In this final chapter, I work *across* the case studies, in a space that is at least partly deterritorialised and transnational. The space was constructed by exploring the perspectives of three interpretive communities across case studies: NGOs and activists, water companies and operators, and regulators (understood broadly to encompass civil servants, independent agencies and international financial institutions). Each of these three interpretive communities was embedded in networks and practices that, up to a point, either transcend or operate with little reference to national political processes and institutions. I then explored these groups' understandings of the meaning and utility of law, working with a communicative and systemic conception of law as encompassing institutions, rules and processes that defined conduct as legal or illegal. This process opened up commonalities across case studies: for example, in both Argentina and New Zealand activists turned to quasi-judicial small claims dispute resolution processes in ways that expanded traditional notions of consumer rights, using them as a lever for influencing decisions about production and management structures that were usually beyond the remit of consumers. Despite the profound differences in material and political context between the countries, activists in both settings viewed law as a means of keeping open political space – the second of three images of law's work that emerged in the partially deterritorialised space of this final chapter.

Each of the three images of law's work explored in this chapter resonated across the three interpretive communities. The first is an image of law as supporting and securing market relations; the second an image of law as a means of keeping open political space; the third an image of law as (ambiguously) constitutive of partnership. The images are in a sense a weaving together of the practices of naming, blaming and claiming, rulemaking, monitoring and enforcement that characterise managed liberalisation (law as supporting and securing market relations), public participatory governance (law as keeping open political space) and the hybrid solutions that are emerging as compromises (law as constitutive of partnership). The chapter will discuss each in turn, beginning with a general overview of what is entailed by the image and then exploring that with a particular focus on a specific practice that occurs in transnational space. The three practices that will concretise and illuminate law's work are international arbitration (for the work of securing and supporting market relations), uncivil disobedience (for the work of keeping open political space) and hybrid public–private partnerships (for the work of constituting partnership).

In each of the three images, law has a polyvalent status as both a strategic resource and a constitutive well of meaning. It is a locus of instrumental power and the construction of collective identity simultaneously. Thus each practice will be placed at the centre of a bifurcated exploration – first of law's status as strategic resource, and then of its place in a more elusive conception of emerging transnational identities. As we shall see, law as a strategic resource is predominantly exploited by political and economic elites, although its capacity to open political spaces can be strategically useful (with some important constraints) for disadvantaged groups which find themselves at the margins of global and national policymaking processes around access to water. As a locus for emergent identities, the question is: are transnational identities built in the process of struggles around access to water? Do these struggles perhaps unite activists from different countries, or build an epistemic community of regulators, or forge common concerns amongst the transnational companies that compete to provide water services? In conditioning collective identities that extend across geographically disparate areas, we will see that legality is paradoxically both friend and foe, in a manner especially charged with ambiguity for those at the margins of global policymaking.

## 6.2   Supporting and securing market relations

An image of law's role in supporting and securing market relations in the context of providing access to water had particularly powerful traction across activists, companies and regulators. Because the provision of drinking water services via large-scale network infrastructure has strong natural monopoly tendencies, market relations are by necessity actively constructed by legal–institutional frameworks. The case studies show that the most important facets of law's role in supporting and securing market relations in access to water were three-fold: competitive tendering procedures when long-term contractual outsourcing of water service delivery was sought; the degree to which legal frameworks regulating the price of water allowed for full cost-recovery for investors; and the conditions under which water services can be disconnected for failure or inability to pay.

Different evaluative positions were taken both within and across groups. Private sector water operators, particularly large multinationals, were perhaps the most obvious affiliates that worked 'with' this market-supporting image, supported by epistemic communities in international financial institutions and contract management professionals from large consulting firms. Regulators, while often occupying in practice more of a hybrid position combining all three images, particularly in relation to tariff-setting, were clearly part of an epistemic community that articulated a rationale for regulatory agencies that was consistent with supporting and securing markets. Regulators from this viewpoint carry out functions that facilitate competitive tendering, cost-recovery and (though more contentious) bill-collection. As the case studies have shown, this varied significantly by political context, with the Chilean regulatory agency most supportive of that viewpoint, Argentina the least, and Bolivia's agency occupying a somewhat embattled position in the crossfire of strong pressures from opposing directions.

Arguably, even some NGOs were oriented to this image of law's work in the sense of working *with* it. For example, organisations such as WaterAid or PS-Eau carried out service provision work in rural and unserved areas, often as a complement to the limits of providing water by competitive market, and in some cases funded by grants from the principal market operators. However, many, if not most, of the NGO and activist groups explored in the case studies, while they acknowledged the power of the law in constituting market conditions, were actively hostile to this image of law's work. The Bolivian case study showed the most comprehensive opposition against the structural dimensions of market-based access to water, while the South African case study highlighted with particular intensity the dark side of market-based policies in respect of disconnection and bill-collections, as the previous chapter showed.

A stance of hostility to the market-supporting image of law was not confined to the interpretive community of activists: with spatial variation, there were water operators who sought to temper the market-based distribution of water services, such as Grenoble's municipal water company, Cochabamba's water company's attempts to instantiate 'social control', or the Waikatere municipal government's water department in Auckland, New Zealand. Some regulators also had an ambiguous attitude to law's market-supporting role, such as the Tucumán agency in Argentina, while in South Africa and New Zealand a sense of political commitment to tempering market-based delivery principles led to an avoidance of building an independent central regulatory agency in the first place.

In terms of the location and site of this aspect of law's work, it is striking that it was at the national (and sometimes the local) level where the bulk of the formal legal and institutional determinants of market structures for the delivery of domestic water services resided. This was true across all the case studies: yet it should not mask the importance of the transnational diffusion of ideas and values, often via the avenues of conditions attached to financing, which have shaped the spread of managed liberalisation. And of course the case studies demonstrated a highly variable penetration of these ideas in different domestic contexts. To draw out the more general salience of this image of law's work at the transnational level, however, it is helpful to return to and focus on the specific issue of international investor arbitration.

### 6.2.1  International investor arbitration

#### From national to transnational

As has emerged in previous chapters, bilateral investment treaties are a crucial aspect of the transnational institutional architecture that focus on legal protection of the property and contract rights of foreign investors. In other words, they help to support and secure market relations when those relations are between actors on different sides of national political borders. Such treaties are controversial by virtue of their potential ability to

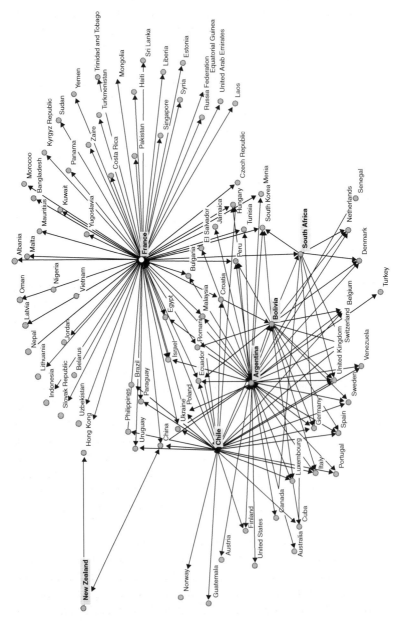

**Figure 4** Network view of bilateral investment treaty commitments by the six case study countries, mid 2003

Note: Created using data from Ginsburg (2005).

trump national and local regulatory protection. In a typical investor–state dispute, the investor claims compensation for damage it has allegedly suffered as a result of a state measure: for example, legislation, regulations, policies or practices of the state that alter the level of authorised tariffs that an investor could charge, or that affect methods of collection for bill payments.

During the 1990s, when the struggles over access to water explored in this book were all catalysed, the number of bilateral investment treaties concluded globally exploded, quadrupling from 500 to almost 2,000 over the decade (Ginsburg 2005). The exposure of the countries from this study was highly variant, as Figure 4 displays visually.

France was the most highly embedded in this form of transnational legal market infrastructure, with sixty-five treaties concluded by mid 2003. Argentina (thirty-eight treaties) and Chile (thirty treaties) were in a zone of medium exposure, while Bolivia (seventeen treaties), South Africa (ten treaties) and New Zealand (two treaties) were to varying degrees minimally exposed. The figures reflect the differential positions that the countries held in the global water services market, with France being a major global investor and Latin America having received the primary share of foreign private sector investment during the 1990s. The medium position of Argentina and Chile reflects their middle-income status and the fact that they invest externally as well as host foreign investors.

As we saw in some of the case studies, the chief influence of investment protection frameworks occurs by reason of the dispute settlement mechanisms provided to foreign operators, and the shadow this casts on national-level trajectories of water service policymaking. The majority of bilateral investment treaties contain clauses which submit the signatories to mandatory arbitration between a disgruntled investor and a host state. In practice, this can mean that a decision by, say, a three-member panel of arbitrators appointed by ICSID, located at the World Bank, can lead to extensive monetary compensation paid by a state to an investor by reason of regulatory and political decisions made in relation to the provision of water services by that investor.

As we saw in the case of Tucumán in Argentina, this is just what occurred, and in Bolivia a similar outcome was narrowly avoided by virtue of a symbolic settlement achieved by means of energetic transnational lobbying by groups hostile to the law's role in supporting and securing transnational markets. Indeed, although the protection of bilateral investment treaties is formally available to both signatories of a treaty, at least in the context of water, the results of actual disputes are skewed against those developing countries embedded in the global treaty system: by mid 2003 Argentina was defending eleven ICSID claims, while South Africa faced none. France, meanwhile, was prosecuting several (including the one based in Tucumán discussed in Chapter 4) and defending none.[1] In the bigger picture, it is clear from trends in ICSID claims that disputes at the transnational level have become increasingly central to the governance of projects involving high capital-cost infrastructure development. Between February 2002 and August 2005, ICSID claims almost doubled, almost half due to high capital infrastructure projects.[2]

## From state to non-state

The architecture of ICSID dispute resolution not only shifts the key playing field for supporting and securing market relations from local–national levels to transnational levels, it also shifts power from state to non-state actors. The ICSID treaty has been described as 'a key turning point in international dispute settlement, signalling the minimization of state intervention … highlighting the individual's own role in acceding to such arrangements … and encourag[ing] the flow of investments in a more certain and predictable legal environment' (Vicuña 2004). 'Certain and predictable' is given content by reference to the norms of market competition, and the reference to 'individuals' in practice means individual legal (usually corporate) entities rather than ordinary individual citizens, since the latter by themselves rarely contract to make major cross-border investments.

The way in which international arbitration resolves disputes while largely sidestepping states challenges the very definition of law. Simply put, in a transnational context, the core of legality is dispute resolution rather than sanction-backed rules. Gunther Teubner has argued that while national law's exemplary form is one of sanctions-backed rules and effective social control, transnational law (he uses the term 'global law')

---

[1] Calculated from ICSID (n.d.). These numbers are likely to represent only a fraction of total claims against the case study countries for two reasons: first, ICSID only publishes a claim once it has been registered by the Secretary General of ICSID, which can take some time; and, second, it does not take into account other fora for investor–state arbitration such as the United Nations Commission on International Trade Law (UNCITRAL) and the International Chamber of Commerce, neither of which has an obligation to publish claims.

[2] The 110 pending or complete ICSID claims in 2002 had increased to 189 by 2005, 81 of which involved large-scale infrastructure: energy projects (40 claims), infrastructure construction projects (28 claims), water and wastewater projects (9 claims) and municipal waste disposal (4 claims): calculated from ICSID (n.d.).

is very different (Teubner 1996). Global law, he argues, is constructed piecemeal when global networks of actors who regard particular norms as valid explicitly or implicitly designate particular actions as legal or illegal. Dispute resolution, not rule-creation, is at the heart of transnational legality for Teubner. The key facet of legality is the communicative dimension of dispute resolution: specifically, the allocation of conflict resolution to a third party who then renders a binary judgement (legal or illegal) that is made public, accepted by those in conflict, and later applied to resolve future conflicts. Moreover, this can be achieved without reference to the state if communicative practices internally differentiate 'spontaneous' (unofficial) and 'organised' (official) law production. These are most advanced at the transnational level in commercial law. So, for example, in international investment arbitration, contracts are the 'spontaneous' unofficial law (generated by parties bottom-up even though often modelled on precedent), while arbitration panels enunciate official law. Apart from the background structure of treaties legitimating this (including the option to turn to national courts to enforce the final judgement), states are not involved.

On the whole these processes are fragmented, resulting in multiple uncoordinated small islands, a patchwork of legal regimes – almost project-specific, save for the influence of model contracts. But we have seen in earlier chapters how powerful they can be. They make available a powerful set of rulemaking, monitoring and enforcement practices for a very restricted set of injuries that relate to supporting and securing market relations. Actors and interpretive communities who name, claim and blame outside the framework of supporting and securing market relations are effectively rendered silent within this space. Moreover, the ICSID dispute settlement mechanism, particularly in comparison to courts, is very restricted in terms of the participation opportunities it affords. International arbitration fora in general are essentially private, traditionally restricting access and participation solely to the investor and the relevant state government, with little or no publicity for the relevant documentation.[3] The case studies have, however, demonstrated pressures for these dispute resolution fora to be reformed.

---

[3] ICSID publishes the existence only of awards registered under the ICSID Convention or the ICSID Additional Facility, and the content only with the consent of the parties to the dispute (ICSID Convention, Article 48(5)). Other fora for investor–state arbitration (e.g. UNCITRAL and the International Chamber of Commerce) have no obligation to publish claims at all. Additional materials relevant to a dispute, such as the submissions of the parties, are not normally published.

Responses and trends

Pressure for reform as demonstrated by the case studies has taken one of two paths. The first has been to push for reform of the investor–state arbitration process directly, primarily via procedural avenues that expand transparency and participation rights for third parties at the formal dispute resolution stage. Although petitions for such an expansion were made by transnational NGO coalitions in relation to the ICSID claim brought by Bechtel regarding the Cochabamba dispute (Chapter 3), they were unsuccessful. However, some four years later similar claims made (albeit in more detailed legal terms) by a different transnational coalition that linked legal, consumer and environmental NGOs[4] did succeed. As discussed in Chapter 4, an ICSID tribunal was convinced for the first time that it had the power to accept amicus curiae briefs from civil society organisations, even in the face of objections from parties. Since then, although no formal system of following precedent exists within international arbitration, other tribunals have nonetheless followed suit, including in a similar dispute over a long-term contract with the private sector to deliver water services in Tanzania.[5]

More broadly, there is widespread support from epistemic communities in public law (Van Harten and Loughlin 2006), supported by the interpretive community of activists and NGOs interviewed for this research, for a broader conception both substantively and procedurally of the public interests at stake in dispute resolution over large infrastructure projects providing essential services. In other words, some space for articulating ('naming and blaming') a broader scope of felt injuries has been won, even if there is still limited scope for the substantive claims in legal terms. But although this may be seen as a tentative hybrid between managed liberalisation and public participatory governance, the dependence of the hybrid on the overall structure of rulemaking, monitoring and enforcement associated with managed liberalisation renders the reforms vulnerable.

For example, there is a general counter-movement to promote 'efficiency' in investor–state protection that is eroding these small gains for public participatory governance even before they have become

---

[4] Specifically two Argentinian legal NGOs (Centro de Estudios Legales y Sociales (CELS); La Associación Civil por la Igualdad y la Justicia (ACIJ)); two Argentinian consumer/public services NGOs (Consumidores Libres Cooperativa Ltda. de Provisión de Servicios de Acción Comunitaria; Unión de Usuarios y Consumidores); and a US-based international environmental NGO (Centre for International Environmental Law (CIEL)).

[5] *Biwater* v. *Tanzania*, Case No. ARB/05/22, Procedural Order No. 5.

particularly embedded (Nottage and Miles 2009). And another trend is noteworthy: private law in the 'spontaneous' dimension of contracting can, via carefully worded clauses, anticipate and block the effects of any reform on the 'official' side of international arbitration. As professional and advocacy groups in the US observed,[6] contracts that post-dated failures of the kind that occurred in Bolivia and Cochabamba have often included clauses shifting the financial implications of political backlash away from the private investor and onto the contracting government. No matter how inclusive the dispute resolution forum may be, in such circumstances clear contractual terms will decide the matter. Given the limitations of this hybrid path of reform, it is perhaps not surprising that Bolivia, the strongest advocate of a public participatory model, has taken a different path of reform. This will be discussed in more detail in the next section, but, as noted in Chapter 3, Bolivia has, as part of this alternative trajectory, withdrawn its participation from the ICSID dispute resolution regime. By taking dispute resolution out of the space of managed liberalisation represented by ICSID, the impetus for change returns to domestic-level political forces, much as it has remained with them in countries like South Africa and New Zealand which have been less directly embedded in the transnational infrastructure supporting and securing market relations.

### 6.2.2    Transnational identities

In closing the exploration of law's work in supporting and securing market relations, the final question is whether or not the work yokes together a wide range of actors in a shared sense of collective identity. This is a powerful and deeply rooted image of law: that it is highly contested is seen in the way some groups only acknowledge it by way of opposition. Conflictual politics can generate collective identity, when conflict is rooted in a shared practical orientation that develops an expressive dimension. But the processes of transnational commercial law at the heart of international arbitration are fragmented, and the shared practical orientations are on the whole more technocratic, instrumental and strategically oriented than they are expressive. The 'patchwork legality' that results is strategically useful in securing predictable market relations, but it is a relatively thin form of shared identity, episodically invoked and only in the context of the competitive social relations of the global market.

---

[6] Gary Wolff and Meena Palaniappan, Pacific Institute, interviewed by Bronwen Morgan, Oakland, California, 1 August 2003.

Perhaps during the 1990s one could have argued that the broader ideological orientation of the Washington Consensus cemented a kind of collective identity around certain configurations of actors: in the global water policy field, this would have been private for-profit firms, contract management professionals, international financial institutions and certain service provision NGOs. But configurations of actors who support the core work of law as being to secure market relations have responded to the contestation of the 1990s by tempering their position somewhat, particularly since 2005 when the original fieldwork at the heart of this book occurred. The limits of private sector participation are more frankly acknowledged than during the 1990s, the need for some form of regulation is much more part of a shared consensus (albeit with little agreement on the form and institutions), and the basic idea of taking account of affordability and equity concerns is more prominent than it once was (Bakker 2009). Yet this has occurred largely without any profound alteration of either the power relations within the global water policy field, nor its basic institutional arrangements.

In such a context, it is perhaps no surprise that the identity most associated with this partial shift, that of the corporate social responsibility of transnational corporations, is not, at least yet, taken seriously by those who have contested this image of law's role as a marker of global citizenship. As Ronen Shamir argues, '"corporate social responsibility" is becoming a corporate commodity in and of itself. It is traded on the market as a moral resource that legitimizes and naturalizes global capitalism, while facilitating a whole new market of products and services' (Shamir 2002: 230). This is consistent with the idea suggested by Teubner's work that global law is almost defined by the way in which it is socially rooted in strategic relations rather than the 'lifeworld' that we associate more with a sense of enduring identity:

> The social source of global law is not the lifeworld of globalized personal networks, but the proto-law of specialised, organisational and functional networks which are forming a global, but sharply limited identity. The new living law of the world is nourished not from stores of tradition but from the ongoing self-reproduction of highly technical, highly specialized, often formally organized and rather narrowly defined, global networks of an economic, cultural, academic or technological nature. (Teubner 1996: 8)

In terms of the overall analytical framework of this book, what has happened is that the particular configuration of rights and regulation embodied by managed liberalisation in the global field of urban water services policy shifted during 1990–2005 in response to practices of 'naming, blaming and claiming' that were rooted in a competing policy model – that of public participatory governance. However, the shift has not extended to the practices of rulemaking, monitoring and enforcement that govern the field, with the result that gestures towards normative compromise are not yet backed by any stable set of shared practical orientations that move beyond the narrower image of law supporting market relations. If the specialised networks of transnational commercial law have a weak expressive dimension in terms of fashioning transnational *political* identities, do the practices engendered in the work of using law to keep political spaces open move further towards collective transnational identities? And what kinds of institutional alternatives to managed liberalisation do they project? The next section will consider these questions in reverse order.

## 6.3   Keeping political space open

As we saw in the previous section, securing and supporting market relations is a dominant aspect of law's work for all of the key interpretive communities in transnational water policy. The image of law keeping open political space is one which responds to that dominant aspect: the core of the image is to keep open political space for articulating the needs of those marginalised by market-based water service delivery policies. Most often, 'law' in this image was concretised in terms of litigating to defend such needs, particularly at national or local levels, but the articulation of legislative or regulatory frameworks based on non-market norms was also an important facet, especially at the transnational level. Thus here, by contrast with Teubner's emphasis on dispute resolution *rather than* norm-building activities, both are important. Indeed, without norm-building activities, litigation of socio-economic rights risks prising open a depoliticised space that facilitates private inter-party disputes but little structural political change. Norm-building global networks may, at present, catalyse less transnational 'hard' law of the kind that designates actions as either 'legal' or 'illegal', as international arbitration does. But they arguably facilitate the development of shared practical orientations around social conventions and moral norms, at least within interpretive communities, that can help to build transnational identities at a thicker level than in relation to law's work of securing and supporting market relations.

There was great variation across case studies in the depth and penetration of this image of law's work. In Chile, for example, this image was painfully residual, and was expressed with hope only by regulators and civil servants, who focused on consumer law as an outlet for those dissatisfied with the outcomes of market-based provision. Activists, NGOs and even private companies were less sanguine: one private company observed that for consumers trying to use the law to their advantage in water policy was 'like speaking to a brick wall'.[7] South Africa and Bolivia represented roughly the opposite end of the spectrum: activists and NGOs in Bolivia had access to an especially rich range of legislative strategies and in South Africa to a fertile array of litigation strategies. Yet even in these cases, activists often remained deeply ambiguous about law's potential for keeping political spaces open. Their main fear was that using law for this purpose risked depoliticisation and individualisation and was open to manipulation by powerful elites, as an image drawn by one of the interviewees in Chapter 5 vividly illustrates:

> People would love to have someone come in on a white horse and save them – people desire that – but that's something that's been deliberately decided against … in that way [the Durban legal activists] have been very reluctant to use legal skills to replace the politics, because it's disempowering – law takes a long time, that kind of [big test-case] law, and people tend to rely on this elite lawyer and if they don't deliver there's nothing to fall back on.[8]

Yet they were rarely willing to jettison law, stressing that it also provided an expressive venue for powerful stories. The importance of law as a means of legitimation here is worth emphasising, as the following quotation illustrates:

> There is this huge ideological project – the local press and the vast majority of academics are all saying 'there is one way of doing things, it's the way that competitive nations do things. We've all got to pull together, these [water activists] are messing it up for us, they're holding us back.' Now getting a court case can really help with the ideological stuff – it helps show these people are not criminal, they are not lazy, [their actions] are actually in line with the values of the new society that was founded.[9]

### 6.3.1    Uncivil disobedience

The political ambiguity of law's work here can be unpacked by exploring its relationship to what Jennet Fitzpatrick calls 'uncivil disobedience'.

---

[7] Castro and Manzano interview.
[8] Pithouse interview.    [9] Pithouse interview.

Her book with this title uses it to explore the commonalities between violent and non-violent populist reform, arguing that violence is structurally embedded in collective understandings of the legitimate boundaries of non-violent pressure for change. She insists that the boundary between 'rule of law' and 'rule of the people' is an analytically murky one that is nonetheless politically charged, so that it can be exploited by those practising uncivil disobedience who thereby restructure the boundary, rearticulating the appropriate limits of the rule of law within a new and compelling moral vision (Kirkpatrick 2008).

I want to suggest that her argument is applicable not only to violent 'uncivil disobedience', but also to practices that are illegal without necessarily turning into outright violence. The two sets of practices that are most salient in the context of access to water debates are illegal reconnection to water networks and mass boycotts of paying bills. These core strategies of the 'water wars' explored in the case studies are visceral aspects of tangible community interconnections. They make and sever physical and economic lifelines that are not only core aspects of the policies explored in this book, but also the metaphorical equivalent of the 'ties that bind' particular communities. They are 'uncivil' even when they are not violent as such, because they breach the terms of the cultural contract which imbricates norms of consumerism and aspirations to social citizenship at the level of everyday practice.

A cultural contract, in Davina Cooper's terms, is a dominant if imaginary framework of beliefs, norms and values governing a given community (Cooper 1994) that functions as a reference point for constructing the boundaries of who has rights and who does not. The mutual trust that is a necessary constitutive part of any functioning market depends on the everyday expectation, held by both buyer and seller, that payment will follow provision. The routinisation of 'responsible consumerism' makes this so obvious as to be taken for granted: in a market economy, the responsibility to pay one's bills is possibly one of the most taken-for-granted norms that permeate our everyday lives, certainly from the perspective of the dominant ideology. But law's judgement on the appropriateness of such behaviour can draw on *competing* notions of the boundaries of proper community behaviour where different cultural contracts underpin the exercise of legal judgement. Cultural plurality in this sense can find legal outlets in the multiplicity of legal venues and legal frameworks that apply to water policymaking, particularly if those practising uncivil disobedience emphasise the material context and structural power relations that produce a different cultural contract. Moreover uncivil disobedience, in challenging the threshold between 'legal' and 'illegal', contests the boundaries of the community itself, redefining who is inside and who is outside.

The South African case study can be used to illustrate these dynamics. Here, as was the case in varying contexts in all of the case studies, the dominant cultural contract of responsible consumerism was firmly embedded. As a local activist lawyer observed:

> There is a very rigid contractual interpretation to the entire thing, that in order for you as a citizen of this country to get services, you have contracted to pay for the amenities that have been provided, and should you not pay, you cannot be allowed the opportunity of continuing to use those services, because you're creating a precedent for the rest of this country, and the more people are paying, then services will benefit.[10]

But, activists went on to argue, the specific material and political–structural context of South African townships legitimated non-payment and the illegal reconnections made by 'moonlight plumbers'. The exigencies of continued material deprivation in the townships combined with a felt crisis of political representation. Municipal councillors may well have once fought alongside the activists during apartheid, but post-apartheid they now found themselves exacting payment through disconnection and repression. The resulting cleavages were shaped by macro-economic structural forces well outside the scope of the seller–buyer relationship, embedded in the politics of international global competition as illustrated in the previous chapter. The practices of uncivil disobedience were aimed at deflecting attention towards exactly these tensions within political representations, and *away* from the mutual expectations of the service delivery environment. They were practices aimed at building new communities based on a shared practical orientation to gaining control over their daily access to basic necessities.

Seen from this perspective, payment boycotts and 'moonlight plumbing' practices were not explicitly rejecting responsible community norms of the kind demanded by market economy service provision so much as enacting a politics of socio-economic rights in the context of a different cultural contract. As Trevor Ngwane, leader of the Anti-Privatisation Forum, said with some passion in relation to the practice of ordinary citizens removing pre-payment meters installed as part of the private management contract by Suez in Johannesburg: 'Oh no, to characterise [the

---

[10] Reddy interview.

removal of pre-payment meters] as vandalism is crazy! That's criminal-izing it because, no no, no, no, I mean, it's a defiance campaign. We take them out, you know, we don't break them and then during a march we collect them and hand them over to Eskom, symbolically.'[11]

And in Durban, where the *public* water company was pursuing a cor-poratisation strategy, township residents marched en masse to the muni-cipal water office waving 10 rand notes, chanting their willingness to pay 10 rand per month and no more for their water. In short, 'uncivil dis-obedience' blended illegality with expressions of ongoing commitment to a revised notion of 'responsible consumer behaviour', one that was explicitly part of a practice of collective representation linked to the his-tory of anti-apartheid activism. The 10 rand marches and the symbolic returns of pre-payment meters co-existed with the technical illegality of payment boycotts and illegal reconnections, pointing to the fact that cur-rent structures of law attempt to close down such practices in the name of illegality, while at the same time enacting an alternative cultural contract that *redefined* the legal/illegal boundary, re-badging vandalism as defi-ance, and redefining criminal behaviour as a defence of full citizenship and community membership.

### 6.3.2   Patchwork legality

Payment boycotts and 'moonlight plumbing' practices enact a politics of socio-economic rights that bears an ambiguous relationship to legal-ity – one that is critical and yet goes beyond critique to imagine what a reformed legality might look like in an alternative political space. This ambiguous simultaneity is possible because competing cultural contracts are visible *within* law: they do not simply oppose themselves to the current legal order. This is vividly illustrated in the patchwork of legalities govern-ing access to water. In all the case studies, multiple legal frameworks were applicable to the issues at stake, both in terms of different areas of law and different levels of governance. In South Africa, as Chapter 5 illustrated, constitutional law arguments allowed activists to reconstruct criminal delinquency as responsible parenting, communicating in the legitimating forum of a courtroom competing norms that challenged the taken-for-granted practices of responsible consumerism.

---

[11] Ngwane interview.

This multivalency was salient not only for activists but also for official state actors: as the director of South Africa's infrastructure investment authority commented: 'transferring financial risk [through contracting-out water service provision] means nothing when you have a constitutional obligation to deliver a service'.[12] Patchwork legality in New Zealand made it possible for activists to press claims for a publicly owned and managed water service within commercial law, administrative law, electoral law and environmental law – this bricolage opened up multiple internal definitions of what counts as 'legal' or 'illegal' and thus provided space for competing cultural contracts. And in both Argentina and New Zealand activists turned to quasi-judicial small-claims dispute resolution processes in ways that expanded traditional notions of consumer rights, using them as a lever for influencing decisions about production and management structures that were usually beyond the remit of consumers.

Patchwork legality is politically ambiguous, however, particularly when shifting between levels of governance. For example, as Chapter 4 showed, in Argentina the shadow of international investment arbitration negated challenges to responsible consumerism by effectively 'trumping' the local articulations of competing cultural contracts. In contrast, Chapter 3 showed an alternative political space emerging in Bolivia, displacing that same framework of international investment arbitration and introducing a new constitutional order. But ambiguity remained: the exigencies of implementing the new rights regime secured by indigenous irrigators brought back into play the regulatory frameworks favoured by international financial institutions. In short, if multiple competing cultural contracts are ever to successfully alter structural power relations, they must be responsive to the different energy, skills and commitment involved in any transition from resistance to organisational governance.

### 6.3.3    Rendering justiciability

Transitions from resistance to positive organisational governance often face a major challenge in avoiding functional incorporation into the regime that was originally resisted, which in these case studies has been managed liberalisation. This challenge can be met if the transition is understood as a process of *rendering justiciability*. Patterns of activity, allocations of resources or distributions of entitlements are rendered

---

[12] Senior official, Municipal Infrastructure Investment Unit, interviewed by Bronwen Morgan, Johannesburg, 6 October 2003.

justiciable when they become *capable of being judged* by institutions, organisations or other holders of structural power that have the power to change the rules of the game. These actors may be courts, governments, corporations, international organisations – the justiciability is not a technical-legal one, but must cross a general threshold of operability. The core point is that it must become possible to imagine the norms articulated through uncivil disobedience as operable dimensions of a new policy order in the future. Three means of doing this emerged across the case studies: socio-economic rights litigation, norm-building activities at national and transnational levels (legislative drafting) and bottom-up community governance.

## Socio-economic rights litigation

Framing, through litigation, the practices of uncivil disobedients in terms of socio-economic rights gave them legal form in policy-relevant ways. This made it possible to extrapolate aspects of these practices into operational dimensions of a new policy order in the future. However, at the level of direct action, where the energy of resistance is predominant, socio-economic rights are not a distinct category from civil and political rights; but when litigation is invoked, such distinctions emerge. And once visible, the case studies illustrated that socio-economic rights are far more at risk than civil and political rights of being domesticated and emptied out of their interrogatory power. The source of this vulnerability is the material and symbolic power embedded in the regulatory frameworks of managed liberalisation. When the organisational governance of socio-economic rights becomes dependent upon, or entwined with, these frameworks, it colonises the capacity of socio-economic rights to decommodify market-based provision or to critically interrogate the structural power underpinning those structures of provision.

A number of examples from the case studies illustrate this vulnerability. New Zealand activists' attempts to manipulate consumer and commercial law provisions in order to challenge the corporatisation of Auckland's water services were unsuccessful, in large measure because of the compatibility of the structures of corporatisation with the rights and regulatory framework of managed liberalisation. Where a stronger alternative legal framework existed, as was the case with the South African constitutional right to water, similar vulnerabilities were able to creep back despite early indications of promise. The first hearing of the *Mazibuko* case, discussed in Chapter 5, which declared both pre-payment meters and the limited volume of free basic water unconstitutional, was superseded on appeal by a decision that provided much more scope for the government to 'manage' the decision in ways that could severely limit its impact on the regulatory policymaking framework.[13] In particular, the order that the pre-payment meters were unconstitutional was suspended by the appeal court for two years in order to give the government time to 'legalise' the pre-payment meter regime. This is a form of rendering justiciability in reverse, welding the potential of litigation to achieve social change to existing rulemaking, monitoring and enforcement frameworks rather than opening up spaces for new ones.

### Norm-building activities at national and transnational levels

Norm-building activities at national and transnational levels are another way of rendering justiciability. The legislative drafting of the Bolivian activists provides one example which was less vulnerable to dependencies on state action. As one interviewee commented, such activities effectively shadowed the state until the activists gained sufficient political power to allow the alternative governance proposals to replace current state law.[14] But norm-building also remains vulnerable to dependency on the detailed legal implementation frameworks of managed liberalisation, as we saw in Chapter 3. This is especially the case in the context of multiple levels of governance where access to crucial economic resources remains governed by competing ideological frameworks, and public participatory approaches have less institutional 'bite' at transnational levels than managed liberalisation.

This may change over time. NGOs and activists involved in the legalisation of the human right to water aspire to create a viable regulatory framework that is consistent with human rights. But although some valuable work has been done in benchmarking existing national legislative frameworks against the standards of the 2002 General Comment on the Right to Water (COHRE et al. 2007), it has thus far had very limited leverage on, for example, lending policies of international financial institutions, model contracts used by transnational investors or national government policy frameworks. The obduracy of the transnational dimension of

---

[13] *Lindiwe Mazibuko & Ors* v. *The City of Johannesburg & Ors*, Case No. 06/13865, High Court of South Africa, Witswatersrand Local Division; *City of Johannesburg and Others* v. *Lindiwe Mazibuko and Others*, Case No. 489/08 [2009] ZA SCA 20 (25 March 2009). The case has been appealed to the Constitutional Court but judgement had not yet been handed down as of December 2009.

[14] Bustamante interview.

managed liberalisation increases the attraction of constructing an alternative transnational framework for political economy at the macro level. This is the path that Bolivia has chosen.

Since the election of Evo Morales as president, when Bolivia withdrew its participation from the ICSID dispute resolution regime, the country has increasingly supported instead the creation of an entirely distinct regional legal architecture in the form of the Bolivarian Alternative for the Peoples of America (ALBA). While the scope of this initiative is extremely wide-ranging,[15] for the purposes of the point made here, it is sufficient to note that it provides an extended framework for the development of an alternative (counter-hegemonic) political economy that inverts the centrality of competitive market relations in favour of a regional complex centred on 'cooperative advantage' and the values of solidarity, complementarity and reciprocity (Muhr 2010). Fair trade agreements replace free trade agreements. Social–humanitarian cooperation, initially focused on education and health but including a commitment to the universal provision of basic essential services, is funded by surpluses generated by the cost savings made through the regional distribution of energy resources.

Although there is as yet no formal multilateral legal dimension to ALBA, a large number of formal bilateral and regional agreements create a legal infrastructure that aspires to articulate an alternative set of rulemaking, monitoring and enforcement institutions for regional governance from those that give priority to securing and supporting market relations. This is a distinctly different path from that of reforming managed liberalisation through hybrid initiatives. But we have already seen in Chapter 3 that even within Bolivia this path currently operates mainly at a macro level that is belied by the more complex compromises of micro-level developments in water services policy. Whether this macro trajectory will prevail sufficiently to enable public participatory governance to diffuse more broadly in the regional space of ALBA is an open question for the future, but there is a marked contrast between tempering managed liberalisation via the legalised implementation of a transnational human right to water and creating an alternative pathway for political–economic cooperation at the macro level.

---

[15] ALBA presently has nine members, including founding members Venezuela and Cuba, and (in addition to Bolivia) Nicaragua, Honduras, El Salvador, Ecuador, Dominica, St Vincent and Antigua-Barbuda. Its activities span ten different areas: political, cultural, energy, economic, financial, military, educational, environmental, social-humanitarian and legal. See Muhr (2010).

Community governance from bottom-up practice

A third way of rendering justiciability is to create models of community governance from bottom-up practice rather than establishing new norms, shifting direct spontaneous action into the rhythms of everyday life. This approach takes us away from the image of law as a tool to pry open political space, and further into difficult questions of the relations between law and partnership, which will be explored in the final section of the chapter. As we shall see, law's role here is deeply ambiguous: law undermines partnership at the operational level as often as it facilitates it, depending on the texture of partnership that develops. Before turning to this, however, I briefly consider whether transnational identities are forged in the work of law opening up political space.

### 6.3.4    Transnational identities

For building identities, the importance of law's image as a means of keeping open political space is its endorsement of conflict. Schaap has recently re-emphasised the importance of a politics that 'substitutes conflict for consensus as the lodestar of democracy' (Schaap 2009: 14), viewing conflict as an unavoidable and constitutive aspect of politics, institutions as the contingent outcome of political struggle, and rights as political action rather than philosophical truth (Schaap 2009). A tension emerges, however, between the strategic and expressive implications of a conflict-centred politics (Schaap 2009). If strategically political struggle is a means for social transformation, expressively it may be an end in itself by virtue of the plurality and freedom it represents. Almost paradoxically, though, when conflict is viewed as strategically central, it can block productive action; while expressive conflict can, arguably, generate practical forward action even though it does not aspire to do so. Let me explain this by following through the implications of uncivil disobedience strategically and expressively.

From a strategic point of view, Schaap argues, acts of uncivil disobedience can create an *external* challenge to the legal/illegal distinction. They are 'disorderly not just in the derivative sense [of] ... illegal but in the primordial sense that ... contests what counts as legal and illegal in the first place' (Schaap 2009: 11). They create an asymmetrical opening that is not (yet) a new legality but that makes possible the kind of productive political conflict that might in time produce a new legality. Yet as forward-looking as this sounds, it grounds the intelligibility of any new legality on abstract principles, and in practice the tension between struggle and routine threatens to undermine the process of building sustained links between uncivil disobedience and the more banal, everyday activities required to reconstruct water service delivery in a more humane or sustainable form – the goal for which the protestors fight. This is reflected in the vulnerabilities discussed earlier that haunt the use of law for opening up political space.

Expressively, then, are different possibilities opened up? David Owen argues that the aesthetic and affective dimension of conflict-centred politics can achieve a break, an opening, a polyvocality, that is denied a politics that premises its intelligibility in terms of abstract principles. A particular speech, a protest, a ritualistic act can be a political act that aesthetically and emotionally makes it possible to continue to work together towards new legalities, even if formal legalities are taming the energy of resistance by reincorporating their challenges. The emphasis is on the shared practical orientation generated by struggling to follow the principles of popular sovereignty and the rule of law within particular historical circumstances – this is the work that (re)constitutes a sense of 'we', a sense of belonging (Owen 2009). The case studies showed some limited evidence of this, rooted in a sense of shared endeavour and mutual support across borders.

In South Africa and New Zealand, activist groups provided mutual support (occasionally financial but more often in the form of political advocacy) in assisting those who are disconnected from their water supplies as a result of payment boycotts. The New Zealand activists hosed down the Bolivian embassy with a fire-engine owned by one of the activist groups to express solidarity with Bolivian activists in Cochabamba. Bolivian and Canadian water activists met face-to-face to share strategies and tactics, and North American press coverage of the Bolivian conflict that reached the Bolivian activists provided a sense of international solidarity that encouraged them to persist with the mass blockades they had imposed on their town, as did news conveyed in a local left-wing Bolivian newspaper about a similar struggle over water privatisation in Tucumán, Argentina.[16] Activists spoke with passion about the energy and sense of purpose that they acquire from these experiences and links:

> Yes, yes, yes, well I mean, we've been at the forefront, New Zealanders and the South Africans, from what I can see in terms of civil disobedience campaigns. So whether that connection is part of our background, and

---

[16] Carlos Crespo, lecturer at the University of San Simón, Bolivian School of Planning, interviewed by Carolina Fairstein, Cochabamba, 3 March 2004.

> it's like solidarity in action, I mean, it's wonderful, and I've had more sup-
> portive emails from South Africa than I've had from unions and people
> in New Zealand. The bond is very strong, especially when you meet the
> people.[17]

They also emphasised the way in which transnational connections can replace national connections alienated by the methods of civil disobedience and unruly dissent:

> Look, remember also that earlier it was like a desert here because people had
> been smashed but everyone still believed in the government, [the current
> South African government] was able to have its agents everywhere, people
> have been confused so, you know, people like myself, we got inspired, you
> know, we could keep our work going on and workshops … it's a support
> structure, personally, yes, yes, and also, comrades around you, you know,
> people meet other people, so if you break ties with [the government] then
> you meet new friends, new comrades. That keeps us going.[18]

These energies, then, have created something of a sense of common endeavour across borders for activists working to open political spaces for the participation of traditionally marginalised groups in urban water services. But what can be institutionally built with such energies, what sorts of more routine, enduring forms of social relations emerge? This is the question to which the final section of this chapter turns.

## 6.4    Law as (ambiguously) constitutive of partnership

A major trend evident in the case studies at the heart of this book has been a move away from the important but simplified dichotomy that structured my initial presentation of transnational governance models in urban water service delivery, to a range of more nuanced hybrid possibilities. Instead of managed liberalisation 'versus' public participatory governance, various mixed public–private hybrids are now consistently offered as appropriate solutions to the policy challenges. This is in part a reflection of the consensus orientation of mainstream policy discourse, which seeks to resolve the tension between different models by searching for workable compromises, often framed in highly technical terms. It is also important to note that many contributors to the policy debate continue to emphasise the need to revive or preserve state-embedded public provision of water services, with all its acknowledged faults and limitations (Bakker 2000; Balanyá et al. 2005; Lobina and Hall 2000).

---

[17]  Bright interview.    [18]  Ngwane interview.

The aim of this section is to present – in a manner that keeps the politics underlying the debate to the fore – two different versions of hybrid approaches. The first is a community-based approach linking community cooperatives, activist NGOs and social consultancies, which resonates more with public participatory governance. The second is a social enterprise approach, linking social enterprise, certification-focused NGOs and regulators, which resonates more with managed liberalisation. The two hybrids overlap, and there is a tendency for efforts to establish the former to mutate into the latter, in part under the pressure of support structures which tend to favour the latter model.

### 6.4.1 Community-based approaches

The oppositional work of law in opening up political space discussed above often focused either on specific reforms or pointed to relatively unarticulated broader alternatives. However, reading across the case studies and focusing on those positive institutional dimensions that are consistent with the energies of that second image of law's work, a combination of community cooperatives, activist NGOs and social consultancies emerges. I use 'community-based' as a catch-all term to capture the mix of public and private that subsists in this hybrid model: it seeks to avoid the state-owned sense of public but also the individualistic market-centred structures of private governance. As Karen Bakker has observed (Bakker 2008), the tendency to use community in very vague ways frequently blurs any distinction between community ownership and management (which is more common in rural or small-scale peri-urban settings) and community-led governance (which is more likely to apply to the urban water supply infrastructure contexts at the core of this book).

Although the original system of 'uses and customs' based on managing rural irrigation in the Bolivian case study probably does illustrate community ownership and management, the attempt to establish 'social control' of the Cochabamba water company is a better example of the type of operational structure envisaged at the core of this hybrid. As we saw in Chapter 3, however, significant challenges to the effective operation of this structure have hobbled its efficacy, pointing to the need for institutional support structures for community-based operations and management. Activist NGOs might be one possible source of such support: for example, as noted in Chapter 3, the international public sector union Public Services International tried to set up a transnational partnership that would have offered technical assistance to the Cochabamba company. In this particular instance, the effort was defeated by a combination of slow uptake and bad timing (the 9/11 crisis intervened at an inopportune point), but the general potential remains, and public–public partnerships have become a staple recommendation of a range of actors who support public participatory governance, including the UN Commission for Sustainable Development (Lobina and Hall 2008; TNI 2006; UNCD 2005).

The support may be more effectively provided by a professional 'social consultancy' such as the non-profit consultancy services firm Service Public 2000, set up by the local mayors' association in France to support small towns in contract negotiations with private sector operators (Chapter 2). Similarly, in South Africa a local consultancy firm, Akira Ltd, set itself up with the express intention of providing support services for infrastructure development that combined South Africa's transformative constitutional commitments in the area of essential services with an in-depth knowledge of financing and contracting issues. In practice, though, the detailed support services provided by this company tended to focus on the detail of the financing and contracting issues, with the constitutional issues as a background commitment. This illustrates a tendency for this hybrid to mutate into the second type of hybrid, whose main contours I now outline.

### 6.4.2    Social enterprise approaches

A social enterprise approach is a hybrid model of governance that links social enterprise, certification-focused NGOs and regulators. It resonates more with managed liberalisation than with public participatory governance, incorporating some of the redistributive and social ideals of the latter into incentive-based governance mechanisms rather than embedding them in community-based dialogue. The 'mixed company' proposal spearheaded by GTZ in the post-Cochabamba water war period in Bolivia is a classic example of the service delivery dimension of this approach: the proposed structure is mainly embedded in commercial and corporate law, and major assets (pipes, facilities, land, etc.) are transferred to the company rather than owned and controlled collectively by user communities, but there is still a 'public' dimension in the sense that the company shares are held jointly by the region's citizens, cooperatives and municipalities. The corporatised public water delivery companies in Auckland and Durban provide additional examples, with this model also being potentially applicable in smaller urban settings.

The 'hybrid' character of this in many ways lies less in the forms proposed for service delivery and more in the notion that entities such as mixed companies can be held to a social agenda by means of pressure from other entities external to them. Where regulators retain an explicitly political and social aspect to their mission (for example, South Africa's recently established National Regulator for Water which remains embedded in a government department), they can monitor and enforce goals such as social tariffs and appropriate disconnection policies. If there is no central regulator, or if the regulator has been structured to have a more market-supporting role, NGOs can also fill this 'social-monitoring' role. For example, in Chile where the regulator is primarily focused on a market-supporting role, one environmental NGO has proposed a social enterprise-style consultancy that would provide certification for environmentally and socially sustainable small-scale water service systems.[19] This idea has more recently been taken up by a coalition of NGOs and other organisations that has called itself the Alliance for Water Stewardship. The Alliance proposes the development of a certification logo somewhat analogous to the popular Forest Stewardship Council one, indicating a minimum level of social and environmental sustainability attained by water service delivery systems.

### 6.4.3  Law, community and partnership

The two hybrid models have much in common. Both advocate a participatory approach to management and a regulatory framework that supports it. In practice both tend to take an individualist discretionary approach to the needs of 'end-users', despite the rhetorical commitments of the community-based model to prioritising collective interests and solutions. The main difference is that community-based approaches draw on tacit knowledges and practices, especially but not only those rooted in tradition and what Frances Cleaver calls a moral ecological rationality (Cleaver 2000). By contrast, social enterprise approaches tend to use modernist, technical knowledge more familiar in the hierarchical corporate bureaucracies of industrial water management, even though they seek to move away from the associated management approaches. Community-based approaches are embedded in holistic relationships; social enterprises are more comfortable with a world of specialised functional differentiation.

---

[19] Manuel Baquedano, director of Chilean environmental NGO, interviewed by Bronwen Morgan and Carolina Fairstein, Santiago, 29 January 2004.

What is striking from the case studies is the vulnerability of the community-based approach. Whether because of the relational difficulties faced by community cooperative structures, particularly in a large-scale urban environment, or because of the thin resources available at the micro level for detailed legal and regulatory support of this approach, it is all too easy for a community-based approach to either fail or to mutate into a social enterprise approach. Is this an issue of power relations? Some might argue that when the community-based model fails, it is because social activists cannot compete in the legal arena; others that the hegemony of market-based liberal capitalism blocks the development of adequate and appropriate legal resources to support the governance model they envisage and aspire to. The fact that the UN's formal support of public–public partnerships rapidly mutated into a vehicle that allows both private companies and public water utilities to participate is an example of the ambiguity of support for a more community-based approach (ADB 2010; UNSGAB 2009). Whatever the explanation, it often seems that if activists operate within the mode of market entities, they then find it easier to translate their interests into terms that resonate with the dominant debate.

Alison Post has argued that the ability to maintain 'relational contracts' is the most important factor promoting longevity and success in private sector participation in highly politicised sectors with large up-front investment (Post 2009). She shows how, in Argentina, private domestic firms that had a number of diverse activities in the territory in which they operate were better able (in comparison to either international firms or narrowly specialised domestic firms) to maintain relationality with host governments because of the broader set of possible exchanges that were possible with government.

The implications of this are that more holistic relationships work better than specialised functional differentiation at promoting the kind of relations that make public participatory governance (or alternative models of economic development more broadly) work. Rural irrigators in Bolivia could negotiate informal and complex arrangements of mutual interdependence in sharing water with each other because they are mutually interdependent in a multitude of ways that facilitate implicit trade-offs, long-term leverage and trust. Once they were embedded in a functionally specialised bureaucratic agency whose specific mission was restricted to delivering water services, they were operating in a context where they had sharply defined legal obligations to a range of constituencies with whom they had little relationship outside the context of water services delivery.

This raised the stakes, defined the issues in much more black-and-white terms and arguably undermined the set of implicit and tacit relationships which support relational contracting. Public participatory governance and its affiliated hybrids, in short, depend on a relatively diffuse and socially embedded sense of community, while managed liberalisation and its affiliated hybrids manufacture contingent, temporary communities that persist for the purpose of specialised activities and then dissolve.

This has implications for the role of law that were reflected in the case studies, particularly in the attitudes of actors who did not cleave strongly to either of the first two images of law explored in this chapter. For a surprising number of these – typically regulators and NGOs who worked in a zone between service provision and advocacy – law had a (negative) tendency to police relationships by defining mutual obligations in a black-and-white manner that individualised and fragmented common problems. They felt, in other words, that law had a corrosive effect on partnership. Law for them undermined the fluid relationships and the processes of support and capacity-building crucial to fostering productive change in the policy field of access to urban drinking water services. Yet we have seen, in the exploration of the previous two images of law's work, that when such fluid relationships do not (yet) exist or have broken down, law is an important resource in two very different ways. Law can do important work in securing sharply defined market relations that will substitute for fluid conceptions of mutual trust. Alternatively, and often in tension with the first, law can work to keep open political space in which to build fresh relationships of mutual interdependency.

There is a fundamental challenge here for the relationship between law, community and partnership. Working in partnership to manage a collective good such as water is at its heart a problem of a poor fit between governing the commons and modern legal systems that have in the last few decades been so powerfully shaped by intensifying global market integration. The move towards hybrid governance models and the stress on public–private partnerships does not resolve an inherent tension in perceptions of what the 'problem of the commons' actually entails. Karen Bakker has pointed to stark differences between activist and academic conceptions of the commons (Bakker 2008). Academic notions of the commons define it narrowly as a set of resources from which it is difficult to exclude individuals and for which use by one individual can reduce the benefits available to others. Thus defined, the management of such resources is amenable to improvement through better governance and optimised institutions and incentives. This perspective, which focuses on the commons as an efficient system for mitigating over-consumption amongst a defined group of users (Ostrom 1990), is able to accommodate relatively easily the practices of naming, blaming and claiming that underpin the work of law in securing and supporting market relations, even though the rulemaking, monitoring and enforcement practices it highlights actually do considerable work to *temper* market relations, and correct for their failures in relation to governing the commons.

In contrast, the activist perspective frames the commons as a set of communal social relations which are universally applicable, the threats to which have intensified in an era of neoliberal globalisation, and the defence of which, via political struggle, is necessary to sustain viable alternatives to capitalism. The stress here on the notion that collective action is embedded in a moral economy of community solidarity and equity (Boelens 2008) fits much more comfortably with the practices of naming, blaming and claiming that underpin law's work in keeping open political spaces, but in many ways sees law in its practical operational dimensions of rulemaking, monitoring and enforcement as peripheral to this essentially political task.

In short, in terms of building positive institutional alternatives, the activist vision of the commons as yet lacks a fully elaborated vision, particularly in terms of rulemaking, monitoring and enforcement, of the specific rights which would underpin its institutions, and the regulatory regime that would implement it. Until this is developed, law's role in constituting the partnerships needed to face the challenges of governing the commons will remain parasitical on a macro-political economy of market relations. Nuanced hybrid models may well be the way of the future in water governance, but they will still be defined at the intersection of rights and regulation.

~

# Epilogue

This book has made three core empirical arguments. First, in the Introduction and Chapter 1 I argued that urban access to safe drinking water is a policy problem that has an increasingly important global dimension, which is illuminated by understanding it in terms of rights and regulation. This perspective helps to trace emerging cross-border patterns of activity without losing sight of the way that these activities are still embedded in, and shaped by, particular national political and cultural contexts.

Second, Chapters 2 and 3 argued that two primary models have emerged in the global policy field as responses to the problem of access to water services in urban settings, each rooted in a particular national setting. France is emblematic of the managed liberalisation model while Bolivia has been a crucial site for the emergence of a public participatory model. However, as shown in Chapters 4 and 5, as aspects of the public participatory model are institutionalised at the micro level, they tend to be colonised by managed liberalisation.

Third, socio-economic rights and 'community control' are commonly invoked in efforts to hold back this colonising tendency, but there are a number of challenges in retaining a political–critical edge to these strategies. Their relationship to law and legality is a site of particular interest in this respect, as explored in Chapter 6, and illuminates different kinds of hybrids between managed liberalisation and public participatory governance. Whether social enterprise approaches (which resonate more with managed liberalisation) or community-based approaches (which resonate more with public participatory governance) will flourish will probably depend on the depth of institutional architecture channelling the energies of the models' supporters, and the degree to which it is supported by powerful transnational interests.

The theoretical arguments made in this book are intended to extend beyond the domain of urban water services, and to illuminate other areas of globalising social policy provision that involve significant capital investment, but also directly impact on the basic needs of individuals. Three facets of the book's theoretical contribution can be highlighted as having this wider resonance in relation to emerging patterns of transnational legal governance.

First, in relation to the *transnational* dimension, regulation and rights – two of the most important building blocks of the architecture of transnational governance – tend towards counter-majoritarianism. Although both rights and regulation have their roots in felt wrongs which could as easily be channelled into democratic political processes, their systemic institutionalisation tends to link them to processes and interpretive communities that erect boundaries between them and democratic political institutions. This is intensified by the inbuilt trajectories of communities of expertise that elaborate detailed rulemaking, monitoring and enforcement regimes for rights and regulation. Combined with the absence of democratic institutions at the level of global governance, these tendencies create at least partial systemic closure.

Second, in relation to *governance*, the most interesting place to explore trajectories of regulation and rights is their *intersection*. Systemic closure tends to seal regulation and rights off from each other, but under certain conditions they come into contact with each other in very interesting ways: primarily in situations of intense political contestation, or when a policy problem emerges in a novel arena with little existing institutional architecture. Their intersection is helpfully explored through the double triad of 'naming, claiming and blaming', and 'rulemaking, monitoring and enforcement'.

Third, in relation to *legality*, the double triad has especially important ramifications in the context of major infrastructure-based provision of basic needs. In such contexts, the stage of activism – naming and blaming – tends to blur civil, political and socio-economic rights. But even when claiming, and especially in the context of rulemaking, monitoring and enforcement, socio-economic rights and civil and political rights take separate trajectories. At this stage, unless socio-economic rights claims engage with regulation, they risk remaining mere rhetoric. But if they step too close to regulation, they lose their critical edge and political force.

Law thus plays an ambiguous role both as a strategic resource and a constitutive well of meaning. Law in civil and political rights can straddle the contradiction embedded in the rhetorical appeal of rights talk, the tension between the cry for autonomy and the building of collective identity, because it can construct that identity *through and by rejecting* the terms of state, or hierarchical, power. Effective socio-economic rights depend at least partially on state action, and the collective identities built around struggling for such rights therefore face greater risks of absorption into, or complicity with, state power.[1] One implication is that less formal, quasi-judicial procedures at local levels can play an important role in channelling direct protest into sustained and more routine political leverage. Legal and quasi-legal dispute resolution particularises and makes concrete very general rules, thereby allowing small sequential wins and losses for otherwise polarised forces. This routinises and at least sometimes also legitimises activist tactics, thereby creating a connection between direct protest and sustained, routine political leverage. Such a connection is at the heart of hopes for progressive political change in globalising social policies where fundamental human need collides with the imperatives of high-cost capital investment.

---

[1] This contrast is over-simplified, since there is a real sense in which civil and political rights are also state-dependent, in the sense that they become operable through an action against the state (and in some cases, particularly in the European context, the state can balance the claim against other priorities). However, the basic contrasting logic still pertains: civil and political rights to some degree limit state power v. rights that compel the use of state power.

# REFERENCES

ADB (Asian Development Bank) 2010. 'Water Operators Partnership Programme': www.adb.org/water/operations/partnerships/GWP-water-operators.asp#a1.

Ayres, Ian and Braithwaite, John 1992. *Responsive Regulation: Transcending the Deregulation Debate*, Oxford: Oxford University Press.

Bakker, Karen 2000. 'The Greening of Capitalism? Privatising Water in England and Wales': www.geog.ox.ac.uk/~jburke/wpapers/wpg00–02.html.

2004. *An Uncooperative Commodity: Privatizing Water in England and Wales*, Oxford: Oxford University Press.

2008. 'The Ambiguity of Community: Debating Alternatives to Water Supply Privatization', *Water Alternatives* 1(2): 236–52.

2009. 'Regulation of Water and Sanitation Services: Insights from The Water Dialogues': www.waterdialogues.org/thematic.htm.

Bakker, Karen and Bridge, Gavin 2006. 'Regulating Resource Use', in Kevin R. Cox, Murray Low and Jennifer Robinson (eds.), *Handbook of Political Geography*, London: Sage, pp. 219–34.

Balanyá, Belén, Brennan, Brid, Hoedeman, Olivier, Kishimoto, Satoko and Terhorst, Philipp (eds.) 2005. *Reclaiming Public Water: Achievements, Struggles and Visions from Around the World*, Amsterdam: Transnational Institute and Corporate Europe Observatory.

Baron, Catherine 2006. 'Mutations institutionnelles et recompositions des territoires urbains en Afrique: une analyse à travers la problématique de l'accès à l'eau', *Développement Durable et Territoires Fragiles*: http://developpement-durable.revues.org/pdf/2940.

Bevir, Mark 2007. 'The Construction of Governance', in Mark Bevir and Frank Trentmann (eds.), *Governance and Consumption: Agency and Resistance*, Basingstoke: Palgrave Macmillan.

Black, Julia 2005. 'What is Regulatory Innovation?' in Julia Black, Martin Lodge and Mark Thatcher (eds.), *Regulatory Innovation: A Comparative Analysis*, Cheltenham: Edward Elgar Publishing, pp. 1–15.

Boelens, Rutgerd 2008. 'Water Rights Arenas in the Andes: Upscaling the Defence Networks to Localize Water Control', *Water Alternatives* 1(1): 48–65.

2009. 'The Politics of Disciplining Water Rights', *Development and Change* 40(2): 307–31.

Braithwaite, John and Drahos, Peter 2005. *Global Business Regulation*, Cambridge: Cambridge University Press.

Castro, Esteban 2005. *Water Power and Citizenship: Social Struggle in the Basin of Mexico*, Basingstoke: Palgrave Macmillan.

CBC Canada 2004. 'Dead in the Water', documentary, CBC-TV, 31 March: see www.cbc.ca/fifth/deadinthewater/.

Chechilnitzky, Alexander 2003. 'AIDIS: 55 anos de fructifera labor', *Revista AIDIS* 33: 4–7.

Cleaver, Frances 2000. 'Moral Ecological Rationality: Institutions and the Management of Common Property Resources', *Development and Change* 31(2): 361–83.

COHRE (Centre on Housing Rights and Eviction) with AADS (American Association for the Advancement of Science), SDC (Swiss Agency for Development and Cooperation) and UN-HABITAT (United Nations Human Settlements Programme) 2007. *Manual on the Right to Water and Sanitation*, Geneva: Switzerland.

Collins, Hugh 2007. 'Utility and Rights in Common Law Reasoning: Rebalancing Private Law through Constitutionalisation', *Dalhousie Law Journal* 30: 1–26.

Conant, Jeff 2009. 'Defeating the Multinationals Is Just the Start of the Problem for Anti-Globalization Movements': www.alternet.org/water/117988/defeating_the_multinationals_is_just_the_start_of_the_problem_for_anti-globalization_movements/.

Conca, Ken 2005. *Governing Water: Contentious Transnational Politics and Global Institution Building*, Cambridge, MA: MIT Press.

Cooper, Davina 1994. 'Out of Place: Symbolic Domains, Religious Rights and the Cultural Contract', in Nicholas Blomley, David Delaney and Richard T. Ford (eds.), *The Legal Geographies Reader: Law, Power and Space*, New York: Guilford Press, pp. 42–51.

Corporate Europe Observatory and Transnational Institute 2010. 'Water Remunicipalisation Tracker': www.remunicipalisation.org.

Crenzel, Emilio Ariel 2003. '*Argentina – Tucuman Case Study*', Argentina: University of Buenos Aires: www.prinwass.org/proreports.shtml.

Crespo, Carlos 2003. 'Water Privatisation Policies and Conflicts in Bolivia: The Water War in Cochabamba 1999–2000', Ph.D. thesis, Oxford Brookes University, Department of Planning.

De Albuquerque, Catarina 2009. *Water, Sanitation, MDG's and Human Rights*, Sofia: UNSGAB: www2.ohchr.org/english/issues/water/iexpert/docs/UNSGAB.22052009.doc.

De Sousa Santos, Boaventura and Rodríguez-Garavito, César 2005. *Law and Globalisation from Below: Towards a Cosmopolitan Legality*, Cambridge: Cambridge University Press.

Department of Water Affairs and Forestry of South Africa 1994. White Paper on Water Supply and Sanitation Policy: www.dwaf.gov.za/Documents/Policies/WSSP.pdf.

1997. White Paper on a National Water Policy for South Africa: www.dwaf.gov.za/documents/Policies/nwpwp.pdf.

Dorf, Michael and Sabel, Charles 1998. 'A Constitution of Democratic Experimentalism', *Columbia Law Review* 98(2): 267–473.

Dubreuil, Céline 2006. *The Right to Water: From Concept to Implementation*, Marseilles: World Water Council: www.worldwatercouncil.org/fileadmin/wwc/Library/RightToWater_FinalText_Cover.pdf.

ECLAC (Economic Commission for Latin America and the Caribbean) 2002. *Foreign Investment in Latin America and the Caribbean*, Santiago, Chile: ECLAC: www.eclac.org/publicaciones/xml/1/12151/LCG2198chapI.pdf.

Engel, Eduardo 2005. 'Consumidores: tres tareas pendientes', *La Tercera*, 20 November, p. 12.

Fairstein, Carolina forthcoming. 'Argentina: Privatisation and Re-municipalisation in Local and International Context', in Malcom Langford and Anna Russell (eds.), *The Right to Water: Theory, Practice and Prospects*, Cambridge: Cambridge University Press.

Felstiner, William, Abel, Richard and Sarat, Austin 1981. 'The Emergence and Transformation of Disputes: Naming, Blaming and Claiming', *Law and Society Review* 15: 630–49.

Finnegan, William 2002. 'Letter from Bolivia: Leasing the Rain', *The New Yorker*, 8 April.

Foerster, Morrison 2002. 'Morrison Foerster Quarterly Report on Water Industry Developments in Latin America': www.mofo.com/news/updates/files/update816.html.

Foster, Vivien 2005. *Ten Years of Water Service Reform in Latin America: Towards an Anglo-French Model*, Washington, DC: The World Bank: http://siteresources.worldbank.org/INTWSS/Resources/WSSServiceReform.pdf.

Foweraker, Joe 2001. 'Grassroots Movements and Political Activism in Latin America: A Critical Comparison of Chile and Brazil', *Journal of Latin American Studies* 33(4): 839–65.

Freeman, Jody 2000. 'The Private Role in Public Governance', *New York University Law Review* 75: 543–675.

French Department of Health 2000. 'Circular DAS/DSFE/LCE n° 2000–320 of June 6': www.santé.gouv.fr/adm/dagpb/bo/2000/00-32/a0322329.htm.

Fritz, Thomas 2006. 'Development Aid and Water Privatisation: The Example of German Development Cooperation in Bolivia': www.fdcl-berlin.de/fileadmin/fdcl/Publikationen/FDCL-Bolivia-Water-Privatisation.pdf.

Gamarra, Eduardo 1995. *Democracy Markets and Structural Reform in Latin America: Argentina, Bolivia, Brazil, Chile, and Mexico,* Boulder, CO: Lynne Rienner.

Ginsburg, Tom 2005. 'International Substitutes for Domestic Institutions: Bilateral Investment Treaties and Governance', *International Review of Law and Economics* 25(1): 107–25.

Global Water Operators' Partnership Alliance n.d. www.unhabitat.org/categories. asp?catid=568.

Gordon, Philip H. and Meunier, Sophie 2001. *The French Challenge: Adapting to Globalization,* Washington, DC: Brookings Institution Press.

Goubert, Jean-Pierre 1989. *The Conquest of Water,* Oxford: Polity Press.

Guérin-Schneider, Laetitia and Nakhla, Michel 2010. 'Emergence of an Innovative Regulation Mode in Water Utilities in France: Between Commission Regulation and Franchise Bidding', *European Journal of Law and Economics:* www.springerlink.com/content/v372vx53261686u5/fulltext. pdf.

Guerquin, François, Ahmed, Tarek, Hua, Mi, Ikeda, Tetsuya, Ozbilen, Vedat and Schuttelaar, Marlies 2003. *World Water Actions: Making Water Flow for All,* London: Earthscan.

Halliday, Terry and Oskinksy, Pavel 2006. 'Globalization of Law', *Annual Review of Sociology* 32: 447–70.

Haut Conseil du Secteur Public 1999. *Quelle régulation pour l'eau et les services publics,* Paris, France: www.ladocumentationfrancaise.fr/rapports-publics/004000299/ext.shtml.

Healy, Kevin and Paulson, Susan 2000. 'Political Economies of Identity in Bolivia, 1952–1998', *Journal of Latin American Anthropology* 5(2): 2–29.

Hilton, Matthew 2009. *Prosperity for All: Consumer Activism in an Era of Globalisation,* Ithaca, NY: Cornell University Press.

Houtzager, Peter and Kurtz, Marcus 2000. 'The Institutional Roots of Popular Mobilization: Transformation and Rural Politics in Brazil and Chile, 1960–95', *Comparative Studies in Society and History* 42(2): 394–424.

HRC (Human Rights Council) 2008. 'Resolution A/HRC/7/L.16', New York: United Nations.

ICHRP (International Council on Human Rights Policy) 2008. *Climate Change and Human Rights: A Rough Guide,* ed. Stephen Humphreys, Vernier, Switzerland: Atar Roto Press.

ICSID (International Centre for the Settlement of Investment Disputes) 2009. http://icsid.worldbank.org/ICSID/Index.jsp.

n.d. 'Search ICSID cases': http://icsid.worldbank.org/ICSID/FrontServlet? requestType=CasesRH&reqFrom=Main&actionVal=ViewAllCases.

IDDC (The International Development Research Centre) n.d. *After the Water Wars: The Search for Common Ground*: www.idrc.ca/en/ev-85928-201-1-DO_TOPIC.html.

INNI (International NGO Network on ISO) 2009. http://inni.pacinst.org/inni/.

International Conference on Water and the Environment 1992. 'The Dublin Statement on Water and Sustainable Development': www.un-documents. net/h2o-dub.htm.

International Office of Water 2009. www.oieau.org/anglais/gest_eau/index.htm.

ISO (International Organization for Standardization) 2007. *Guidelines 24512-2007 for the Management of Drinking Water Utilities and for the Assessment of Drinking Water Services; and Guidelines 24510-2007 for the Assessment and for the Improvement of the Service to Users*, Geneva: ISO.

Kara, Jan and Quarless, Diane 2002. *Guiding Principles for Partnerships for Sustainable Development ('Type 2 Outcomes') to be Elaborated by Interested Parties in the Context of the World Summit on Sustainable Development (WSSD)*, New York: United Nations: www.un.org/esa/sustdev/partnerships/guiding_principles7june2002.pdf.

Keck, Margaret and Sikkink, Kathryn 1998. *Activists Beyond Borders: Transnational Advocacy Networks in International Politics*, Ithaca, NY: Cornell University Press.

Kerf, Michel and Izaguirre, Ada K. 2007. *Revival of Private Participation in Developing Country Infrastructure: A Look at Recent Trends and Policy Implications*, Washington, DC: World Bank.

Khumprakob, Melissa 2004. 'The Vivendi–Argentina Water Dispute', *Sustainable Development Law and Policy* 5(1): 64–9.

Kirkpatrick, Colin and Parker, David 2004. *Infrastructure Regulation: Models for Developing Asia*, Tokyo, Japan: Asian Development Bank Institute.

Kirkpatrick, Jennet 2008. *Uncivil Disobedience: Studies in Violence and Democratic Politics*, Princeton, NJ: Princeton University Press.

Kooy, Michelle and Bakker, Karen 2008. 'Splintered Networks: The Colonial and Contemporary Waters of Jakarta', *Geoforum* 39(6): 1843–58.

Kriel, Ross 2003. 'Facing Local Government Post-Demarcation: Impact of the Regulatory Framework on the Private Sector – Case Studies and Analysis', on file with author.

Langevin, Philippe, 2008. 'La Loi Oudin–Santini sur la cooperation internationale dans les domaines de l'eau et de l'assainissement': www.medcoop.com/uploads/lettres/EXE_No44.pdf.

Levin, Thomas and Kampf, Andrea 2009. *Human Rights Meets Water: A Conversation*, Eschborn: GTZ Deutsche Gesellschaft für Technische Zusammenarb.

Lindseth, Peter 2005. '"Always Embedded" Administration: The Historical Evolution of Administrative Justice as an Aspect of Modern Governance', in

Christian Joerges (ed.), *The Economy as a Polity: The Political Constitution of Contemporary Capitalism*, London: Routledge, pp. 117–36.

Litfin, Karen T., Milner, Helen V. and Ruggie, John G. (eds.) 1995. *Ozone Discourses: Science and Politics in Global Environmental Cooperation*, New York: Columbia University Press.

Liu, Sida and Halliday, Terence C. 2009. 'Recursivity in Legal Change: Lawyers and Reforms of China's Criminal Procedure Law', *Law and Social Inquiry* 34(4): 911–50.

Lobel, Orly 2007. 'Form and Substance in Labour Market Policies', in Bronwen Morgan (ed.), *The Intersection of Rights and Regulation: New Directions in Socio-legal Scholarship*, Aldershot: Ashgate, pp. 23–40.

Lobina, Emanuele and Hall, David 2000. 'Public Sector Alternatives to Water Supply and Sewerage Privatization: Case Study', *Water Resources Development* 16(1): 35–55.

2007(a). *Water Privatisation and Restructuring in Latin America*, Greenwich, London: www.psiru.org/reports/2007–09–W-Latam.doc#_Toc180224506.

2007(b). 'Experience with Private Sector Participation in Grenoble, France, and Lessons on Strengthening Public Water Operation', *Utilities Policy* 15: 93–109.

2008. 'The Comparative Advantage of the Public Sector in the Development of Urban Water Supply', *Progress in Development Studies* 8(1): 85–101.

Maldonado, Gonzalo Rojas 2004. *H2O: La guerra del Agua: testimonia desde la linea de fuego*, La Paz: Bolivia: Fondo Editorial de los Diputados.

Marin, Philippe 2009. *Public–Private Partnerships for Urban Water Utilities: A Review of Experiences in Developing Countries* Washington, DC: World Bank.

Marin, Philippe and Izaguirre, Ada K. 2006. *Private Participation in Water: Toward a New Generation of Projects?*, Washington, DC: World Bank.

Medalla, Eva 2006. 'Water Ministry Awaits Budget, Negotiates International Funding – Bolivia': www.bnamericas.com/story.jsp?idioma=I&sector=4&noticia=345473.

Mehta, Lyla 2008. *Contexts and Constructions of Scarcity*, New Delhi: Oxford University Press.

Merry, Sally 2003. 'Constructing a Global Law – Violence against Women and the Human Rights System', *Law and Social Inquiry* 28(4): 941–77.

Micheletti, Michele 2008. 'The Moral Force of Consumption and Capitalism – Anti-Slavery and Anti-Sweatshop', in Kate Soper and Frank Trentmann (eds.), *Citizenship and Consumption*, Basingstoke: Palgrave Macmillan, pp. 121–36.

Ministry of Foreign Affairs 1997. 'Suez-Lyonnaise des Eaux: Birth of a Services Giant', *Label France*, 10.

Morgan, Bronwen 2004a. 'Water: Frontier Markets and Cosmopolitan Activism',
    *Soundings: A Journal of Politics and Culture* 27: 10–24.
    2004b. 'The Regulatory Face of the Human Right to Water', *Journal of Water
    Law* 15: 179–87.
    2006a. 'Turning Off the Tap: Urban Water Service Delivery and the Social
    Construction of Global Administrative Law', *European Journal of
    International Law* 17: 215–47.
    2006b. 'The North–South Politics of Necessity: Regulating for Basic Rights
    Between National and International Levels', *Journal of Consumer Policy*
    29(4): 465–87.
    2006c. 'Emerging Global Water Welfarism: Access to Water, Unruly Consumers
    and Transnational Governance', in Frank Trentmann and John Brewer
    (eds.), *Consumer Cultures, Global Perspectives*, Oxford: Berg, 279–310.
    2007. 'Local Politics and the Regulation of Global Water Suppliers in South
    Africa', in Dana Brown and Ngaire Woods (eds.), *Making Global Self-
    Regulation Effective in Developing Countries*, Oxford: Oxford University
    Press, 201–26.
    2008a. 'Consuming Without Paying: Stealing or Campaigning? The Civic
    Implications of Civil Disobedience around Access to Water', in Kate
    Soper and Frank Trentmann (eds.), *Citizenship and Consumption*,
    Basingstoke: Palgrave Macmillan, 71–86.
    2008b. 'Building Bridges Between Regulatory and Citizen Space: Civil Society
    Contributions to Water Service Delivery Frameworks in Cross-National
    Perspective', *Law, Social Justice and Global Development Journal (LGD)*,
    2008 (1): www.go.warwick.ac.uk/elj/lgd/2008_1/morgan.
Muhr, Thomas 2010. 'Nicaragua: Constructing the Bolivarian Alternative for the
    Peoples of our America (ALBA)', in Ulrike Schuerkens (ed.), *Globalization
    and Transformations of Social Inequality*, New York: Routledge, pp. 115–34.
Munger, Frank 2008. 'Globalisation, Investing in Law, and the Careers of Lawyers
    for Social Causes: Taking on Rights in Thailand', *New York Law School
    Review* 53(4): 745–802.
Murillo, Maria Victoria 2009. *Political Competition, Partisanship, and Policymaking
    in Latin America*, New York: Cambridge University Press.
Murray, Andrew and Scott, Colin 2002. 'Controlling the New Media: Hybrid
    Responses to New Forms of Power', *Modern Law Review* 65(4): 491–516.
Nickson, Andrew and Vargas, Claudia 2002. 'The Limitations of Water
    Regulation: The Failure of the Cochabamba Concession in Bolivia', *Bulletin
    of Latin American Research* 21(1): 99–120.
Nottage, Luke R. and Miles, Kate 2009. '"Back to the Future" for Investor–State
    Arbitrations: Revising Rules in Australia and Japan to Meet Public Interests',
    *Journal of International Arbitration* 25(1): 25–58.

OHCHR (Office of the United Nations High Commissioner for Human Rights) n.d. (a) 'Committee on Economic, Social and Cultural Rights': www2.ohchr. org/english/bodies/cescr/.

n.d.(b). 'Independent Expert on the Issue of Human Rights Obligations Related to Access to Safe Drinking Water and Sanitation': www2.ohchr.org/english/ issues/water/iexpert/Ind_expert_DeAlbuquerque.htm.

Olivera, Oscar and Lewis, Tom 2004. ¡Cochabamba! *Water War in Bolivia*, Cambridge: MA: South End Press.

ONEMA 1999. *Creation of an Observatory on the Performance of Public Water and Water-Treatment Services*: www.onema.fr/IMG/EV/EV/plus/Fiche-Observatoire.pdf.

Ostrom, Elinor 1990. *Governing the Commons: The Evolution of Institutions for Collective Action*, New York: Cambridge University Press.

Owen, David 2009. 'The Expressive Agon: On Political Agency in a Constitutional Democratic Polity', in Andrew Schaap (ed.), *Law and Agonistic Politics* Farnham: Ashgate, pp. 71–86.

Pezon, Christelle 2007. 'The Role of "Users" Cases in Drinking Water Services Development and Regulation in France: An Historical Perspective', *Utilities Policy* 15(2): 110–20.

Pezon, Christelle and Bonnet, Frédéric 2006. *Déroulement des procédures de délégation des services publics d'eau et d'assainissement,* Paris, France: École Nationale du Génie Rural des Eaux et des Forêts (ENGREF).

Polanyi, Karl 2001. *The Great Transformation: The Political and Economic Origins of our Time*, 2nd edn, Boston, MA: Beacon Press.

Post, Alison 2009. 'Liquid Assets and Fluid Contracts: Explaining the Uneven Effects of Water Privatization', PhD dissertation, Department of Government, Harvard University.

Roth, Dik, Boelens, Rutgerd and Zwarteveen, Margreet (eds.) 2005. *Liquid Relations. Legal Pluralism and Contested Water Rights*, New Brunswick, NJ: Rutgers University Press.

Russell, Anna 2009. 'The Right to Water', D.Phil. thesis University of Oxford, Faculty of Law.

Santiago, Charles 2003. 'A Shared Vision: The EU Water Policy and European Water Corporate Interests', Berlin: Heinrich Boll Foundation.

Saytanides, Adam 2003. 'Bolivia Offers Cautionary Tale for FTAA Negotiators': www.inthesetimes.com/article/650/bolivia_offers_cautionary_tale_for_ ftaa_negotiators/.

Schaap, Andrew (ed.) 2009. *Law and Agonistic Politics*, Farnham: Ashgate.

Scott, Colin 2006. 'Privatization and Regulatory Regimes', in Michael Moran, Martin Rein and Robert E. Goodin (eds.), *The Oxford Handbook of Public Policy*, Oxford: Oxford University Press, pp. 651–68.

SEMAPA 2003. *Semapa: a un ano de la institucionalizacion*: SEMAPA annual report 2002–3, Cochabamba, Bolivia.

Shamir, Ronen 2002. 'The Commodification of Corporate Social Responsibility – South Africa Case Study': unpublished paper on file with author.

Shapiro, Martin 2001. 'Administrative Law Unbounded: Reflections on Government and Governance', *Indiana Journal of Global Legal Studies* 8: 369–400.

Shiva, Vandana 2002. *Water Wars: Privatization, Pollution and Profit*, Cambridge, MA: South End Press.

Shultz, Jim 2006. 'Bechtel vs Bolivia – The People Win', *Democracy Centre Online* 69: www.democracyctr.org/newsletter/vol69.htm.

2008. 'The Cochabamba Water War and its Aftermath', in Jim Shultz and Melissa Draper (eds.), *Dignity and Defiance: Stories from Bolivia's Challenge to Globalization* Berkeley: University of California Press, pp. 9–44.

Shultz, Jim and Draper, Melissa 2008. *Dignity and Defiance: Stories from Bolivia's Challenge to Globalisation,* Berkeley: University of California Press.

Silva, Gisele, Tynan, Nicola and Yilmaz, Yesim 1998. 'Private Participation in the Water and Sewerage Sector – Recent Trends', *Public Policy for the Private Sector* 147: http://rru.worldbank.org/documents/ publicpolicyjournal/147silva.pdf.

Simpson, Robin 2006. 'Universal Access in the Water and Sanitation Sector', in *Liberalisation and Universal Access to Basic Services,* Paris, France: OECD Publishing, pp. 97–134.

Smets, Henri 2007. 'Implementing the Right to Water in France', paper presented at the Workshop on Legal Aspects of Water Sector Reforms, International Environmental Law Research Centre (IELRC), Geneva, 20–21 April 2007: www.academie-eau.org/admin/fichier_publication/80– 2007_Implementing_the_right_to_water_in_France_April_2007– 1271952822fichier_publication0.pdf.

Somers, Margaret 2008. 'Towards a New Sociology of Rights: "Buried Bodies" of Citizenship and Human Rights', *Annual Review of Law and Social Sciences* 4: 385–425.

Spronk, Susan 2007. 'Struggles against Accumulation by Dispossession in Bolivia: The Political Economy of Natural Resource Contention', *Latin American Perspectives* 34(2): 31–47.

Suez Environnement 2007. 'Human Rights and Access to Drinking Water and Sanitation', in *Contribution to Office of the High Commissioner of Human Rights' Consultation According to Human Rights Council Decision 2/104,* Geneva: Human Rights Council.

Swyngedouw, Erik 2004. *Social Power and the Urbanization of Water: Flows of Power,* Oxford: Oxford University Press.

Teubner, Gunther 1983. 'Substantive and Reflexive Elements in Modern Law', *Law and Society Review* 17: 239–85.

1996. 'Global Bukowina: Legal Pluralism in the World Society', in Gunther Teubner (ed.) *Global Law without a State*, Aldershot: Dartmouth, pp. 3–30.

Tickell, Adam and Peck, Jamie 2003. 'Making Global Rules: Globalisation or Neoliberalisation?' in Jamie Peck and Henry Wai-Chung (eds.), *Remaking the Global Economy: Economic–Geographical Perspectives*, London: Sage, pp. 163–81.

TNI (Transnational Institute) 2006. *Public Water for All: The Role of Public–Private Partnerships*, Amsterdam: Transnational Institute and Corporate Europe Observatory.

Udaeta, Maria Esther, Bustamente, Rocio, Sanchez, Loyda, Alurralde, Juan Carlos and Cossio, Vladimir 2007. *Group on Social Consensus Building for Drafting of Laws: The Case of Bolivia Irrigation Law No 2878*, La Paz: Swiss Agency for Cooperation and Development.

UN-HABITAT (United Nations Human Settlements Programme) n.d. 'Global Water Operators' Partnership Alliance': www.unhabitat.org/categories. asp?catid=568.

UNCESCR (United Nations Committee on Economic Social and Cultural Rights) 2002. *Substantive Issues Arising in the Implementation of the International Covenant on Economic, Social and Cultural Rights – General Comment No. 15 (2002) – The Right to Water (Arts. 11 and 12 of the International Covenant on Economic, Social and Cultural Rights)*, UNCESCR 29th Session (11–29 November 2002), New York: United Nations.

UNCSD (United Nations Economic and Social Council, Commission on Sustainable Development) 2005. *Freshwater Management: Policy Options and Possible Actions to Expedite Implementation, Report of the Secretary General, Thirteenth Session, Document E/CN.17/2005/2*, New York: UN Commission on Sustainable Development: http://daccess-dds-ny.un.org/ doc/UNDOC/GEN/N04/647/82/PDF/N0464782.pdf?OpenElement.

UNDP (United Nations Development Programme) 2000. *Human Development Report*: http://hdr.undp.org/en/media/hdr_2000_back1.pdf.

UNECE (United Nations Economic Commission for Europe) 1992. *Protocol on Water and Health to the Convention on the Protection and Use of Transboundary Watercourses and International Lakes*, Geneva: UNECE www.unece.org/env/water/.

United Nations Millennium Project Task Force on Water and Sanitation 2005. *Health, Dignity and Development: What Will It Take?*, New York: United Nations: www.unmillenniumproject.org/reports/tf_watersanitation.htm.

UNSGAB (United Nations Secretary General's Advisory Board on Water and Sanitation) 2006. *The Hashimoto Plan*, New York: UNSGAB: www.unsgab. org/docs/HAP_en.pdf.

2009. 'Welcome to UNSGAB Website!': www.unsgab.org/.

Van Harten, Gus and Loughlin, Martin 2006. 'Investment Treaty Arbitration as a Species of Global Administrative Law', *European Journal of International Law* 17: 121–50.

Vicuña, Francisco Orrego 2004. *International Dispute Settlement in an Evolving Global Society*, Cambridge: Cambridge University Press.

Walker, Christopher 2006. 'Toward Democratic Consolidation? The Argentine Supreme Court, Judicial Independence and the Rule of Law', *Florida Journal of International Law* 14: 746–806.

World Bank 2005. 'Infrastructure Development: The Roles of the Public and Private Sectors: World Bank Group's Approach to Supporting Investments in Infrastructure', *World Bank Guidance Note*, Washington, DC: World Bank.

World Water Forum 2009. worldwaterforum5.org/index.php?id=192.

Zibechi, Raúl 2009. 'Cochabamba: From Water War to Water Management': *America's Program*: www.alternet.org/water/140393/cochabamba:_from_war_to_water_management/.

# INDEX

access to water
  analytical framework, 23–4
  recognition of right of access, 4
activism
  justiciability of, 165–6, 188–94
  specific countries *see specific*
      *countries*
  transnational identity built through,
     192–4
  as 'uncivil disobedience', 184–7
ALBA, 114–17
America, Latin *see* Latin America
Americanisation, globalisation as, 1–2
arbitration, international
  fora, pressure to reform, 179, 180–1
  national to transnational, 175–8
  non-state actors, 178–9
  role, 10
  specific countries *see* Argentina;
     Bolivia; France; South Africa
  transnational legal analysis, 175–81
Argentina
  access to water, level of, 119
  activism
    Chile compared, 126
    disputes, 126–8
    level of, 119
  arbitration, international, 138–9,
     177–8
  background, 118–20
  BITs, 177
  'blaming' process, 34–6, 41–2
  case study structure (table), 19–20
  chapter summary, 18–21
  'Chicago boys', influence, 119
  Chile contrasted
    activism, 126

international dimensions, 138–9
  regulatory agencies, 120–6
  summary, 118–20
'claiming' process, 43
contractual disputes, 34
disputes
  consumer activism, 126–8
  pattern of disputation
    *see* 'popcorn politics' *below*
economic climate, 119
'enforcement' process, 38
hybrid model of governance,
    emergence, 119–20
institutionalised right to water, 41
investment by multinational
    corporations, 118–20, 121
litigation, use of, 144
managed liberalisation model
  emergence, 118–19
  success, 119–20
patchwork legality, 188
'popcorn politics'
  operation, 133–8
  as pattern of disputation, 120
regulatory agencies
  development and structure,
    118–19, 120, 121, 122–3,
    124–5
  market relations, supporting and
    securing, 174, 175
summary of developments, 141–5
Asia, investment in East Asia, 8

banks *see* international financial
    institutions
Bilateral Investment Treaties (BITS),
    69–70, 96

# CAMBRIDGE STUDIES IN LAW AND SOCIETY

Printed in Great Britain
by Amazon.co.uk, Ltd.,
Marston Gate.